W9-ADK-463

ANSYS®*Workbench*™ *Tutorial*

Structural & Thermal Analysis using the ANSYS Workbench Release 11.0 Environment

Kent L. Lawrence
Mechanical and Aerospace Engineering
University of Texas at Arlington

ISBN: 978-1-58503-397-3

PUBLICATIONS

Schroff Development Corporation

www.schroff.com
www.schroff-europe.com

Kent L. Lawrence is Professor of Mechanical and Aerospace Engineering, University of Texas at Arlington where he has served as Graduate Advisor, Chair of the Department, and supervised the graduate work of over one hundred masters and PhD students. He is a Life Fellow of ASME, the author of the book *ANSYS Tutorial*, SDC Publications, 2002, 2003, 2004, 2005, 2006 and coauthor with Robert L. Woods of the text *Modeling and Simulation of Dynamic Systems*, Prentice-Hall, 1997.

© 2007 by Kent L. Lawrence. All rights reserved.

No part of this book may be reproduced in any form or by any means without written permission from the publisher.

The author and publisher of this book have used their best efforts in preparing this book. The efforts include the testing of the tutorials to determine their effectiveness. However, the author and publisher make no warranty of any kind, expressed or implied, with regard to the material contained in this book. The author and publisher shall not be liable in any event for incidental or consequential damages in connection with the use of the material contained herein.

ANSYS, ANSYS Mechanical, ANSYS Multiphysics, Workbench, and any and all ANSYS, Inc. product and service names are registered trademarks or trademarks of ANSYS, Inc. or its subsidiaries located in the United States or other countries. All other trademarks or registered trademarks are the property of their respective owners.

Examination Copies:

Books received as examination copies are for review purposes only and may not be made available for student use. Resale of examination copies is prohibited.

Electronic Files:

Any electronic files associated with this book are licensed to the original user only. These files may not be transferred to any other party.

ISBN: 978-1-58503-397-3

Dedicated to:

CABL, always there and always an inspiration,

and

James H. Lawrence, Jr., the family's first engineer.

PREFACE

The exercises in the **ANSYS Workbench Tutorial** introduce the reader to effective engineering problem solving through the use of this powerful modeling, simulation and optimization tool. Topics that are covered include solid modeling, stress analysis, conduction/convection heat transfer, thermal stress, natural frequencies and buckling. It is designed for practicing and student engineers alike and is suitable for use with an organized course of instruction or for self-study.

The ANSYS Inc. finite element method software (such as ANSYS Mechanical, ANSYS Academic Teaching, ANSYS Academic Research, etc) is one of the most mature, widely distributed & popular commercial & academic computer aided engineering (CAE) programs available. The ANSYS Workbench environment provides the user with a powerful, intuitive alternative to the "classic" or "traditional" ANSYS GUI. ANSYS Workbench is today the move forward strategy for ANSYS Inc, as development of the traditional GUI is minimal.

I am most appreciative of the continued support of research and teaching efforts in our universities provided by ANSYS, Inc and for the encouragement to pursue this project given by Paul Lethbridge of ANSYS.

Heartfelt thanks go to Prof. Dereje Agonafer, ever a supporter of this effort, who together with Mukund Narasimhan, Ajay Menon, and Abhijit Kaisare provided helpful examples, comments, and suggestions for use herein.

Stephen Schroff of SDC Publications urged me to try the tutorial approach in class with the Roger Toogood Pro/E Tutorial book and has been very helpful to me in the preparation of the ANSYS related materials. To Stephen I am most indebted as well as to Ms. Mary Schmidt of SDC for her careful assistance with the manuscript. Hats off also to the University of Alberta group for setting the bar for tutorial standards.

Special thanks go as usual to Carol Lawrence, ever supportive and always willing to proof even the most arcane and cryptic stuff.

The tutorials/exercises in this book can be completed by users with access to ANSYS Inc. release 11.0 product that contains ANSYS structural & thermal capability together with ANSYS Design Modeler or alternate solid modeler. Examples are: ANSYS Mechanical & ANSYS Design Modeler, ANSYS Academic Research, ANSYS Academic Teaching Advanced, ANSYS Academic Teaching Introductory, ANSYS Academic Teaching Mechanical. Note that the ANSYS release 11.0 academic products contain ANSYS Design Modeler, however, commercial product users must ensure they have purchased ANSYS Design Modeler (it's a separate commercial product) or access to an alternate solid modeler.

Please feel free to point out any problems that you may notice with the tutorials in this book. Your comments are welcome at **lawrence@uta.edu** and can only help to improve what is presented here. Additions and corrections to the book will be posted on **mae.uta.edu/~lawrence/ANSYSWBtutorial**, so you can check there for any errata to the version that you are using.

Kent L. Lawrence

CONTENTS

INTRODUCTION

CHAPTER 1 – SOLID MODELING FUNDAMENTALS

CHAPTER 2 – PLACED FEATURES, ASSEMBLY

CHAPTER 3 – MODELING TECHNIQUES

CHAPTER 4 – SIMULATION I

CHAPTER 5 - SIMULATION II

CHAPTER 6 – WIZARDS & TOOLS

CHAPTER 7 – HEAT TRANSFER & THERMAL STRESS

CHAPTER 8 – SURFACE & LINE MODELS

LESSON 9 – NATURAL FREQUENCIES & BUCKLING LOADS

Introduction

I-1 OVERVIEW

Engineers routinely use **Solid Modelers** together with the **Finite Element Method (FEM)** to solve everyday problems of **modeling** for **form/fit/function**, **stress**, **deformation**, **heat transfer**, **fluid flow**, **electromagnetics**, etc. using commercial as well as special purpose computer codes. This book presents a collection of tutorials for **ANSYS Workbench**, one of the most versatile and widely used of the commercial solid modeling, simulation and optimization programs.

The tutorials discuss in turn solid modeling, stress analysis, conduction/convection heat transfer, thermal stress, vibration and buckling. Mesh creation and adjustment as well as transferring models from CAD solid modelers other than DesignModeler are also included.

The tutorials progress from simple to complex. Since each tutorial can be mastered in a short period of time, the entire book quickly provides a complete, basic introduction to the concepts and capabilities of the extensive ANSYS Workbench software suite.

I-2 THE PROCESS

The part/product analysis process can be divided into three distinct phases

1. **SOLID MODELING** – Build a digital representation of the part/system.

2. **SIMULATION** – Apply materials, loads and constraints; specify the analysis type; determine response quantities.

3. **OPTIMIZATION** – Determine optimum settings for the parameters that control the design.

The execution of these three steps is conveniently encapsulated in the ANSYS Workbench environment as we shall see in the chapter tutorials that follow.

I-3   THE TUTORIALS

A short description of each of the ANSYS Workbench Tutorials follows.

Chapter 1 - Solid Modeling Fundamentals- A simple cross section is used to introduce basic solid modeling concepts with ANSYS DesignModeler by extruding, revolving and sweeping the section.

Chapter 2 - Placed Features, Assembly – This chapter covers creation of features whose shape is predetermined. Among these are: Holes, Rounds, Chamfers, and Patterns. A simple assembly modeling exercise is also included.

Chapter 3 – Modeling Techniques – Examples include modeling techniques that illustrate the flexibility inherent in the feature-based parametric modeling of DesignModeler. We consider the use of Parameters, other CAD systems, as well as Surface and Line models.

Chapter 4 – Simulation - In this Chapter we consider stress response of a plate with a central hole, stress response to various FEM mesh densities, and the use of convergence criteria for controlling solution accuracy.

Chapter 5 – Simulation II - This chapter covers stress and deflection simulation response of some three-dimensional solids representative of typical mechanical parts. We consider the simulation of a Pressure Vessel, an Angle Bracket, and a Clevis Yoke.

Chapter 6 – Wizards & Tools - ANSYS Simulation provides a number of Tools and Wizards to assist with successful simulation projects. This Chapter illustrates the use of these typical applications. In particular we discuss the use of Wizards for simulation problem setup and Tools for simulation result assessment.

Chapter 7 – Heat Transfer & Thermal Stress - In this chapter we demonstrate the use of ANSYS Simulation for determining temperature distributions for conduction/convection problems and subsequently employing temperature distributions to find thermal stresses.

Chapter 8 – Surface & Line Models – Discussed here are structural and thermal simulation response problems that can be analyzed with surface models or with line models. These include: Plane Stress, Plane Strain or Axisymmetric problems, Plate (shell) problems, as well as Line-body (beam element) problems.

Chapter 9 – Natural Frequencies & Buckling Loads - In this Chapter we discuss the use of ANSYS Simulation to determine the natural frequencies and normal modes of structural parts and systems. The determination of buckling load estimates for such objects is also covered. In particular we illustrate the determination of Natural Frequencies, corresponding Mode Shapes, and Buckling Load estimates.

The chapters are necessarily of varying length and can be worked through from start to finish. Those with previous ANSYS Workbench experience may want to skip around a bit as needs and interests dictate. Also note that a solid modeler other than DesignModeler can be used in many of the tutorials.

I-4   THE ANSYS Workbench INTERFACE

Figure I-1 shows the ANSYS Workbench interface with options across the top that you select to start a **New Project, Geometry**, **Simulation**, **Finite Element**, **Advanced CFD** or **Meshing** session.

Alternatively, the **pull-down menu** allows you to select the type of file to be opened from **Workbench Projects, Simulations, DesignModeler Geometry, DesignXplorer Studies, Finite Element Models** or **Meshing** models. Files relevant to the pull-down selection are listed in order of most recently opened for easy access.

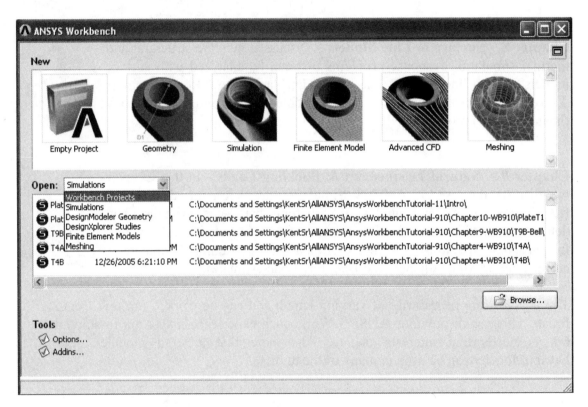

Figure I-1 ANSYS Workbench Interface.

In addition one may use the **Browse** option to locate and open an existing file.

A **Workbench Project** can consist of a **DesignModeler file**; a DesignModeler file together with its associated **Simulation file**; or Modeling plus Simulation plus **Optimization files**, etc., as shown in the next figure.

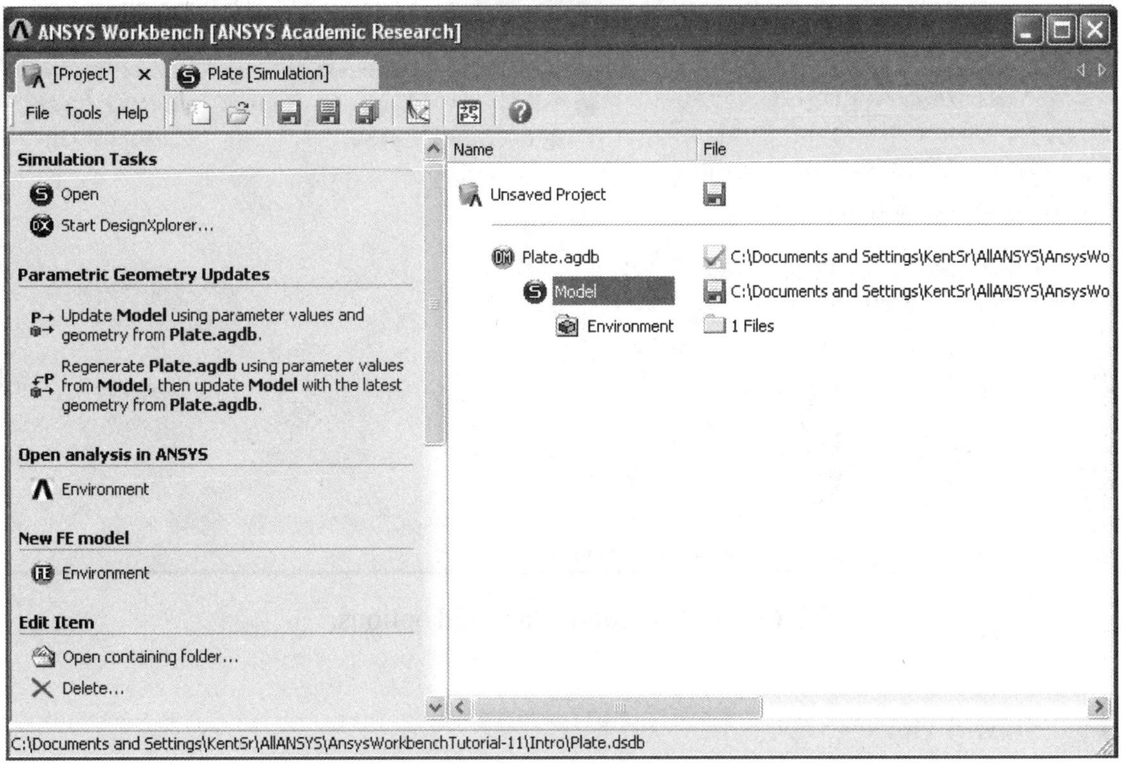

Figure I-2 ANSYS Workbench Project interface.

To open an item, select the file in the right-hand portion of the screen and select open on the left side. **Module Tabs** along the top of the screen allow you to switch between applications.

Also note in the figure above the two-way communication and update available between the modules. "Update Model using parameter values and geometry from Plate.agdb". Here **agdb** is the file extension for DesignModeler; **dsdb** is the extension for Simulation files, etc.

This feature allows changes made in one module to be immediately incorporated in the model for another module; more on this later in the tutorials.

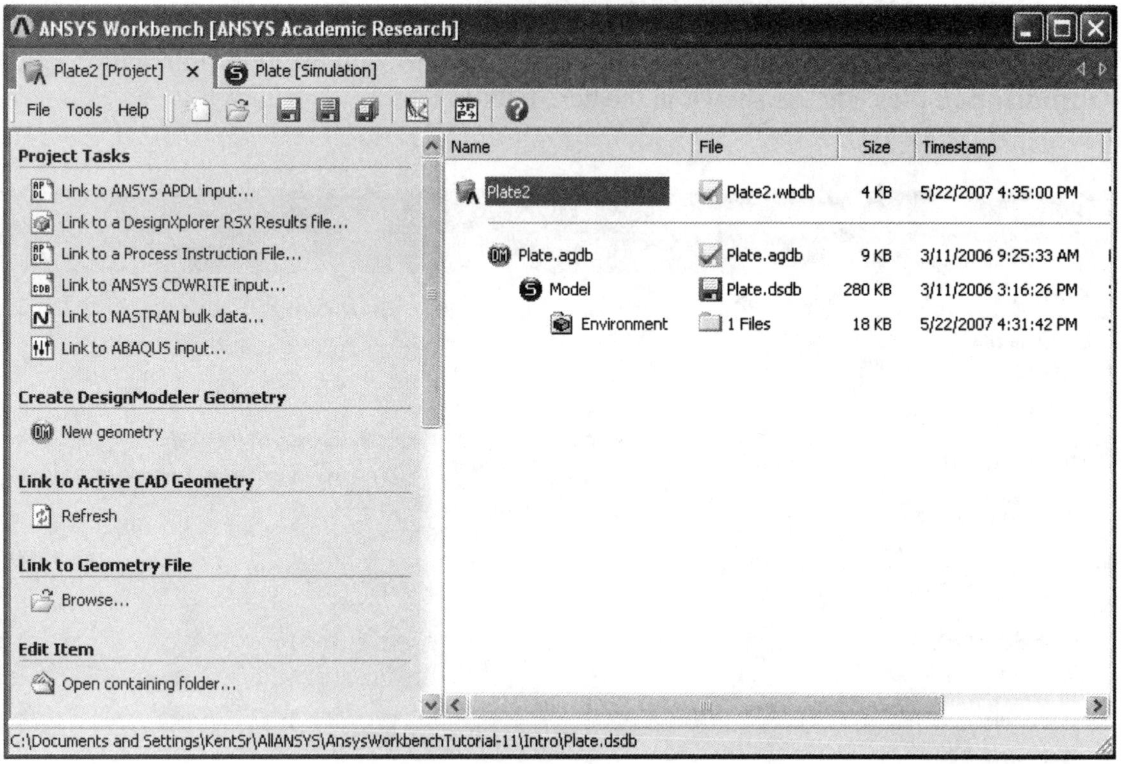

Figure I-3 Module tabs and options.

I-5 SUMMARY

The tutorials in this book explain some of the many engineering problem solution options available in ANSYS Workbench. It is important to remember that while practically anyone can learn which buttons to push to make the program work, the user must also give careful consideration to the assumptions inherent in the modeling process and give equally careful evaluation of the computed results.

In short, model building and output evaluation based upon the sound fundamental principles of engineering and physics are the keys to using any program such as ANSYS Workbench correctly and successfully.

Chapter 1

Solid Modeling Fundamentals

1-1 OVERVIEW

A simple L-shaped cross section is used to introduce basic solid modeling concepts with ANSYS DesignModeler. These tutorials explore solid modeling by:

- ◆ Extruding

- ◆ Revolving

- ◆ Sweeping

A number of additional parametric, feature-based modeling possibilities and formulations are demonstrated in this chapter.

1-2 INTRODUCTION

Solid modeling can be accomplished in a number of ways, and one favorite method involves starting with a two-dimensional shape and manipulating it to create a solid. That is the approach we will use for many of the object models created in this book. Figure 1-1 shows an L-shaped cross section that has been variously **extruded**, **revolved**, or **swept along a curve** to produce the solid object models shown.

Figure 1-1 Extruding, revolving, sweeping an L-shaped section.

In the following we use this simple L-shaped section to illustrate the three fundamental solid modeling approaches mentioned above.

1-3   TUTORIAL 1A – EXTRUSION

Follow the steps below to create a solid model of an extrusion with an L-shaped cross section.

1.   Start ANSYS Workbench

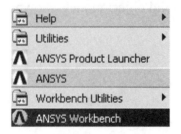

Figure 1-2 Start ANSYS Workbench in Windows.

The startup menu allows you to retrieve old files, begin a new DesignModeler geometry, start a Simulation or initiate a New Project. Select **New geometry**.

2.   Select **New > Geometry**

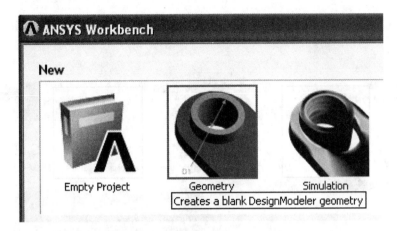

Figure 1-3 ANSYS Workbench startup menu.

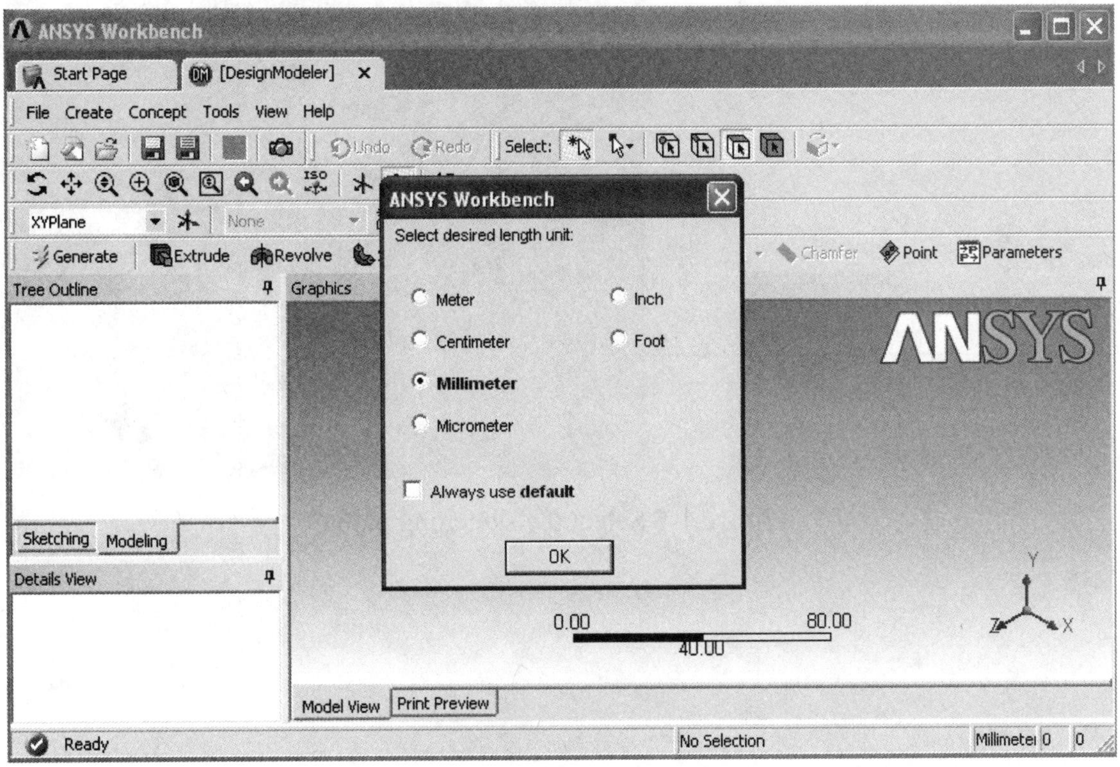

Figure 1-4 DesignModeler interface.

3.   **Select OK** – To work in millimeter units.

We will **sketch** the L-shaped cross section on the XY Plane. Make it **35 mm high, 20 mm wide** with **5 mm thick legs**.

4.   **Select XYPlane** as in the figure below. Then **click** on the **Look at icon** to view the XYPlane.

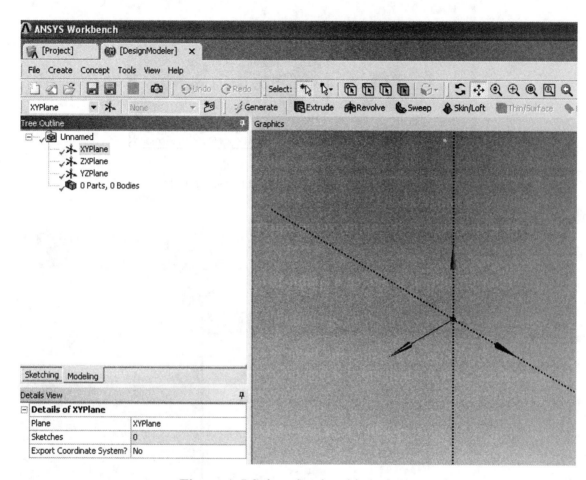

Figure 1-5 Select the sketching plane.

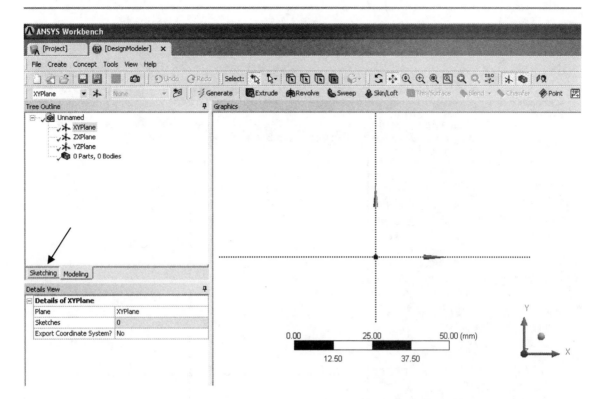

Figure 1-6 View of the sketching plane.

5. **Sketching**. Change from Modeling to Sketching by selecting the Sketching tab.

Select **Draw > Line**.

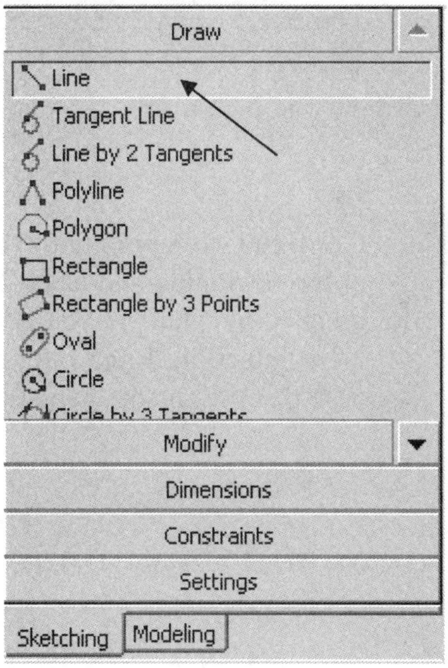

Figure 1-7 Sketching tools.

6. **Use the line drawing tool to draw the left vertical edge of the L-shape**. Left click at the beginning and again at the end of the line. The **V** indicates that you've got it exactly **vertical**.

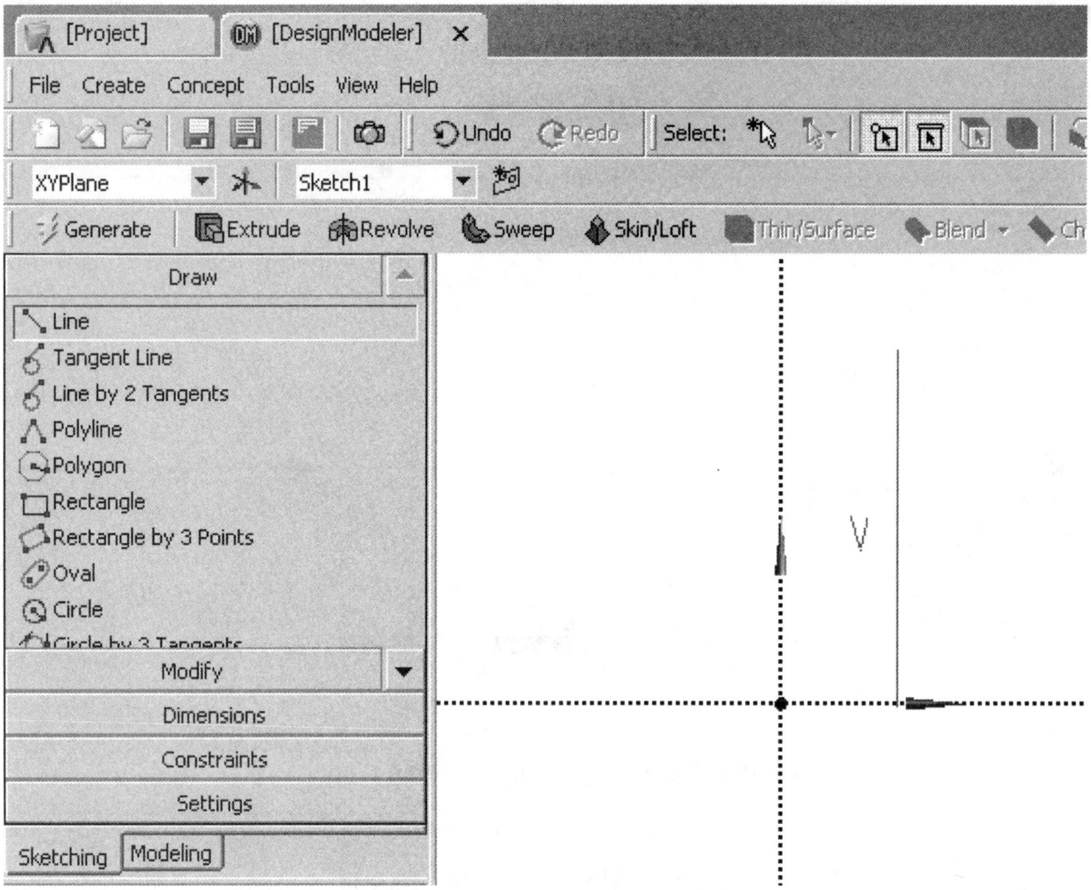

Figure 1-8 Left edge of the L-shape.

7. **Continue sketching** until you have something like what is shown below. Left click at the beginning and again at the end of each line. (Notice that the top edge is not quite horizontal.) If you need to change something, use **Undo** to back up or use **New Selection**, **Edge** filter to select a line, press the delete key and redraw it. Also note that the cursor changes shape when it is snapped onto another point or axis.

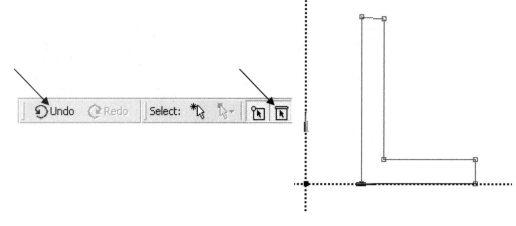

Figure 1-9 L-section sketch.

Use **constraint** options **horizontal** to make the top edge horizontal and **equal length** to make sure that the vertical and horizontal legs of the L are of the same thickness.

8.   Sketching > Constraints > Horizontal –
       Left click the top edge.

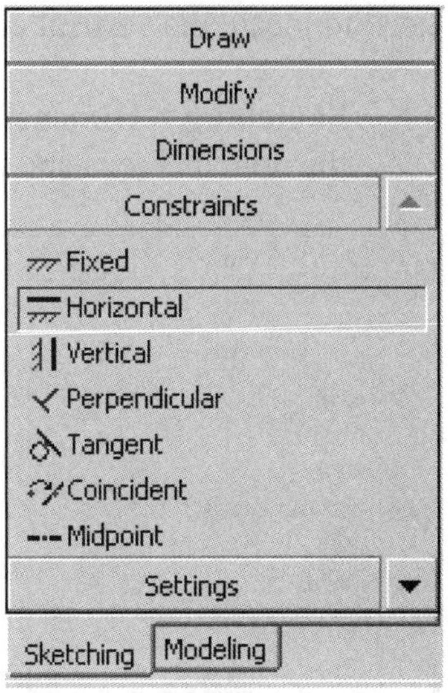

Figure 1-10 Sketching constraints.

9.   Sketching > Constraints > Equal length –
       Left click the top edge and then the right edge.

The figure is just a sketch so far, and a number of different dimensioning schemes could be used to produce the section we want. We will use the **Sketching > Dimensions** options to give it the desired properties.

10.   Sketching > Dimensions > General – Left click and (hold down the button) on the left vertical edge of the section and drag the dimension to a convenient location. The V1 means this is the first vertical dimension for this sketch.

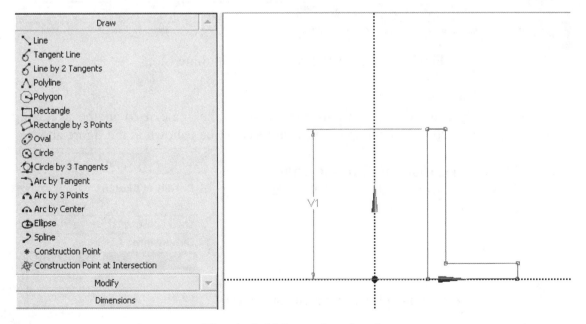

Figure 1-11 L-section sketch.

Continue with general dimensioning to specify H2 and V4. Don't dimension the top edge; it has to be equal to V4. The bottom edge is located directly on the X axis but we need to locate the vertical edge with respect to the Y axis.

11.   **Sketching > Dimensions > Horizontal** – Left click the left vertical edge then click the dotted Y axis and drag the H3 dimension to a convenient location.

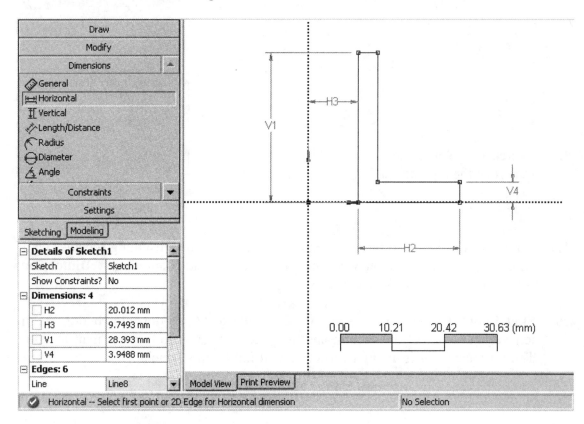

Figure 1-12 L-section sketch with all dimensions.

The current values for the dimensions depend upon the scale used in the sketching process, e.g., H2 = 20.012 mm in the **Details of Sketch1** box shown in the figure above.

12.   **Edit the dimensions to give them the desired values.** – Click on a value, enter the change and press return.

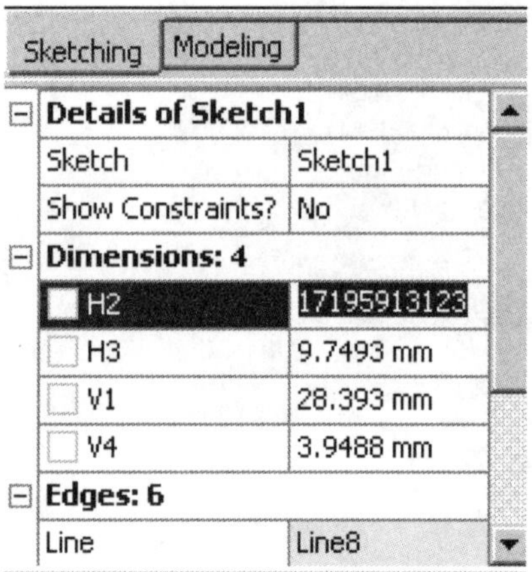

Figure 1-13 Default dimension values.

13. **View > Ruler** (Top menu) to turn off the ruler display. Use the middle mouse roller to zoom in and out.

To reposition the section on the screen, **right click** in the graphics area of the display and select one of the following options: **Cursor Mode, View,** or **Zoom to Fit**.

The result is shown in the figure below.

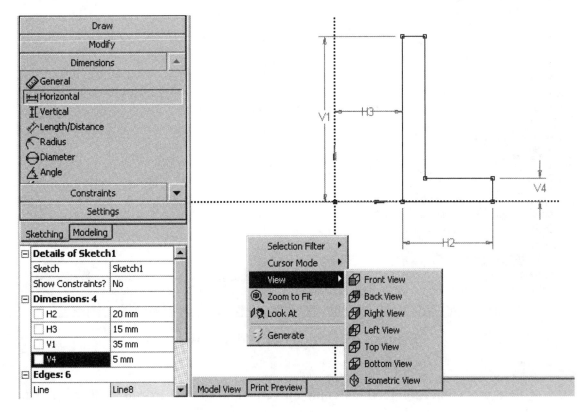

Figure 1-14 Edited dimension values.

To perform the extrusion, switch back from Sketching to Modeling. If it is not already highlighted, click **Sketch1** in the **Tree Outline** to highlight it.

14. **Modeling > Sketch1 > Extrude**

The L-shaped section will be extruded along the positive Z axis by the amount specified in the **Depth** field shown in the **Details of Extrude1** box (next figure). **Edit this value** (45 mm) to give the solid an extrude **depth** of **100 mm**.

The tree structure shows the components from which the solid model is created.

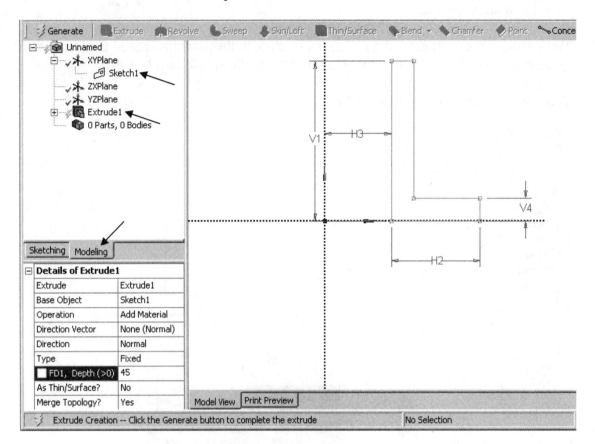

Figure 1-15 Section ready for extrusion.

15. **Click** the **Generate** icon to complete creation of the extruded shape model.

In the graphics area of the display, **right click > View > Isometric** (or hold down the middle mouse button and rotate the object).

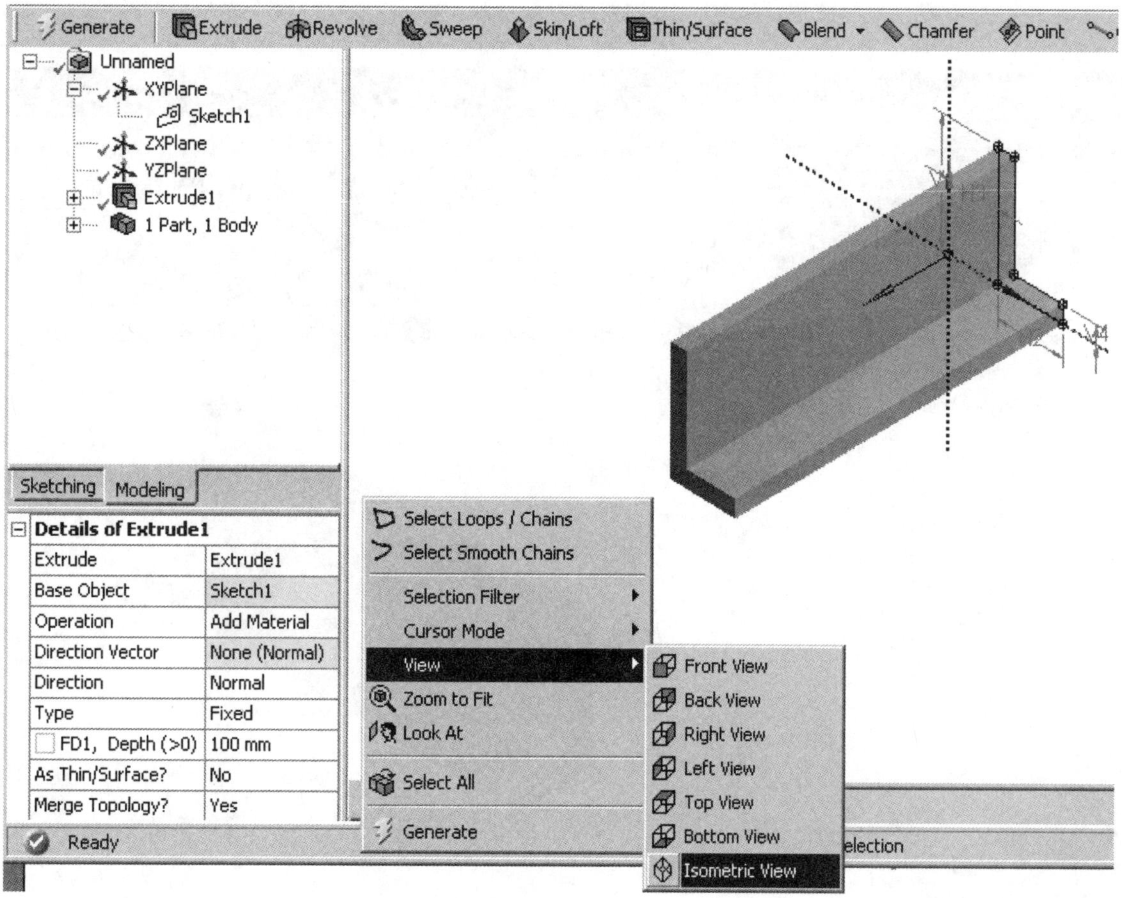

Figure 1-16 Extrusion.

16. **Click** on the **Display Plane** icon ![plane icon] to turn off the axes display and highlight the last item in the model tree (Solid) to display the volume, surface area, faces, edges and vertices in this model.

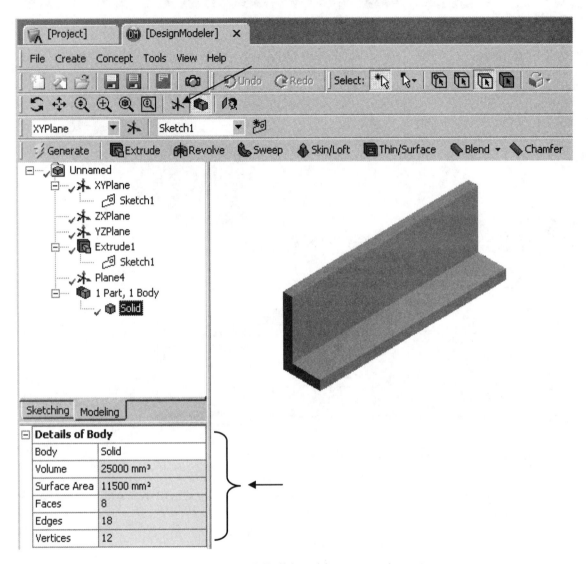

Figure 1-17 Solid and its properties.

17.   **Save your work** – Use the **Save As** option to save the extrusion using a name (e.g. T1A) and location of your choice.

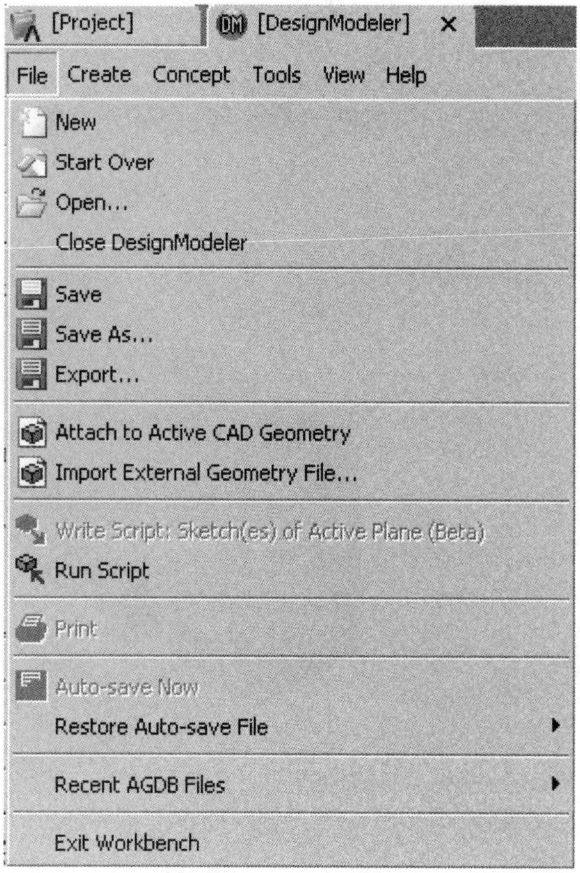

Figure 1-18 File menu.

Basic solid modeling notions have been used thus far to demonstrate creating a solid by extruding a two-dimensional section. In the next tutorial we will revolve the same L-shape to create a solid of revolution.

1-4   TUTORIAL 1B – REVOLUTION

We can reuse the extrusion model after it has been safely saved somewhere. Start from the screen shown below if the extrusion is still in memory, or start Workbench and reload the extrusion.

First modify the tree structure.

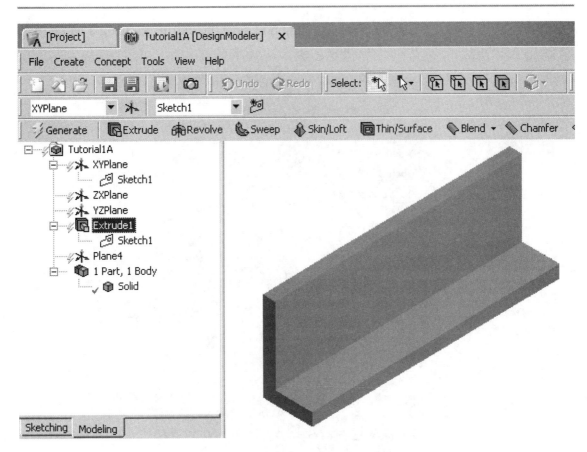

Figure 1-19 Select the extrusion.

1.   **Click on Extrude1** and **press Delete**. Click **Yes** to the query. The extrusion is deleted and the new tree structure shows 0 Parts and 0 Bodies.

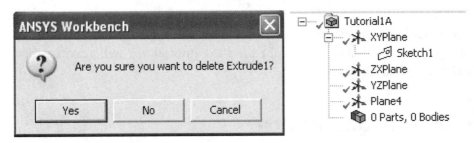

Figure 1-20 Delete the extrusion.

2.   Use **Save As** to save this work using a **new file name**, say **Tutorial1B**.

3.   **Click** on **Sketch1**, the **Display Plane** icon and the **Look at Plane** icon

We obtain the view of the same sketch we had earlier.

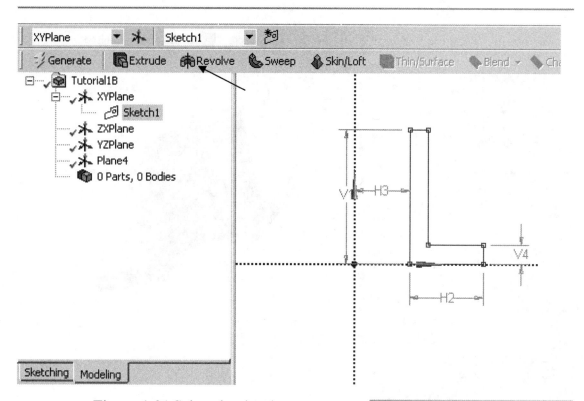

Figure 1-21 Select the sketch.

4. Be sure **Sketch1 is highlighted** and **click Revolve**.

5. **Click Axis > Select the Y axis > Apply** in **Details of Revolve1 box** (below right).

6. **Select Angle > Enter 120 deg**.

7. **Click Generate** [⫶ Generate]

The L-shaped section is rotated about the Y axis by 120 degrees to create the solid of revolution shown next. **Direction** options change the rotation direction.

Figure 1-22 Revolve1 tree.

Details of Revolve1	
Revolve	Revolve1
Base Object	Sketch1
Axis	Apply Cancel
Operation	Add Material
Direction	Normal
☐ FD1, Angle (>0)	120 °
As Thin/Surface?	No
Merge Topology?	Yes

| Generate | Extrude | Revolve | Sweep | Skin/Loft | Thin/Surface | Blend ▾ |

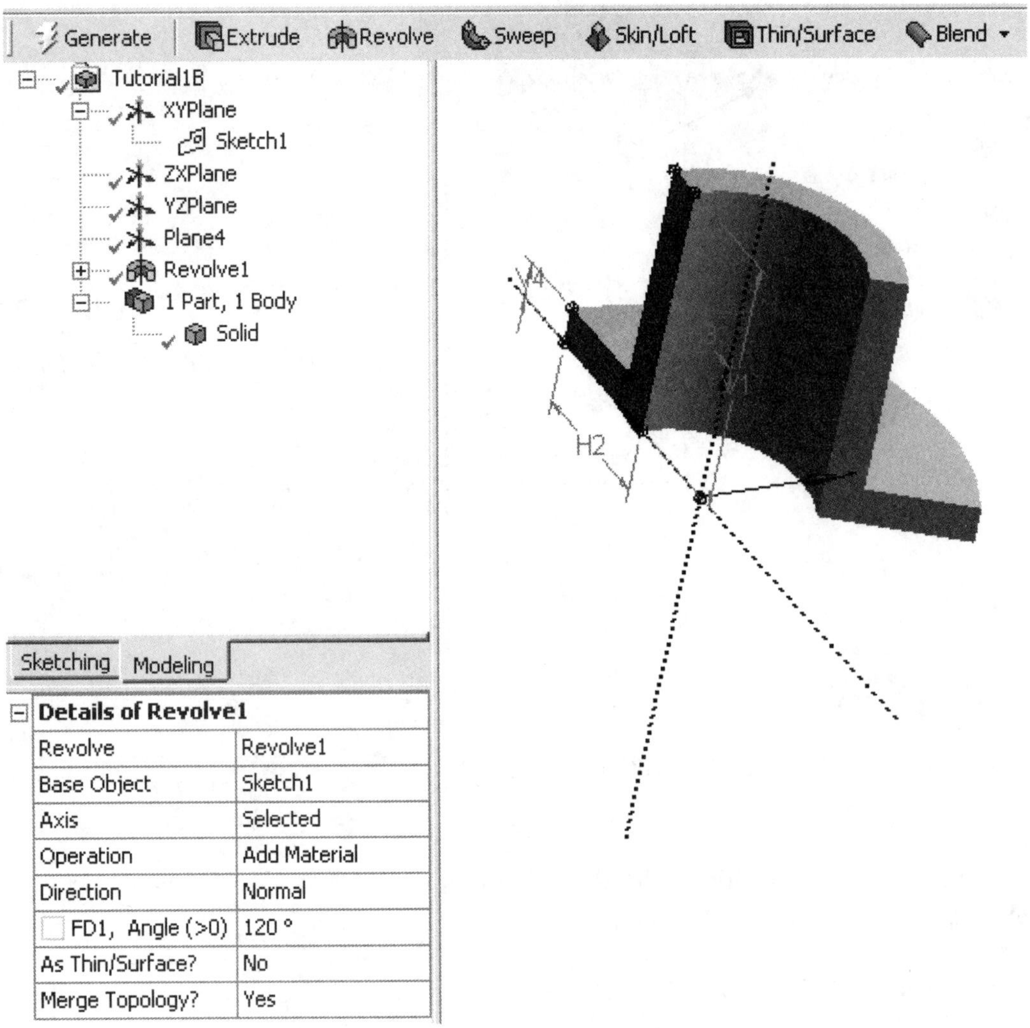

- ☑ Tutorial1B
  - ☑ XYPlane
    - Sketch1
  - ☑ ZXPlane
  - ☑ YZPlane
  - ☑ Plane4
  - ☑ Revolve1
  - ☑ 1 Part, 1 Body
    - ☑ Solid

Sketching Modeling

Details of Revolve1	
Revolve	Revolve1
Base Object	Sketch1
Axis	Selected
Operation	Add Material
Direction	Normal
FD1, Angle (>0)	120 °
As Thin/Surface?	No
Merge Topology?	Yes

Figure 1-23 Solid of revolution.

8.   **Save** to archive your work.

Next we will take the same cross section and sweep it along an arbitrary path to create the third kind of modeling discussed in this chapter.

1-5   TUTORIAL 1C – SWEEP

1.   **Start ANSYS Workbench. Sketch the 20 x 35 mm L-shape on the XYPlane** as before. We get the figure shown below. Save this file as tutorial1c or T1C or something convenient.

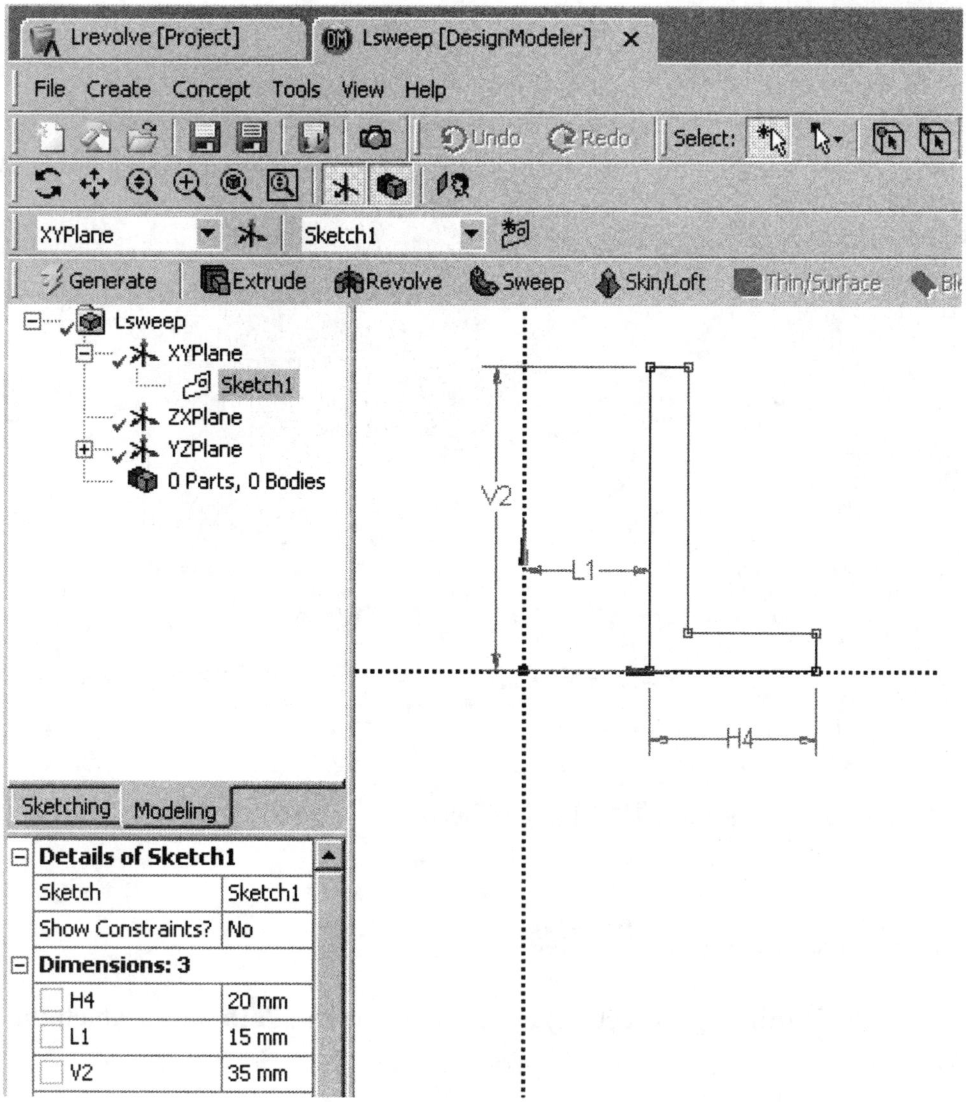

Figure 1-24 Cross section sketch.

We now want to sketch a path along which the L-shape will be swept to produce a solid. We will use a simple curve to define this path.

2.   **Select the YZPlane** and **Select Sketching**.

3.   **Use the Line option to sketch a simple two-segment line in the YZPlane** similar to the one below.

Turn on the **Ruler** and use the **middle scroll wheel** to **Zoom** out so that your line is about

150 to 200 mm in length. If you make a mistake, click the New Select button [Select:], click the line and press delete. (I deleted several before settling on the one shown, so my sketch is numbered Sketch6. Not to worry if your number is different.)

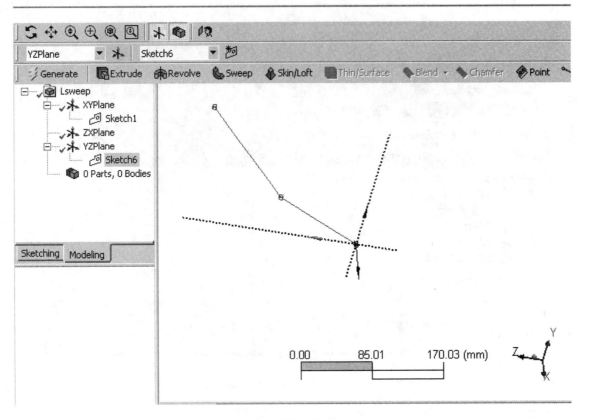

Figure 1-25 Path of sweep.

4. **Select Sweep** to create the solid.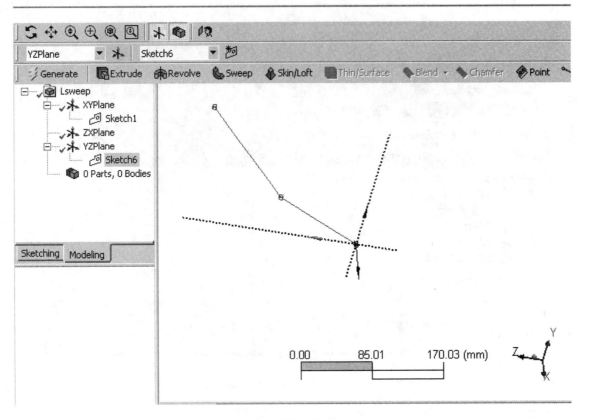

We need to specify the **Profile** (cross section) of the solid and the **Path** along which the profile will be swept.

5. In the Tree Outline click **Sketch1**, then in **Details of Sweep1** > click on **Profile > Apply**.

6. In the Tree Outline click **Sketch6**, then in **Details of Sweep1** > **Path** > **Apply** (Sketch6 in the figure above; your path sketch number may be different.)

See the figure below.

Details of Sweep11	
Sweep	Sweep11
Profile	Apply | Cancel
Path	Not selected
Operation	Add Material
Alignment	Path Tangent
☐ FD4, Scale (>0)	1
☐ FD5, Turns	0
As Thin/Surface?	No
Merge Topology?	No

Details of Sweep11	
Sweep	Sweep11
Profile	Sketch1
Path	Sketch6
Operation	Add Material
Alignment	Path Tangent
☐ FD4, Scale (>0)	1
☐ FD5, Turns	0
As Thin/Surface?	No
Merge Topology?	No

Figure 1-26 Profile and path selection.

7.   **Generate** to obtain the solid shown next.

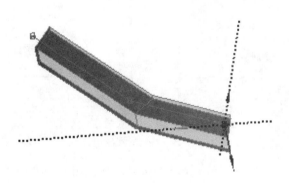

Figure 1-27 Swept solid.

Notice that the profile is not necessarily perpendicular to the path as when we used **Extrude** to create a solid. Also the path can be a more complex curve as in the example of Figure 1-1 where a spline was used for the path.

1-6 SKETCHING

A wide variety of sketching tools are available to help in creating two-dimensional sections. We used the line drawing option and the equality constraint option in the tutorials above. Some of the other sketching features are shown below.

The next illustration shows the **Draw** and **Modify** options. The **Draw** menu includes **Line**, **Tangent Line**, **Line by two Tangents**, **Polyline**, **Polygon**, **Rectangle**, **Oval**, **Circle**, **Arc**, **Ellipse**, **Spline** and **Construction Point**.

The **Modify** menu includes **Fillet**, **Chamfer**, **Trim**, **Extend**, **Split**, **Drag**, **Cut**, **Copy**, **Paste**, **Move**, **Replicate** and **Offset**.

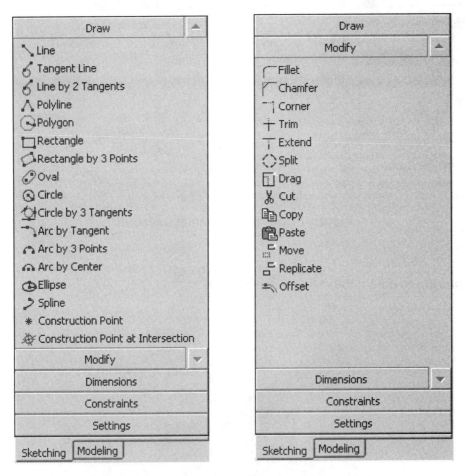

Figure 1-28 Draw and Modify sketching options.

We will have the occasion to illustrate the use of many of these options in what follows.

Menu selections for assigning **Dimensions** and enforcing **Constraints** are shown in the next figure.

In addition to a **General** dimension specification, dimensions can be assigned which are **Horizontal, Vertical, Length/Distance, Radius/Diameter,** or an **Angle**. Select **Semi-Automatic Dimensioning** if you want DesignModeler to select a dimensioning scheme automatically. You then have the option to accept, add or delete dimensions to meet your specific design needs.

Constraints that can be enforced for sketching entities include **Horizontal, Vertical, Perpendicular, Tangent, Coincident, Midpoint, Symmetric, Parallel, Concentric, Equal Radius, Equal Length** and **Equal Distance**.

As sketching proceeds DesignModeler will attempt to detect and enforce constraints that seem to be part of the design intent of the sketch. The **Auto Constraints** option allows you to turn these on and off as desired. **Cursor** triggered constraints are local, while **Global** constraints relate to all entities in the sketching plane.

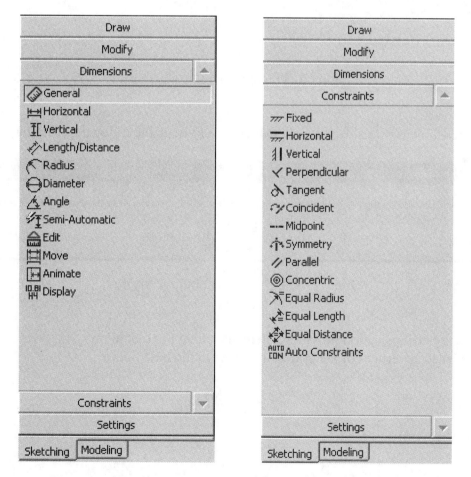

Figure 1-29 Dimensions and Constraints sketching options.

Dimensioning is the process of defining how geometry is to be constructed.

In that regard, sketches must be **unambiguously** defined; that is, they cannot have too many dimensions or too few dimensions specified. The figure below shows two different dimensioning schemes for a simple shape.

H6
V8
V9
H1
L3
L4
V2
H1

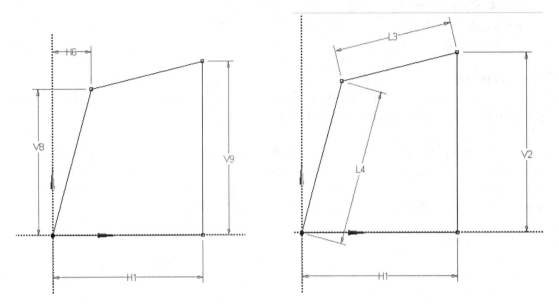

Figure 1-30 Dimensioning schemes.

If you over-dimension a sketch, DesignModeler will issue the following warning:

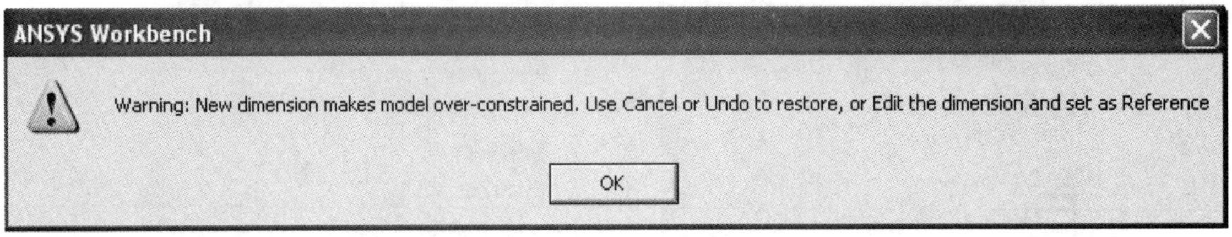

ANSYS Workbench
Warning: New dimension makes model over-constrained. Use Cancel or Undo to restore, or Edit the dimension and set as Reference
OK

Figure 1-31 Over-constraint message.

Finally, the **Settings** option provides a **grid** sketching aid that allows you create drawing entities placed at vertices of the grid as indicated in the next figure.

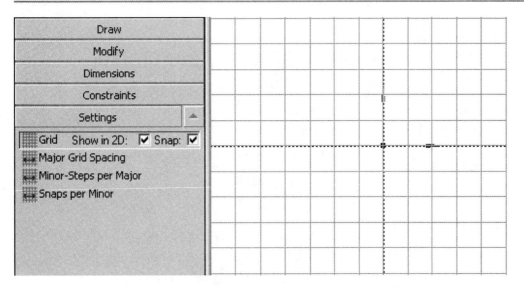

Figure 1-32 Settings options and a sketching grid.

1-7　SUMMARY

Three tutorials in Chapter 1 introduce basic solid model creation in ANSYS DesignModeler and provide examples from which more complex shapes can be developed. In the next chapter we will extend these ideas and introduce additional modeling features.

1-8　PROBLEMS

1-1　Identify some common objects (such as an unsharpened pencil, drinking glass, etc.) and develop models of them using the ideas presented in this chapter.

1-2　Use a "Z" shaped section to create a solid by extrusion, another by revolving, and another by sweeping. Select your own units and dimensions.

1-3　Measure the exterior dimensions of a light bulb, estimate the wall thickness of the glass and base, and create a model by revolving the sketch.

1-4　Create the shape shown and extrude it to form a solid. Choose your own dimensions. Use the Sketching **Trim** option to help in the sketch development. Save it and we'll use it in a simulation problem later in the text.

Figure P1-4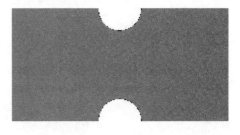

NOTES:

Chapter 2

Placed Features, Assembly

2-1   OVERVIEW

In this chapter we illustrate DesignModeler creation of features whose **shape** is **predetermined**. Among these are

- ♦ Holes

- ♦ Rounds

- ♦ Chamfers

- ♦ Patterns

In addition to these topics, at the end of the chapter we illustrate simple **assembly modeling** in ANSYS DesignModeler.

2-2   INTRODUCTION

Feature-based solid modeling involves the creation of part models by combining various features. The features illustrated in Chapter 1 are sometimes called **sketched features** because they were based upon sketched cross sections we created. Sketched features can have virtually any shape we desire. The basic parts of Chapter 1 can also be called **base features** since we started from scratch each time and created a new part.

We can add features to base features to create more complex parts. If these added features have predetermined shapes they are often called **placed features** because all we need to do is specify the location or placement of the new feature on an existing base feature.

The figure below shows the L-shaped Extrusion created earlier with a **hole**, a **round** and a **chamfer** added to it. This demonstrates the manner in which features can be added to a base feature in order to create more complicated and useful parts with the shapes desired for specific tasks.

The tutorials that follow illustrate how to add these placed features to the basic parts created in Chapter 1.

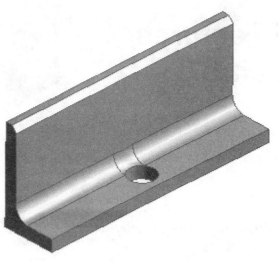

Figure 2-1 Extrusion with placed features.

2-3   TUTORIAL 2A – ADDING A HOLE TO THE EXTRUSION

Follow the steps below to cut a hole in the top face of the short leg of the Chapter 1 extrusion.

Start ANSYS Workbench and reload the L-section Extrusion

1.   **ANSYS > Workbench > DesignModeler Geometry > Browse > Tutorial1A** (or the file name you chose)

Now save this file under a new name for this tutorial

2.   **File > Save As > Tutorial2A** (or another name you select)

We want to create the hole on the top surface of the short leg of the extrusion. We will create a new plane on which to place the circle that generates the hole.

3.   **Selection Filter: Model Faces (3D)**

4.   **Click on the top surface of the short leg.**

Figure 2-2 Surface selected.

5.   Create > New Plane (from the top menu)

A new plane is added to the tree structure (Plane6 in this illustration; your plane number may be different) and an axis system is provided.

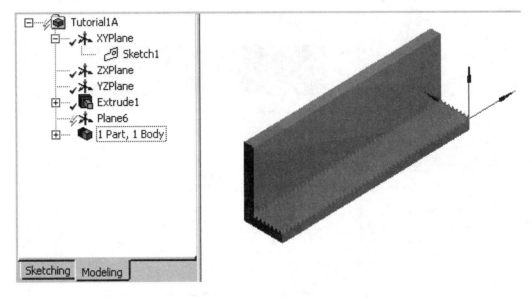

Figure 2-3 New plane is created.

6.   Click Generate Generate

7.   Select Plane6 > then **click** on the **Look at icon** to view the Plane6.

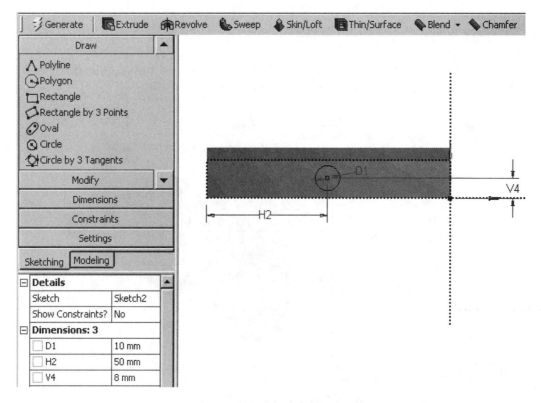

Figure 2-4 'Look at' new plane.

We want to place a **10 mm diameter** circular hole **half way** along the length of the 100 mm leg and **8 mm** from the edge.

8.   Sketching > Circle Draw a circle on the top face as shown in the figure below.

Figure 2-5 Circle sketch.

9. **Dimensions > Diameter** – Place D1 as shown.

10. **Dimensions > Horizontal** – Place H2 as shown.

11. **Dimensions > Vertical** – Place V4 as shown.

Edit the dimension values to 10 mm, 50 mm, and 8 mm as shown in the figure above. (The number attached to each dimension, the 2 in H2, is an internal numbering scheme and depends upon the sketching sequence. Your numbers may be different.)

12. **Modeling > Click** on **Sketch** in the tree structure (Sketch2 in the figure)

13. **Extrude** 　Extrude

14. **Operation > Cut Material**

(Remove material instead of adding it.)

15. **Type > Through All**

(Cut completely through the thickness, through all.)

Details of Extrude3	
Extrude	Extrude3
Base Object	Sketch2
Operation	Add Material ▼
Direction Vector	Add Material
Direction	Cut Material
Type	Imprint Faces
	Add Frozen
☐ FD1, Depth (>0)	30 mm
As Thin/Surface?	No
Merge Topology?	Yes

Details of Extrude3	
Extrude	Extrude3
Base Object	Sketch2
Operation	Cut Material
Direction Vector	None (Normal)
Direction	Normal
Type	Fixed ▼
☐ FD1, Depth (>0)	Fixed
As Thin/Surface?	Through All
Target Bodies	To Next
	To Faces
Merge Topology?	To Surface

Figure 2-6 Extrude details.

16. **Generate** (to complete the feature.) Generate

The completed hole is shown in the next illustration.

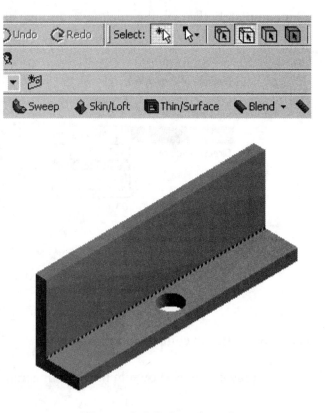

Figure 2-7 Circular hole.

Keep this part in memory since we have more work to do on it.

2-4   TUTORIAL 2B – ADDING A ROUND TO THE EXTRUSION

A gradual transition between surfaces is variously called a **fillet**, a **round** or a **blend**. DesignModeler uses the blend terminology, and a blend is a placed feature. In this tutorial we will place a fixed radius blend at the inside corner of the L where the top surface of the short leg meets the inside vertical surface.

Save your part using a new name.

1.   File > Save As > Tutorial2B

Set the selection filter.

2.   Selection Filter: Edges

3.   Select the inside edge of the part.

Figure 2-8 Select the edge.

4. **Create > Fixed Radius Blend**

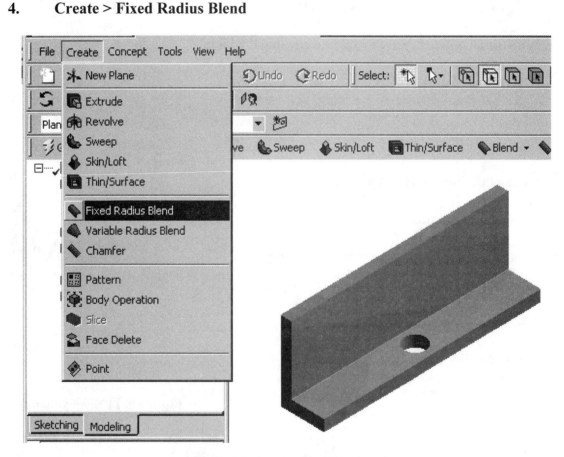

Figure 2-9 Selecting the blend option.

5. **Geometry > Apply**
(Use the default 3 mm radius.)

6. **Generate**

Figure 2-10 The blend completed.

2-5   TUTORIAL 2C – ADDING A CHAMFER TO THE EXTRUSION

Creating the chamfer is pretty much like creating the blend.

1.   **Save As > Tutorial2C**
      (Save the part under a new name if you wish)

2.   **Selection Filter: Edges**

3.   **Select the top inside edge of the part**.

4.   **Create > Chamfer**

5.   **Details of Chamfer > Geometry > Apply**
      (Change the sizing to 2.5 mm.)

6.   **Generate**

7.   **Save your work**.

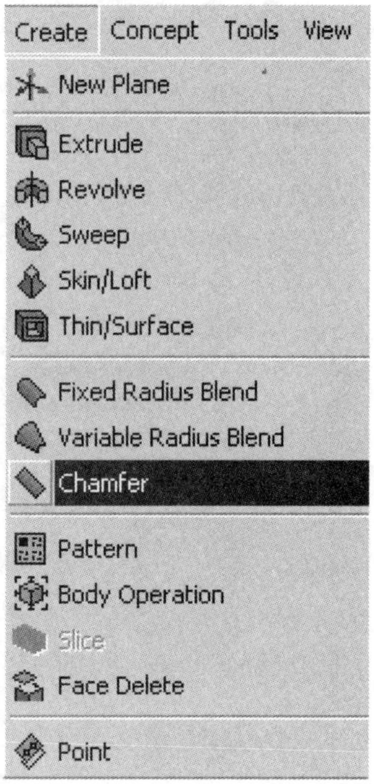

Figure 2-11 Select chamfer.

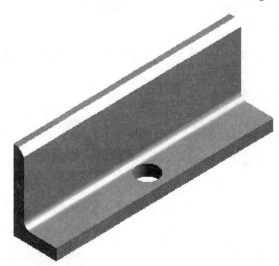

Figure 2-12 The chamfer completed.

2-6   TUTORIAL 2D – PATTERNS

Next we will use a **pattern operation** to create a solid model of circular plate with a symmetric bolt pattern. First extrude a circle to create a **50 mm diameter** plate that is **10 mm** in **thickness** as shown in the next figure. Start a new part file.

1. **Sketch a 50 mm diameter circle** with center at the origin of the **XYPlane**. Click on the sketch then on **Extrude** and set the extrusion depth to be **10 mm**. Click Generate to complete the base feature disk.

2. **Sketching > Dimensions > Display >** check both **Name** and **Value**.

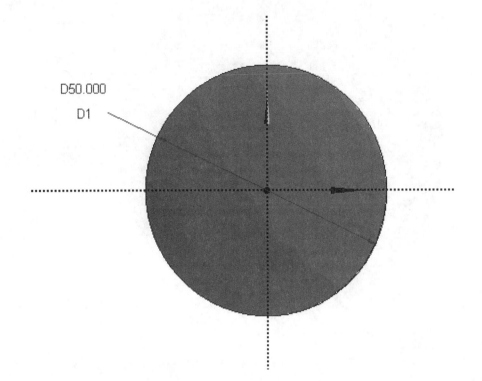

Figure 2-13 Base feature disk.

3. **Create > New Plane** Create a new plane for sketching on the **top or bottom surface** of the base disk

4. **Sketch an 8mm diameter circle** on this plane. Dimension as shown in the next figure.

5. **Sketch an 18 mm line** from the **center of the base feature** to the **center of the small circle**. Dimension as shown below. We'll use this line for angular reference.

6. **Locate the line with an angular dimension**. Click first on the horizontal axis, then on the line. Drag to place the dimension as shown.

7. **Switch to Modeling. Select the sketch and then Extrude > Cut Material > Through All** to create a hole.

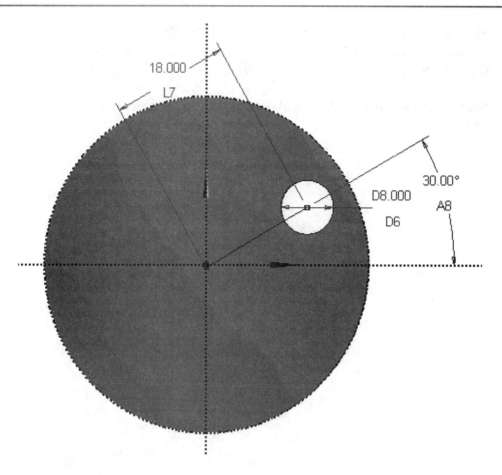

Figure 2-14 Placement of small hole.

8. **Add a 1 mm chamfer to the top edge of the 8 mm hole.** See figure on next page.

9. **Sketch a short line along the Z axis** in the ZXPlane. Sketch3. We will use this for the pattern angular direction reference later.

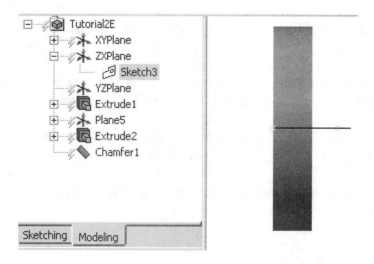

Figure 2-15 Create a line along the Z axis.

10. **Click Selection Filter: Model Faces (3D)**

11. **Select the inside surface of the hole**; then **Ctrl > Select** the **surface** of the **chamfer** so both items will be in the pattern.

Figure 2-16 Select the chamfer and hole.

12. **Create > Pattern**

13. **Geometry > Apply** (in details of Pattern1).

14. **Pattern Type > Circular**

15. **Selection Filter: Edges**

16. **Axis > Click on Sketch3** and select the **short Z axis line > Apply**

17. **Angle > Evenly Spaced**

18. **Number of Copies > 6** (Creates 7 instances total.)

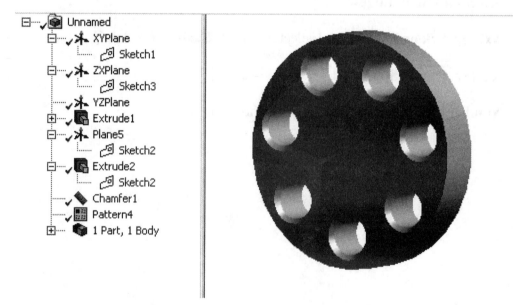

Figure 2-17 Pattern parameters.

19.   **Click Generate**

The resulting hole pattern is shown next. The **selected edge** is used as the **axis** for determining the positive direction of incrementing the angular placement (taken according to the right-hand rule).

Figure 2-18 Circular pattern of chamfered holes.

Once again don't be surprised if the suffix numbers of the entities (Sketch, Extrude, etc) in your tree structures differ from those in the figures. Same with the lighting bolts indicating need for generation. Some experimentation with generation, views, etc. was conducted to obtain the figures presented here. If you have a problem, delete the problem object in the tree and start again.

(The positive direction for incrementing the angular placement is along the selected edge according to the right-hand rule. **Change Evenly Spaced to 35 degrees > 6 Copies** and see what solid is produced.)

Linear patterns are created using similar steps. The direction of the pattern can be along an existing edge or perpendicular to a surface.

2-7 TUTORIAL 2E – CLEVIS ASSEMBLY

The next figure shows an assembly model of the clevis device that is the subject of this final tutorial in this chapter.

Figure 2-19 Clevis assembly.

1.   Start DesignModeler, Select Inches Units, and start sketching on the XYPlane

The yoke is 4.5 inches in overall length, 2.5 inches at its widest point, and the opening is 2.0 inches in width. Use the sketching tools to create the figure shown next with dimensions as indicated. **Arc by Tangent, Modify > Trim**, and other tools will come in handy. If you make a mistake, just delete the item in question and redraw, or just start over.

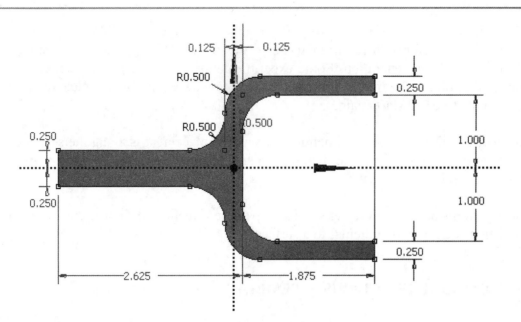

Figure 2-20 Clevis sketch.

2.   **Create the sketch** shown above and **extrude it symmetrically 0.5 inch**. (Total height will be 1.0 inch, 0.5 above the sketch plane, 0.5 inch below.)

3.   **Create a new sketching plane** on one of the yoke fingers and **sketch the opening** shown. The two semicircles are separated by 0.25 inch. Tangent line and trim will be useful.

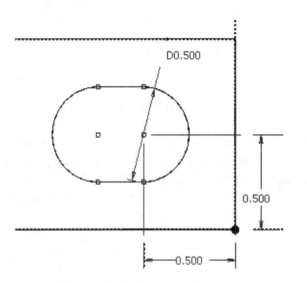

Figure 2-21 Slot sketch.

4.   **Extrude this sketch through all, removing material.**

We obtain the solid model shown next.

Figure 2-22 Complete clevis.

To this we want to add the stem and pin to complete the assembly. First **hide the clevis**.

5.   **1 Parts, 1 Body > Solid > Right Click > Hide Body**

6.   We'll create the **stem** first. **View the XZ sketch plane** and **sketch the rectangle and circle** below for creation of the **brick-shaped stem extrusion.** Use **General** for the linear dimension definitions.

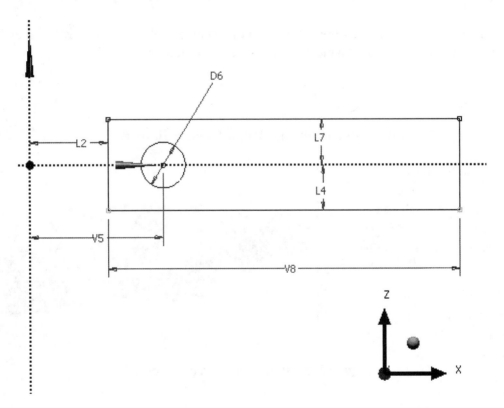

Figure 2-23 Stem sketch.

Refer to Figure 2-20 and give the L2 and V5 placements dimensions the values shown below.

Details of Sketch3	
Sketch	Sketch3
Show Constraints?	No
Dimensions: 6	
☐ D6	0.5 in
☐ L2	0.875 in
☐ L4	0.5 in
☐ L7	0.5 in
☐ V5	1.5 in
☐ V8	4 in

Figure 2-24 Stem sketch dimensions.

7.   **Switch to Modeling**, **Select the sketch** of the **Rectangle** with **Circle**, Click
       Extrude.

8.   **Details of Extrude > Operation > Add Frozen, Direction > Both – Symmetric**,
       and **Depth > 1.0** (See below.)

The **Add Frozen** option adds the stem as a new, separate object and does not merge the
new geometry into the existing clevis. The two parts remain separate.

9.   **Generate**

10.   **2 Parts, 2 Bodies > Solid** (Clevis) > **Right Click > Show Body**

Details of Extrude10	
Extrude	Extrude10
Base Object	Sketch3
Operation	Add Frozen
Direction Vector	None (Normal)
Direction	Both - Symmetric
Type	Fixed
☐ FD1, Depth (>0)	1 in
As Thin/Surface?	No
Merge Topology?	Yes

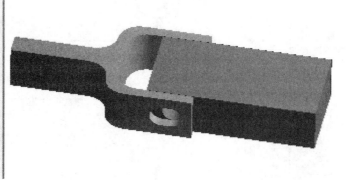

Figure 2-25 Stem extrusion and clevis.

Lastly we need to create the fastening pin that holds the assembly together. Create a new
plane to sketch on.

11.   **Click XZ Plane > Click** the **new plane icon** ✳ on the third line of icons >
       Generate

Figure 2-26 New plane icon.

12. **Right click on graphics screen > View > Bottom** to get the view shown below.

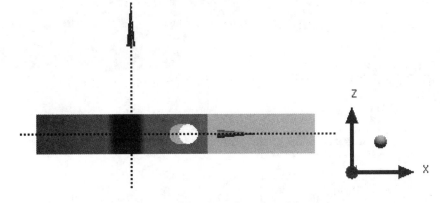

Figure 2-27 View for sketching pin.

13. **Sketch > Circle**

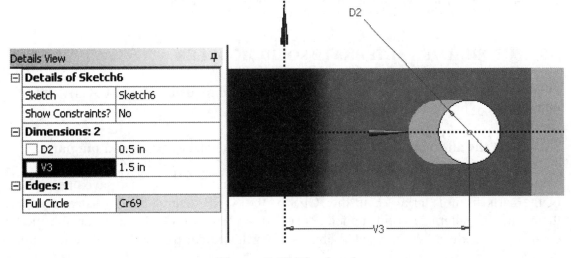

Figure 2-28 Pin sketch.

Put the center of the circle on the X Axis; Dimension its diameter and location from the Z Axis. Set the diameter to **0.5 inches** and the horizontal distance from the Z Axis to **1.5 inches**. (See Figure 2-20.)

Now create the pin extrusion using this sketch.

14. **Switch to Modeling**, **Select the sketch** of the **Circle**, Click **Extrude**.

15. **Details of Extrude > Operation > Add Frozen; Direction > Both – Symmetric; Depth > 1.25**

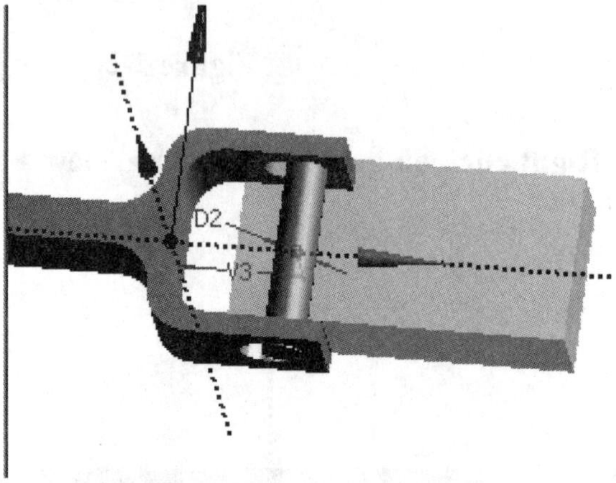

Figure 2-29 Final clevis, stem, pin assembly.

At any time use the middle mouse button to rotate the view so you can see the sketch plane with respect to the rest of the model and turn the axis and dimensions on/off by clicking the icon on the second row. ✳

16. **Save your work.** We'll use an assembly such as this later.

2-8   TUTORIAL 2F – ALTERNATE SOLID MODELER

Finally we outline the steps to utilize an alternate solid modeler (Pro/E, CATIA, etc.) for the creation of the clevis assembly.

1. **Start the alternate solid modeler and create the clevis, stem, and pin parts.**

You can start over completely in the alternate solid modeler or you can save one or more of the parts from Tutorial 2E in the IGES or the STEP neutral file format and import them into the alternate solid modeler. (To extract an individual part from the model created above, delete the unwanted objects from the model tree and save the remaining desired object with a new name.)

2. **Create** the **Assembly** in the **Alternate solid modeler.**

With the alternate solid modeler running and the assembly you created in the alternate modeler as the active session in that modeler, (Windows systems):

3. Start ANSYS DesignModeler

4. File > ▣ Attach to Active CAD Geometry > Generate ⌑ ⫶⁷ Generate

The next figure shows the clevis assembly as created in Pro/ENGINEER. In DesignModeler the stem and the pin parts were deleted and the clevis was saved as a file in the IGES format. The clevis IGES file was then imported into Pro/E and saved as a Pro/E 'prt' file. The stem and pin parts were created in Pro/E, and the assembly was created in Pro/E and opened as the active session in Pro/E. Finally the Pro/E assembly was attached in DesignModeler using steps 3 and 4 above.

Figure 2-30 Assembly attached from an active Pro/E session.

Another approach is to save the assembly in the alternate solid modeler as an IGES or STEP file then to import the IGES or STEP assembly file into DesignModeler.

IGES (**I**nitial **G**raphics **E**xchange **S**pecification) and STEP (**St**andard for the **E**xchange of **P**roduct Model Data) are industry agreed upon neutral file formats for the exchange of modeling information.

During installation of ANSYS Workbench, be sure to install the geometry interfaces to the alternate solid modelers you are using. For Pro/E, for example, it is necessary to indicate the path to the Pro/E executable.

2-9 SUMMARY

The three tutorials in Chapter 2 illustrate basic placed feature creation and simple assembly modeling in ANSYS DesignModeler. In the next chapter we will extend these ideas to more complex parts and introduce additional solid modeling options.

2-10   PROBLEMS

2-1   Use the ideas presented above to add holes, blends and chamfers to the parts you created as end-of-chapter problems for Chapter 1.

2-2   Create a linear pattern of holes in a straight line on a rectangular plate of your design.

2-3   Use the holes in the exercise above to create a multiple hole pattern in the other direction of the plate.

Figure P2-2   **Figure P2-3**

2-4   Create a solid model of the object shown using the dimensions on page 5-2.

2-5   Create a solid model of the object shown using the dimensions on page 8-12.

Figure P2-4   **Figure P2-5**

Chapter 3

Modeling Techniques

3-1 OVERVIEW

This Chapter discusses modeling techniques that illustrate the flexibility inherent in the feature-based parametric modeling of DesignModeler. We consider the use of

♦ Parameters

♦ Other CAD systems

♦ Surface and line models

3-2 INTRODUCTION

The defining dimensions in the sketches, extrusions, revolves, sweeps, and placed features discussed in the previous Chapters were described using fixed numerical values according to the situation. In **parametric design modeling** we wish to assign **parameters** to these quantities so that they can be varied to fit various design requirements. It is also possible to write equations that relate the required variation in certain parameters in terms of other parameters. For example, it might be important for a hole always to be centered in a bracket even if different designs require that the bracket width change with application. Tutorial 3A illustrates this use of parameters.

DesignModeler is a full-featured parametric design modeling system that provides for importation of models from other CAD systems and also allows the user to export models to other CAD systems. One vehicle for doing this is the use of the standard neutral file formats IGES (**I**nitial **G**raphics **E**xchange **S**pecification) and STEP (**St**andard for the **E**xchange of **P**roduct Model Data), agreed upon standards for the transfer of models between systems.

Parts in DesignModeler are composed of Bodies whereas Assemblies may be composed of Parts. We illustrate these concepts also in this Chapter.

3-3   TUTORIAL 3A – PARAMETERS

The steps below illustrate the use of **parameters** and **parametric equations** to define relationships required for the execution of a particular design. The part in question is shown in the figure below. Here we wish the long leg of the bracket always to be 1.5 times the short leg. The bracket thickness is to be constant. These invariant design requirements are accomplished using parametric relations in DesignModeler.

1.   **Start ANSYS Workbench** and use **polyline** to **sketch on the XYPlane an L-section 25 mm x 15 mm x 2 mm thick. Sketching > Dimensions > Display** check **Name** and **Value**.

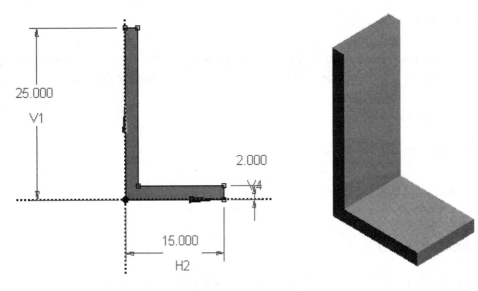

Figure 3-1 Bracket.

2.   **Select the sketch** and **Extrude it 10 mm** (Save a copy of this model for use later.)

Details of Sketch1	
Sketch	Sketch1
Show Constraints?	No
Dimensions: 3	
☐ H2	15 mm
☐ V1	25 mm
☐ V4	2 mm

Details of Extrude1	
Extrude	Extrude1
Base Object	Sketch1
Operation	Add Material
Direction Vector	None (Normal)
Direction	Normal
Type	Fixed
☐ FD1, Depth (>0)	10 mm
As Thin/Surface?	No
Merge Topology?	Yes

Figure 3-2 Sketch and extrusion details.

The figure above shows the details of the sketch and extrusion. The sketch and extrude details boxes give us manual control over the size of the part. Edit any one of the dimensions shown in these detail boxes then click **Generate**, and you see the part size change immediately.

However in this exercise we want to access the dimensions used for this part and turn some of them into parameters that will provide greater control over the part dimensions and the interrelation between them.

3.   **First click on Sketch1** to bring up the details window then **Click the check box** just to the left of the dimension **V1** in the **Details of Sketch1**. (Your numbers may be different.)

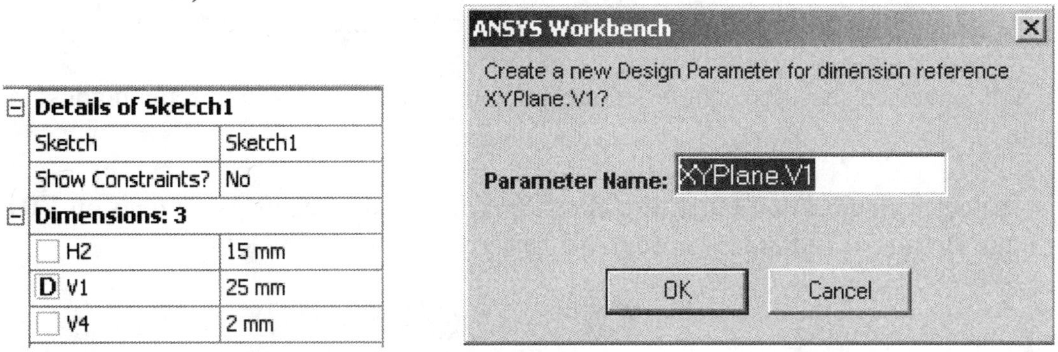

Details of Sketch1	
Sketch	Sketch1
Show Constraints?	No
Dimensions: 3	
H2	15 mm
D V1	25 mm
V4	2 mm

ANSYS Workbench

Create a new Design Parameter for dimension reference XYPlane.V1?

Parameter Name: XYPlane.V1

OK   Cancel

Figure 3-3 Dialog box for parameter XYPlane.V1.

XYPlane.V1 is the dimension of the long leg of the bracket. Notice the D automatically placed in the check box to indicate that this quantity is '**Driven**' by **parameters** and **parameter relations**. It is usually most useful if the parameters are given names meaningful to the part. The XYPlane.V1 parameter will be named '**LongLeg**'. (**XYPlane.H2** will be named '**ShortLeg**' and Extrude1.FD1 will be named '**BracketWidth**'.)

Enter **LongLeg** in the **Parameter Name box** and **Click OK**.

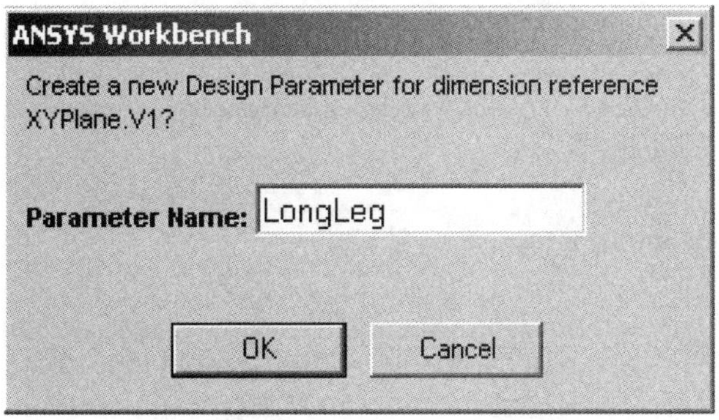

ANSYS Workbench

Create a new Design Parameter for dimension reference XYPlane.V1?

Parameter Name: LongLeg

OK   Cancel

Figure 3-4 XYPlane1.V1 parameter.

Do the same for XYPlane.H2 and enter the name **ShortLeg**.

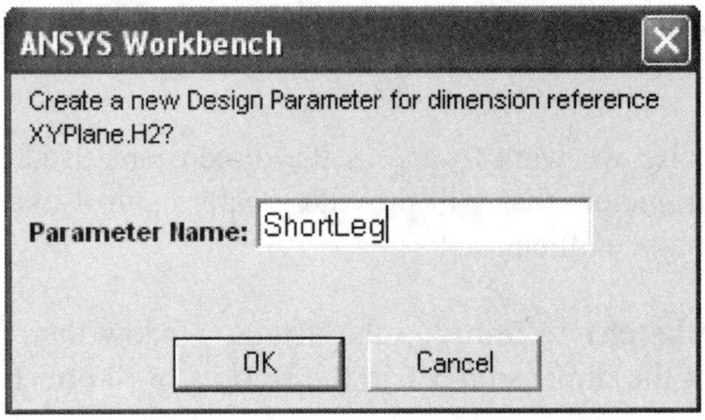

Figure 3-5 Dialog box for parameter XYPlane.H2, ShortLeg.

We will leave the check box for V4 alone since the thickness V4 is to remain constant at 2 mm.

4. **Select Extrude1** and **Click the check box** just to the left of the dimension **FD1** in the **Details of Extrude1**. Accept this Design Parameter; **Click OK**.

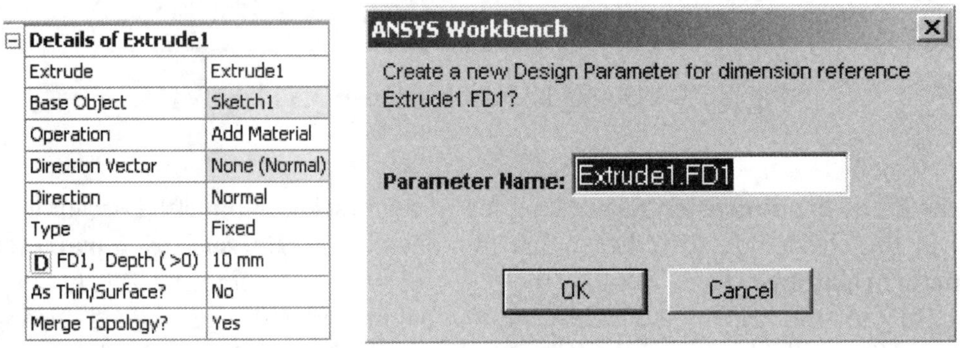

Figure 3-6 Dialog box for parameter Extrude1.FD1.

Extrude1.FD1 is the **parameter** for the length of the extrusion. Enter **BracketWidth** in the Parameter Name box and **Click OK**.

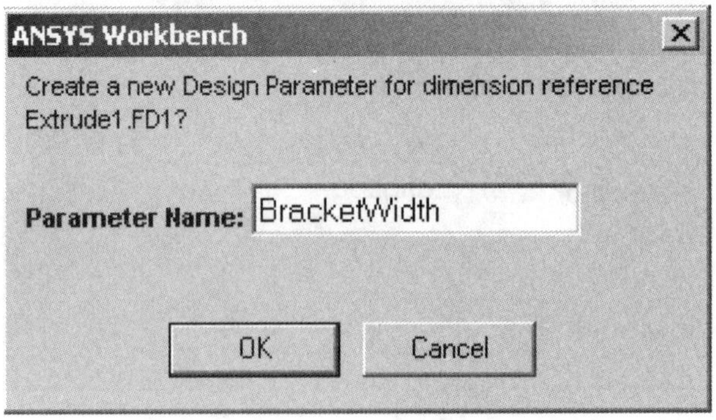

Figure 3-7 Extrude1.FD1 parameter.

We now have defined all of the parameters we want for the bracket dimensions. To view these, click the **Parameters icon** 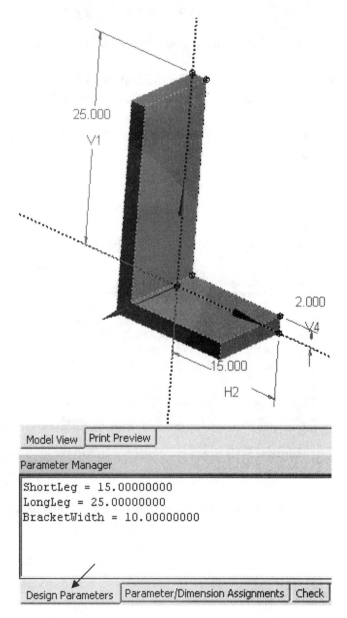 , or use the **tools menu**.

5.   **Tools > Parameters**

The parameters we have defined and their values are now shown at the **bottom of the screen** under the **Design Parameters Tab**.

Figure 3-8 Initial dimensions.

6.   **Click** the **Parameter/Dimension Assignments Tab**.

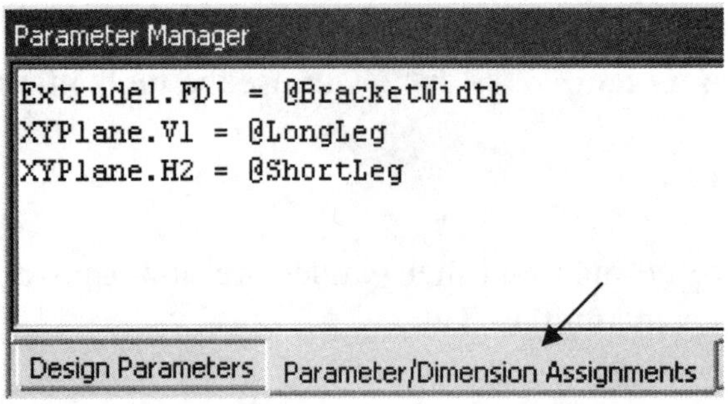

```
Parameter Manager

Extrudel.FD1 = @BracketWidth
XYPlane.V1 = @LongLeg
XYPlane.H2 = @ShortLeg




 Design Parameters   Parameter/Dimension Assignments
```

Figure 3-9 Parameter/Dimension Assignments tab.

The Parameter/Dimension Assignments window displays equation assignments used to drive the model dimensions. The design parameters are given an "@" prefix.

We can edit information in this window and add to these definitions in order to impose the relations between dimensions that we desire. Comments are preceded by the "#" character.

In the example under consideration we want the XYPlane.V1 dimension to be 1.5 times the ShortLeg dimension and the other values as defined. Enter these relations in the Parameter/Dimension Assignments window as shown below.

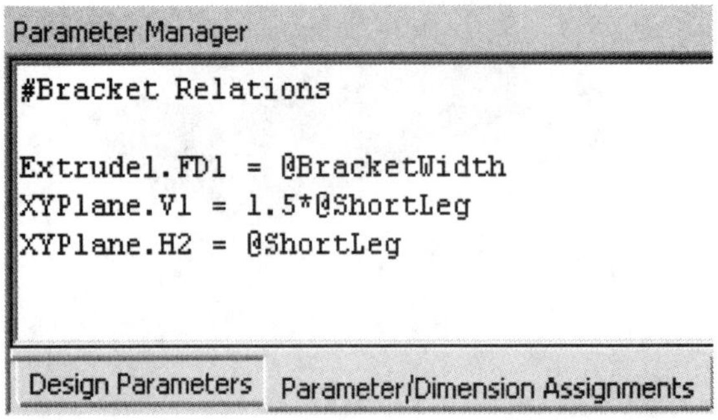

```
Parameter Manager

#Bracket Relations

Extrudel.FD1 = @BracketWidth
XYPlane.V1 = 1.5*@ShortLeg
XYPlane.H2 = @ShortLeg



 Design Parameters   Parameter/Dimension Assignments
```

Figure 3-10 Bracket relation equations.

Then press **Generate** to create the bracket with new size variables as shown in the figure below.

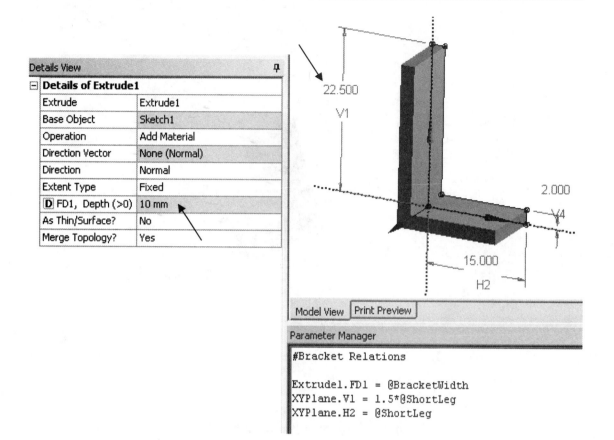

Figure 3-11 Newly sized bracket.

Notice that the H2 dimension remains at 15 mm and the height (long leg) is adjusted to 22.5 mm. These relations persist and are enforced for any subsequent changes we make to ShortLeg. For example, click on the Design Parameters Tab to edit the values shown. If we change the **ShortLeg** to **5 mm** and click **Generate**, we get the part shown next.

```
Parameter Manager
ShortLeg =   5.00000000
LongLeg = 25.00000000
BracketWidth = 10.00000000

Design Parameters  Parameter/Dimension Assignments  Check
```

Figure 3-12 Edit dimension values.

The H2/V1 proportions will change according to the relations assigned, but the bracket thickness will remain 2 mm. Change back to the original dimensions when you are finished.

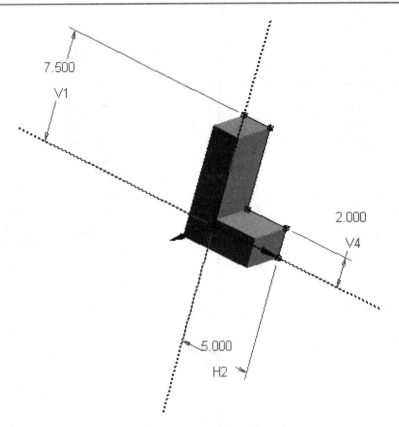

Figure 3-13 Newly sized bracket.

7.   **Click** the **Parameter/Dimension Assignments Tab**

The Check Tab is used to check the syntax of the relations you have entered. For example if @LongLeg appears on the left of an assignment equation, a syntax error will be created, and the part will not be generated correctly.

```
Parameter Manager

### DesignModeler Parameter/Dimension Assignments Output
  1 | Comment    |          | #Bracket Relations
  2 | Comment    |          |
  3 | Feature Dim | 10.0000 | Extrude1.FD1 = @BracketWidth
  4 | Plane Dim   |  7.5000 | XYPlane.V1 = 1.5*@ShortLeg
  5 | Plane Dim   |  5.0000 | XYPlane.H2 = @ShortLeg

### DesignModeler Design Parameter Assignments Output
  1 |             |  5.0000 | @ShortLeg              |
  2 |             | 25.0000 | @LongLeg               |
  3 |             | 10.0000 | @BracketWidth          |

 Design Parameters | Parameter/Dimension Assignments | Check | Close
```

Figure 3-14 Check Tab.

8.   **Close** the **Parameter Manager** window when you finish this exercise. **Save T3A.**

Design parameters appear as the CAD parameters in **Simulation** if their names contain the **Parameter Key** defined when starting the simulation. The **default parameter key** is **DS**. If all design parameters are to be sent to the associated simulation, make the parameter key blank when you start the simulation.

3-4   OTHER CAD SYSTEMS

DesignModeler provides support for a number of other widely used CAD systems. When using Windows-based systems, you can bring a model currently being edited in a CAD session on your computer (Pro/E, CATIA, etc.) into DesignModeler by using the **Attach to Active CAD Geometry** option as mentioned earlier. The model then appears as an object in the feature tree of your DesignModeler session.

Alternate CAD system geometry interface support includes **Autodesk Inventor**, **Autodesk Mechanical Desktop**, **CATIA**, **Pro/ENGINEER**, **Solid Edge**, **SolidWorks**, and **Unigraphics**.

The **IGES** and **STEP** neutral file exchange formats for 2D or 3D CAD product models, drawings, or graphics is also supported by DesignModeler. The bracket model shown here was created in Pro/ENGINEER, saved in the IGES format, then imported in DesignModeler using

File > Import External Geometry File > bracket.igs > Generate

Figure 3-15 IGES import.

Models created in DesignModeler can also be **exported** in the IGES or **STEP** format for use with other CAD, graphics, or analysis software. Use the following sequence to export the file in the current DesignModeler session.

File > Export > IGES (*.igs, *.iges)   (or **STEP**)

3-5   SURFACE AND LINE MODELS

Surface models are necessary if one wishes to perform simulation using simplified planar or 3D surface models, and line models are needed when line elements are being used in engineering simulations. The important shell and beam engineering bending models are supported in Workbench DesignModeler and Workbench Simulation by providing for the DesignModeler creation of surface models subsequently analyzed using ANSYS plate element technology and the creation of line models to which beam cross sections are attached. Planar surfaces are also used to support simulation of Plane Stress, Plane Strain and Axisymmetric modeling.

3-6   TUTORIAL 3B – PLANAR SURFACE MODELS

We will use the L section solid of Tutorial 3A to create a planar surface model in this tutorial. Later we will use this same solid to create a three-dimensional surface model.

1.   **Start DesignModeler** and **Open the file for Tutorial 3A.** The part is 15 x 25 x 2 x 10 mm long.

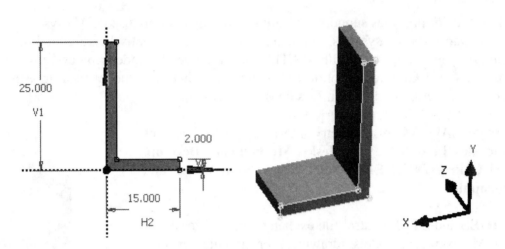

Figure 3-16 L-shaped section.

2.   **Select the sketch in the tree outline.**

3.   **Concept > Surfaces from Sketches**

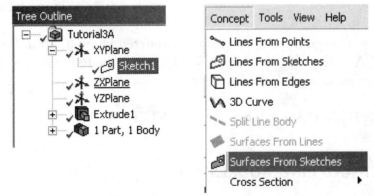

Figure 3-17 Surfaces from sketches.

4.   **Details of SurfaceSk1; Base Objects > Apply, Thickness > 1**

Details View		⊐
Details of SurfaceSk1		
Surface From Sketches	SurfaceSk1	
Base Objects	Apply	Cancel
Operation	Add Material	
Orient With Plane Normal?	Yes	
Thickness (>=0)	1 mm	

Tree Outline
- Tutorial3A
  - XYPlane
    - Sketch1
  - ZXPlane
  - YZPlane
  - Extrude1
  - SurfaceSk1   ✕ Delete
  - 1 Part, 1 Bo   ⚡ Generate

Figure 3-18 Generate the surface.

5.   Right Click SurfaceSk1 > Generate

This creates the surface model, and the solid we started with is no longer needed and may be deleted.

6.   Select Extrude1 > Delete > OK

The surface model is shown in the figure to the right. Notice that no thickness is shown. However the 1 mm thickness we supplied will be carried as a constant into the Simulation module for analysis.

7.   Save this model as T3C.

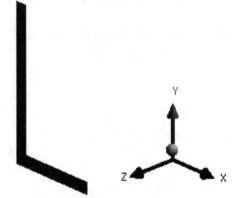

Figure 3-19 Surface model from Sk1.

Three-dimensional surface models also can be developed from sketches using the methods described next.

3-7   TUTORIAL 3C – 3D SURFACE MODELS

Again use the L section solid of Tutorial 3A.

1.   Start DesignModeler and Open the file for Tutorial 3A once again.

We want to capture the middle surface of the bracket.

2.   Tools > Mid-Surface

Figure 3-20 Mid-Surface tool.

3.   **Details of MidSurf2 > Face Pairs**

4.   Use **Ctrl Select** to sequentially pick **all** the front and back face **pairs** on the bracket model > **Apply**.

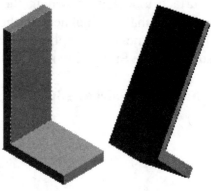

Figure 3-21 Mid-Surface face pairs.

5.   **Generate** ⚡ Generate to create the surface.

Notice that this is a **three-dimensional surface model**.

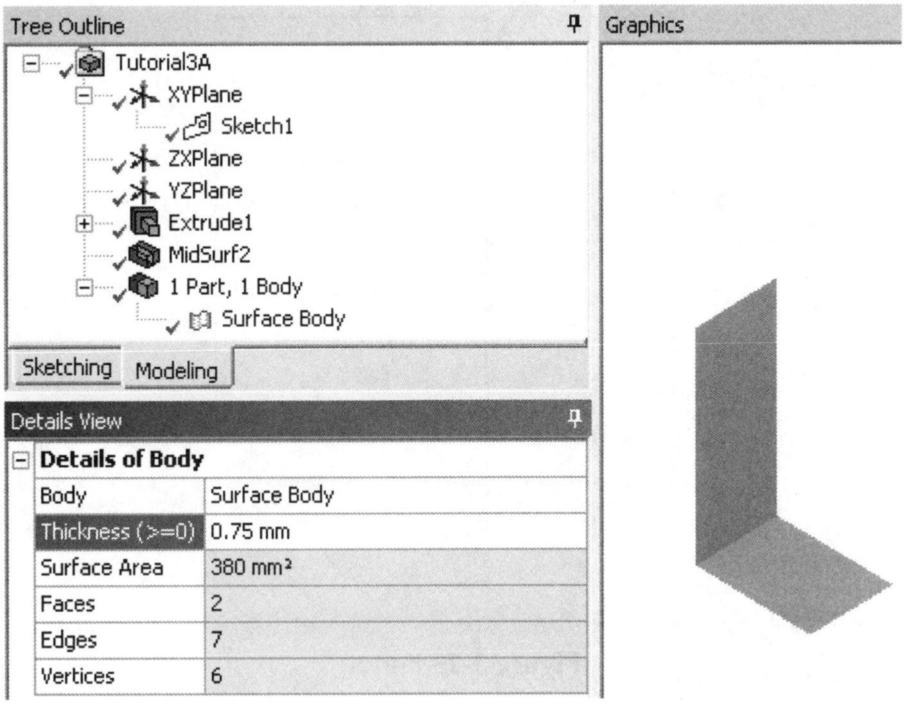

Figure 3-22 3D surface model of the L shaped section.

The **thickness of the Surface Body** is independent of the solid whose mid surface was used and is set by the user in **Details of Body** box as shown above. This thickness value (0.75 mm in our example) is carried into the simulation analysis and used for the calculations there. More detail on this is given in Chapter 8.

3-8 TUTORIAL 3D – LINE BODY MODELS

In the final tutorial of this chapter we develop a line body model to which a cross section is assigned. This model is then used in the Simulation module to compute structural response using beam element modeling.

1. **Start** a **New Model in DesignModeler** and **begin a sketch on the XY Plane**.

2. **Set** the **units to in-lbf-sec** and use lines to **Sketch a portal 120 inches high** and **72 inches wide** (two verticals and one horizontal line across the top).

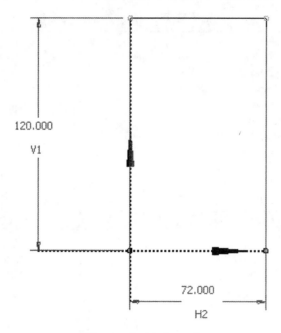

Figure 3-23 Portal.

3.   **Modeling > Select the Sketch**

4.   **Concept > Lines from Sketches > Base Objects > Apply** (The sketch is the base object.)

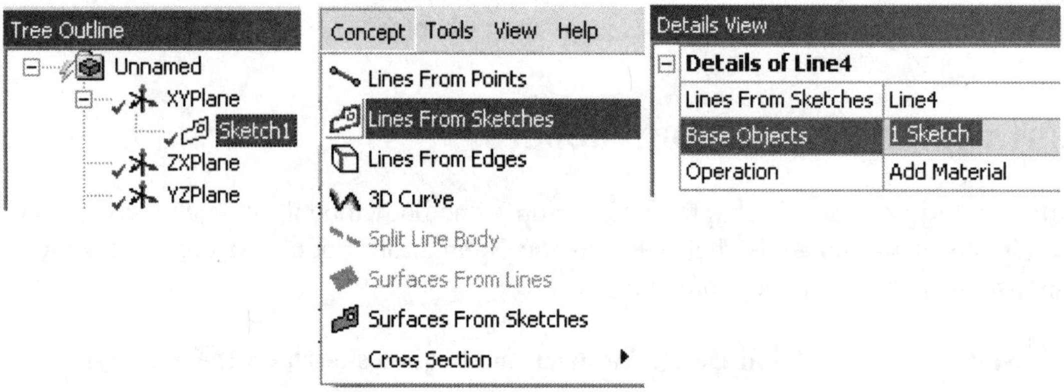

Figure 3-24 Lines from sketches.

5.   **Generate** This generates the line body. Next we **assign a cross section** to this line.

6.   **Concept > Cross Section > Channel**

We take the default size which is the **3 x 6 x 1 inch section** shown below and **assign it to the Line Body** as shown in the second figure below.

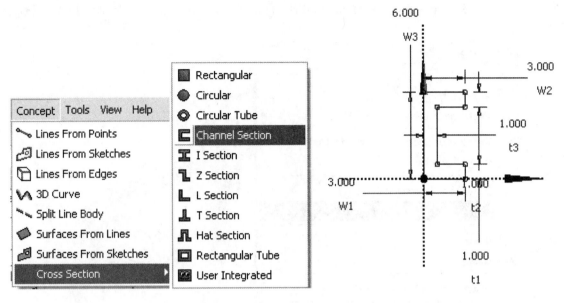

Figure 3-25 Channel section.

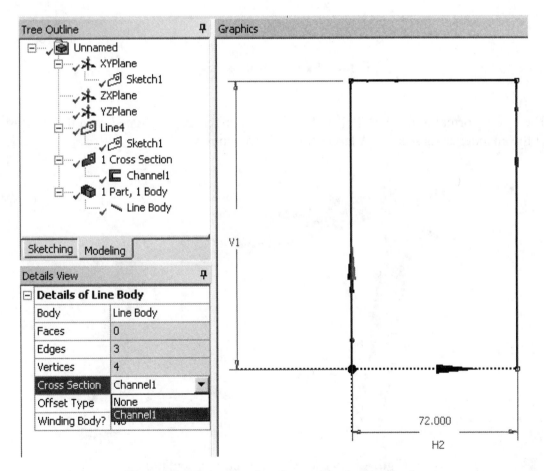

Figure 3-26 Assign the channel to the line body.

7.   **View > Show Cross Section Solids** (Displays the orientation of the section.)

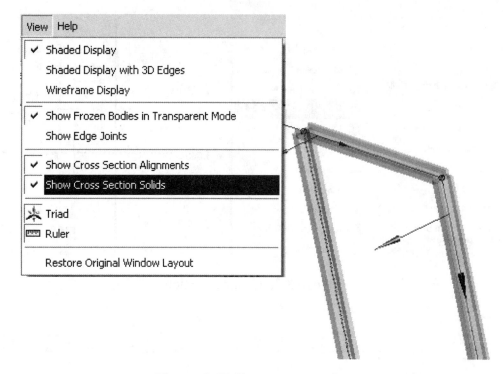

Figure 3-27 Show cross section.

The arrow normal to the portal plane (green on your screen) is aligned with the long edge of the channel cross section. A larger image is shown next.

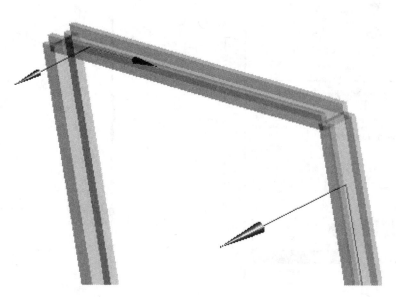

Figure 3-28 Close-up of section orientation.

We would like the legs of all of the channel sections to point inward.

8.   **Turn on** the **Edge Selection Filter** and **Ctrl Pick the Left, Top** and **Right Line-Body Edges**.

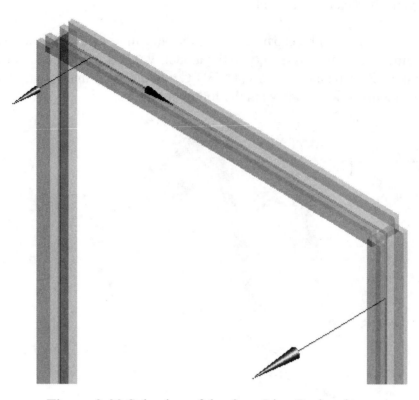

Figure 3-29 Selection of the three Line-Body edges.

9.   **Reverse Orientation? > Yes**

Details View	📌
Line-Body Edges: 3	
Alignment Mode	Selection
Cross Section Alignment	Plane Normal
Alignment X	0
Alignment Y	0
Alignment Z	1
Rotate	0 °
Reverse Orientation?	No ▼
	No
	Yes

Figure 3-30 Reverse orientation of 3 cross sections.

10.   **Save your work**.

Other orientations of the cross section of any of the edges can be made by changing the direction of its cross section alignment vector (the green arrow). Do this by adjusting the X, Y, Z Alignment vector components.

This Line-Body model can be expanded using the sketching methods described earlier to add more elements and dimensionality to the model. We add vertical and horizontal lines sketched in the YZ Plane and a Concept > 3D Curve diagonal line joining the two outer vertices. This modification is shown in the following figure.

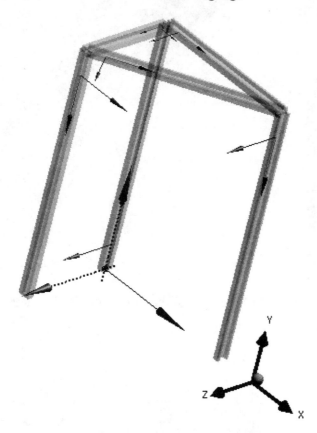

Figure 3-31 Expanded line-body model.

In Chapter 8 we will attach this model in the ANSYS Simulation module to analyze the structure using beam elements.

3-9 SUMMARY

Chapter 3 tutorials introduce the use of DesignModeler parameters and briefly discuss how to make use of other CAD systems and how to create models that are not solid models (lines and surfaces) for use in down-stream simulations.

3-10 PROBLEMS

3-1   Create parameter relations for the model of Problem 2-4 so that the height of the model is 6 times the wall thickness and the exterior radius is 3 times the wall thickness. The wall thickness and interior fillet remain unchanged. (See **Figure 5-1**) Are there size changes that produce invalid solid models?

3-2   Parameterize any of the DesignModeler parts created earlier in your study and examine the effect on the dependent parameters of changing a base dimension value. Are there size changes that produce invalid solid models?

3-3   Create parameter relations for the model of Problem 2-5 so that the large hole is placed at half the height of the part and always centered. The other dimensions remain unchanged. (See **Figure 8-20**) Are there size changes that produce invalid solid models?

3-4   Import an IGES or STEP file from another CAD system. If one is not available, export and save an IGES or STEP file from DesignModeler, start a new DesignModeler session and try importing that IGES or STEP file.

3-5   If another CAD system is available, use DesignModeler to attach the geometry for a part that is in an active session of that CAD system.

NOTES:

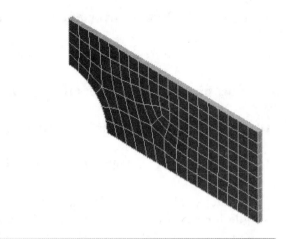

Chapter 4

Simulation I

4-1 OVERVIEW

ANSYS Workbench Simulation provides tools for the user to simulate the **Structural**, **Thermal**, or **Magnetostatic** behavior of engineering systems. In this Chapter we consider

♦ Stress response of a plate with a central hole.

♦ Stress response to various FEM mesh densities.

♦ The use of convergence criteria for controlling solution accuracy.

4-2 INTRODUCTION

Evaluating the response of a part or system in Workbench Simulation involves accessing the Geometry, assigning the Materials, applying the Loadings, Solving the system Equations, Reviewing/Reporting the Results, and Updating the model if desired. An outline of this process is shown below.

1.   **Attach geometry or open a *.dsdb Design Simulation file.**

2.   **Assign Materials.**

3.   **Establish Contact Conditions if applicable.**

4.   **Preview the Mesh and set up Mesh Controls if desired.**

5.   **Apply Loadings.**

6.   **Select Results to be computed and displayed.**

7.   **Solve the system governing equations.**

8.   **Review the Results.**

9.   **Set problem Parameters if desired.**

10.   **Create Reports of the simulation response if appropriate.**

11.   **Update the CAD model if necessary.**

These steps can be carried out manually by an experienced user, or a Workbench Simulation Wizard can be used to assist with the overall simulation process. The step by step manual approach is used in the tutorials in this chapter.

To develop confidence in the process we start in Tutorial 4A by solving a simple structural static response problem the stress result for which we can check separately by a hand calculation.

4-3   TUTORIAL 4A – PLATE WITH CENTRAL CIRCLUAR HOLE

In this tutorial we will use ANSYS Simulation to compute the maximum stress in a thin steel plate with a central hole. The plate is loaded in the long direction by a tensile force of **400 N**. Its dimensions are **1000 mm long**, **400 mm high** and **10 mm thick**. The central circular hole is **200 mm in diameter** as shown in the figure below.

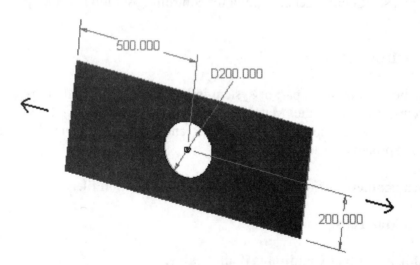

Figure 4-1 Thin plate with central hole.

First we need a solid model of the plate, and this can be created with DesignModeler or another solid modeling system. Since the central horizontal and vertical axes of the plate are on planes of plate and loading symmetry, we only need to analyze a quadrant of the part to obtain the stress distribution.

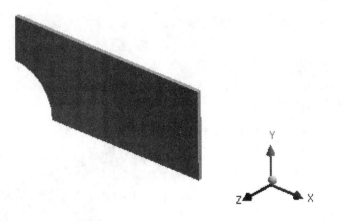

Figure 4-2 Quadrant of plate.

We follow the steps outlined above skipping those not needed in this tutorial.

1. **GEOMETRY:** Start **ANSYS Workbench,** begin a **new Project** and use **DesignModeler** to create the solid model of the upper right quadrant of the plate as shown. **Save** the project and geometry model as **T4A**.

2. **Close DesignModeler**

3. With **T4A highlighted** on the project page, select **New simulation** Ⓢ

T4A [Project] ×	T4a [DesignModeler]
File Tools Help	
DesignModeler Tasks	Name
Ⓓ Open	T4A
Ⓓ Open copy	
New mesh	Ⓓ T4a
Ⓢ New simulation	

Figure 4-3 Project view details.

The Workbench display now shows the **Simulation** that is associated with this **Project**, and the tree structure on the left contains project items that include **Model**, **Geometry**, and **Mesh**. See the figure below.

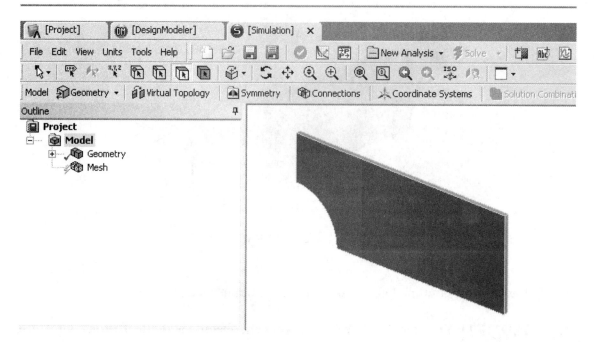

Figure 4-4 Plate quadrant.

Since the geometry was created using mm, the length units for the simulation should be mm also. **Check the units.**

4.   **Units > Metric (mm, kg, N, C, s, mV, A)**

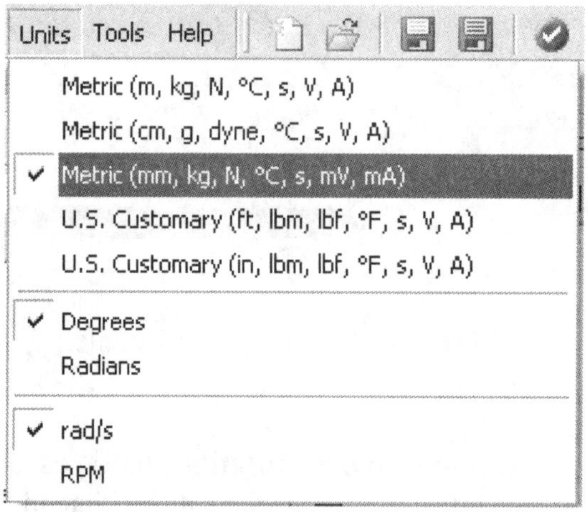

Figure 4-5 Check the units settings.

5.   **ASSIGN MATERIALS: Click on + Geometry > Solid**

6.   **Highlight Material** in the **Details of "Solid"** window.

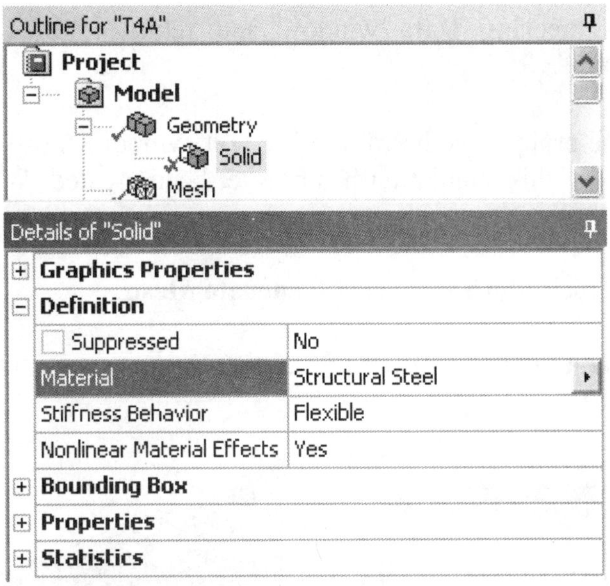

Figure 4-6 Material assignment.

7.   In the top row of menu items click **Data** [icon] to view the **Material Properties Data**.

Structural Steel is the **default material** for simulation problems in Workbench and its properties are summarized in the window shown below.

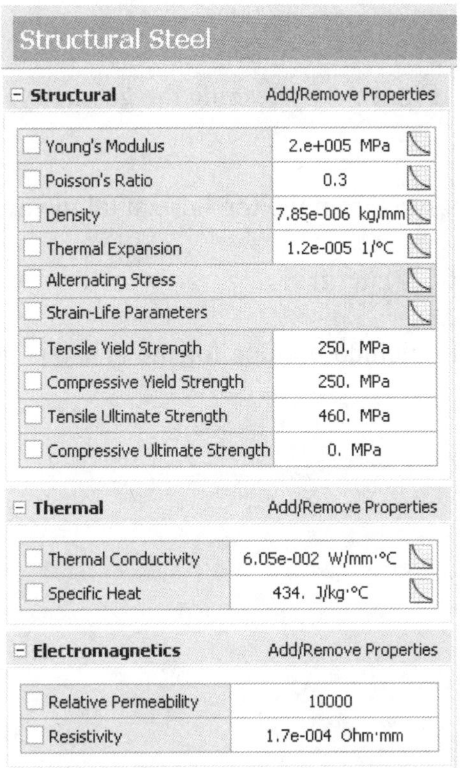

Figure 4-7 Material properties for structural steel.

8. **Close** the **Engineering Data** window and return to the simulation window.

[Engineering Data]   ✕

The Mesh item in the project tree has a lighting bolt symbol next to it indicating that the finite element mesh for this simulation has not yet been created. Workbench simulation will automatically develop a finite element mesh appropriate to the problem.

9. **MESH:** Right click **Mesh** and select **Generate Mesh**

The default mesh that is created consists of 126 three-dimensional 'brick' elements and is shown in the next figure.

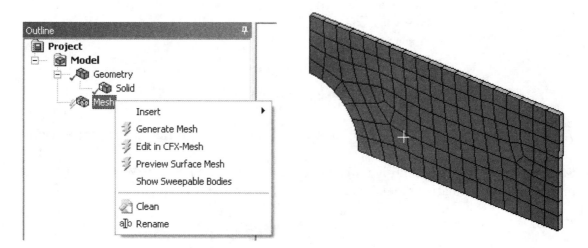

Figure 4-8 Meshing the geometry.

Select a static structural analysis from the top horizontal menu **New Analysis**.

10. **New Analysis > Static Structural**

The outline tree expands to include options for the analysis and solution information as shown in the figure below.

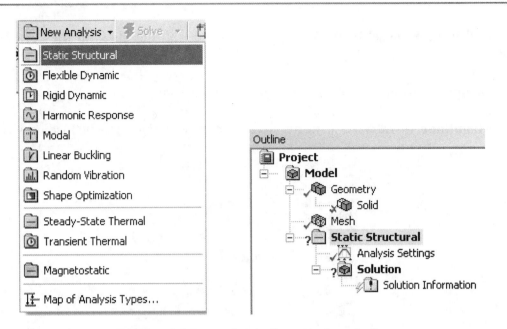

Figure 4-9 Insert Static Structural analysis.

Continue defining the simulation problem by identifying **loads** and **boundary conditions**. First use a **pressure** to apply the tensile load to the thin plate. Select **Static Structural** in the Outline tree and the **Environment** menu is displayed.

Environment Inertial ▾ Loads ▾ Supports ▾ Conditions ▾ CFX Loads ▾

Figure 4-10 Structural environment menu.

A distributed tensile loading of 1 MPa over the end is equivalent to the 400 N load.

11. APPLY LOADINGS: Click **Environment** > **Loads** > **Pressure**

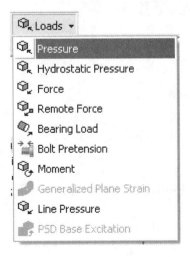

Figure 4-11 Structural loads menu.

Be sure that the **Face** selection option is highlighted 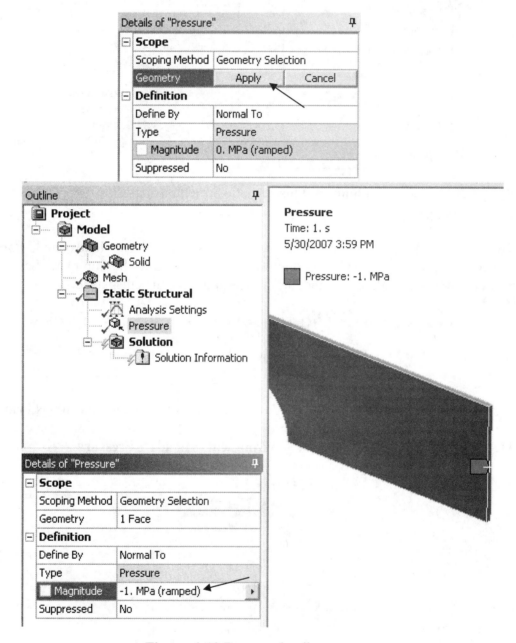 and **click on the area** on the right end of the solid model.

12.   **Geometry > Apply** (Note: It's easy to forget this step.)

13.   **Magnitude = –1.0 MPa** (The negative pressure will give a tensile loading.)

Figure 4-12 Pressure loading.

Next apply the displacement constraints; rotate the plate so that you can see the **bottom, and small end**. These are surfaces on planes of symmetry and no point on these surfaces can move across the plane of symmetry. Symmetry requires that we constrain the displacements perpendicular to these surfaces. We can use the **Frictionless Support** condition to do that. We restrain the **back surface** also so as to prevent rigid body motion in a direction perpendicular to the plane of the plate. See the figure below.

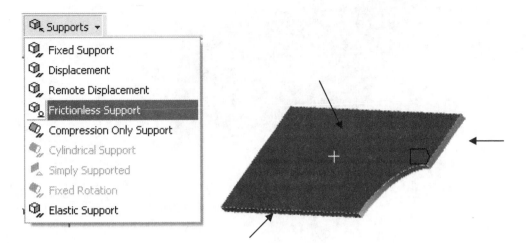

Figure 4-13 Displacement constraints.

14.   Environment > Supports > Frictionless Support

15.   Ctrl > Left click to select the **three** surfaces > **Apply**

Details of "Frictionless Support"	
Scope	
Scoping Method	Geometry Selection
Geometry	3 Faces
Definition	
Type	Frictionless Support
Suppressed	No

Figure 4-14 X displacement constraint.

Check your work by clicking on each of the items under Environment in the model tree to be sure the loadings and constraints are applied as desired. Or click **Static Structural** to see all of the constraints you have applied.

If you find something wrong, just highlight the item in the model tree and edit it in the 'Details' box to correct the error, or delete the item from the outline tree and apply the condition again.

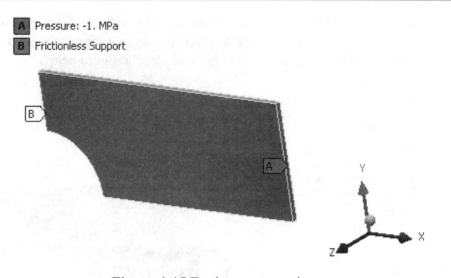

Figure 4-15 Environment settings.

To complete the model building process we need to specify what **result** quantity or quantities we would like to have calculated and displayed. In this problem we are most interested in the **stress** in the **X direction**.

Solution Deformation ▾ Strain ▾ Stress ▾ Probe ▾ Tools ▾

Figure 4-16 Solution result options menu.

16.   Solution > Stress > Normal > Orientation > X Axis

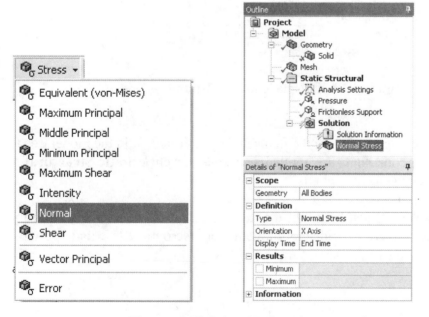

Figure 4-17 Select X-direction normal stress output.

Notice that Solution and Normal Stress items have a lightning bolt indicator meaning that we need to highlight one or the other and select ⚡Solve to complete the simulation solution.

17.   Solve ⚡Solve

The solution progress is shown in the **ANSYS Workbench Solution Status** window.

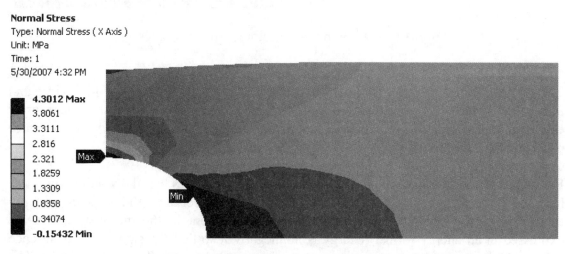

Figure 4-18 Solution status.

Click on the normal stress to view the computed stress results.

18.   Solution > Stress > Normal Stress (In the graphics window: Right click > View > Front). Also click **Max, Min** icons [MAX] [MIN]

Normal Stress
Type: Normal Stress (X Axis)
Unit: MPa
Time: 1
5/30/2007 4:32 PM

4.3012 Max
3.8061
3.3111
2.816
2.321
1.8259
1.3309
0.8358
0.34074
-0.15432 Min

Figure 4-19 X direction normal stress.

The solution for the X direction normal stress shows a **maximum value** of **4.30 MPa**.

To check this result, find the stress concentration factor for this problem in a text or reference book or from a web site. For the geometry of this example we find $K_t = 2.17$. We can compute the maximum stress using (K_t)(load)/(net cross sectional area). Using the pressure $p = -1.0$ MPa we obtain:

$$\sigma_{x\,MAX} = 2.17 * p * (0.4)(0.01)/[(0.4 - 0.2) * 0.01] = 4.34 MPa$$

The computed maximum value is **4.30 MPa** which is less than **one per cent in error** (assuming that the published value of K_t is exact).

Before we leave this tutorial let's compute and display the stress **error estimate** for this problem. Insert a stress error in the solution item in the project tree.

19.   **Solution > Stress > Error > Solve**   [Solve]   (or **Evaluate** results)

Computed results are shown in the next figure.

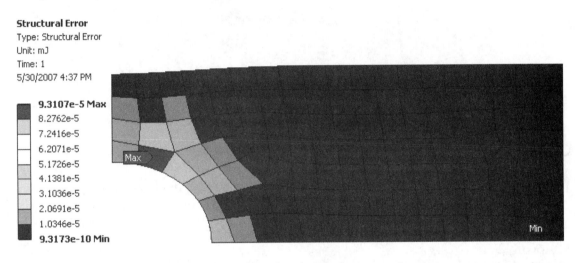

Structural Error
Type: Structural Error
Unit: mJ
Time: 1
5/30/2007 4:37 PM

9.3107e-5 Max
8.2762e-5
7.2416e-5
6.2071e-5
5.1726e-5
4.1381e-5
3.1036e-5
2.0691e-5
1.0346e-5
9.3173e-10 Min

Max

Min

Figure 4-20 Computed structural error estimates.

The error estimates shown above can be used to help identify regions of high error and thus show where the model would benefit from a more refined mesh. These error estimates are used in Workbench automatic adaptive meshing and convergence procedures we discuss later.

For now we note that the Structural Errors shown are **estimates** based upon the difference between a smoothed stress distribution within the object and the stresses actually calculated by the finite element method for each element in the mesh. The data are expressed in an energy format (energy is nonnegative) so that the sign of the difference between the estimated stress and the computed stress does not influence the results. The estimated error is displayed for each element.

For accurate solutions the difference between the smoothed stress and the element stress is small or zero, so small values of Structural Error are good. We know the above solution is reasonably accurate because we compared our result with tabulated results. The small error estimates shown above reflect this.

20. Save your work and close the T4A Workbench Project.

4-4 TUTORIAL 4B – PLATE WITH CENTRAL SQUARE HOLE

Suppose we take the plate of Tutorial 4A and replace the circular hole with a 200 mm square hole. The upper right quadrant of the model is shown below.

1. **Open a new Workbench Project; create the model shown below and save as T4B.**

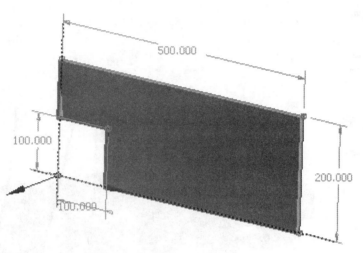

Figure 4-21 Plate with square hole.

2. With **T4B highlighted** on the project page, **select New simulation**. 🅢

3. **Mesh > Preview Mesh** The next figure shows the default mesh for this problem.

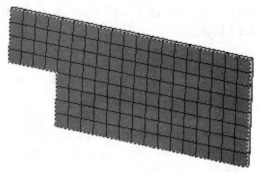

Figure 4-22 Default mesh for the plate with square hole.

The default mesh consists of 136 brick elements as shown above.

4.   **Apply the displacement boundary conditions and pressure loading as in TutorialT4A.**

Include the X direction normal stress and the structural error in the computed quantities.

5.   **Solution > Stress > Normal > Details of "Normal Stress" > Orientation > X Axis**

6.   **Solution > Stress > Error**

7.   **Solve** [Solve] and view the normal stress solution.

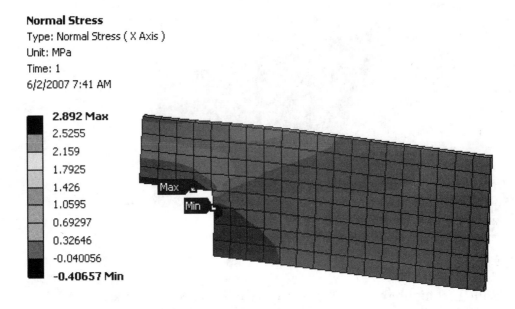

Normal Stress
Type: Normal Stress (X Axis)
Unit: MPa
Time: 1
6/2/2007 7:41 AM

2.892 Max
2.5255
2.159
1.7925
1.426
1.0595
0.69297
0.32646
-0.040056
-0.40657 Min

Figure 4-23 Normal stress in. the X direction.

8.   **Right click and select the front view.** The smooth stress contours show a maximum stress of **2.9 MPa**.

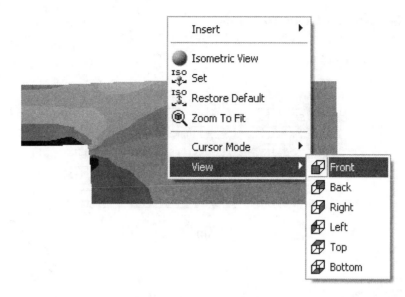

Figure 4-24 Front view.

The default mesh consists of elements that are 25 mm by 25 mm and 10 mm thick. Suppose we reduce the element size and examine the effect on the computed stresses. In the outline tree click on **Mesh**, then in **Details of "Mesh" change** the **element size** from **25 mm** to **10 mm**.

9.   **Mesh > Details of "Mesh"**

10.   **Element Size > 10 mm**

Details of "Mesh"	
Defaults	
Physics Preference	Mechanical
Relevance	0
Advanced	
Relevance Center	Coarse
Element Size	10. mm
Shape Checking	Standard Mech...
Solid Element Midside Nodes	Program Contro...
Straight Sided Elements	No
Initial Size Seed	Active Assembly
Smoothing	Low
Transition	Fast
Statistics	
Nodes	1090
Elements	136

Figure 4-25 Set the element size.

11.   **Right click Mesh > Generate Mesh**

The new mesh is shown below.

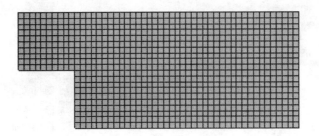

Figure 4-26 10 mm element mesh.

12.   **Solve** 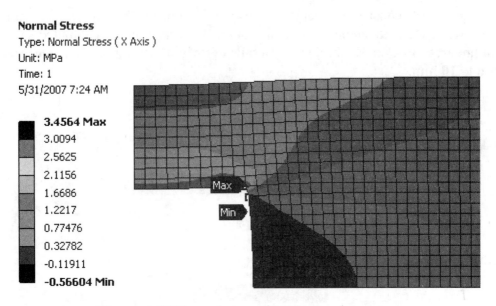 and view the normal stress solution.

The computed **maximum** normal stress is **3.4 MPa**, an increase of **17 per cent**.

Normal Stress
Type: Normal Stress (X Axis)
Unit: MPa
Time: 1
5/31/2007 7:24 AM

3.4564 Max
3.0094
2.5625
2.1156
1.6686
1.2217
0.77476
0.32782
-0.11911
-0.56604 Min

Max

Min

Figure 4-27 Normal stress for 10 mm elements.

Let's reduce the mesh size to **5 mm**.

13.   **Details of "Mesh" > Element Size > 5 mm** (This creates a model with 7200 elements.)

14.   Again **Solve** and view the normal stress solution.

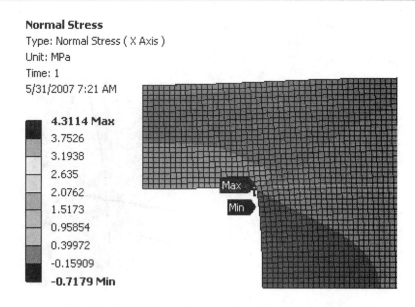

Figure 4-28 Normal stress for 5 mm elements.

The newly computed maximum normal stress in the X-direction is **4.3 MPa**, an increase over the previous value of **26 per cent**, and the stress contours are quite a bit different. So what is happening?

The maximum stress results we just computed are due the stress singularity at the corner of the square hole. The corner has a zero radius of curvature where the two edges meet, and as the radius of an interior corner or other notch approaches zero, the computed stress approaches an infinite value. If the material is ductile and the loads are static, the high stresses at this singularity may not be of concern in the actual use of the part. If the material is brittle or the loading is repetitive (fatigue situation), then it is important to model the actual geometry and thus determine the actual stress value in the vicinity of the notch.

The singularity is also displayed if we plot the **Structural Error**; see next figure. The maximum value of error estimate occurs at the interior corner and there are **twelve orders of magnitude** difference between the error value at the singularity and almost all of the rest of the object. In contrast the max/min error difference for the part in tutorial T4A was only one order of magnitude.

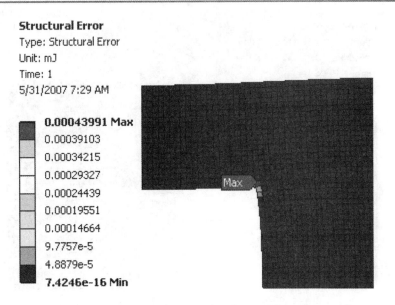

Figure 4-29 Structural error the 5 mm element mesh.

During manufacture of a real plate the edges of the hole cannot be made to meet with a zero radius at the corner. It also may be that a specific corner radius is needed for the function of the part. Suppose for our plate the actual **corner radius** is **15 mm.** Make this change in the ANSYS DesignModeler model of the plate or the solid modeler you are using.

15.   Click on the **Project tab**.

16.   Then **click on the DesignModeler T4B file**.

Working in DesignModeler we will add the fillet radius. Select **Open copy**.

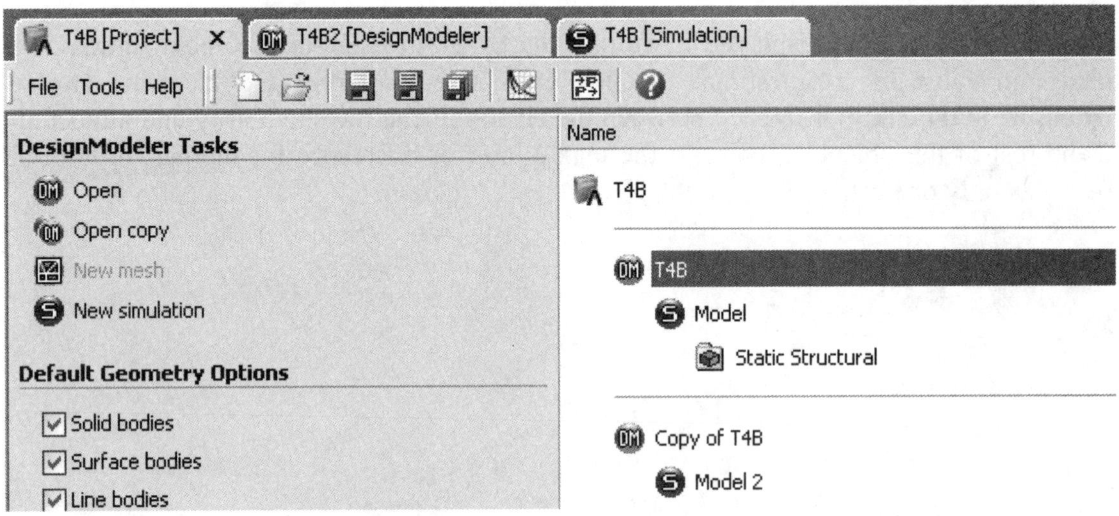

Figure 4-30 Project tab view.

17. **Sketching > Sketch1** (or name of your sketch) **> Modify > Fillet > Radius > 15 mm**

Click the two interior corner lines at points near the corner to indicate tangency of the fillet.

18. **Modeling > Extrude2** (or your object name) **> Generate**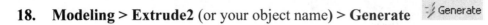

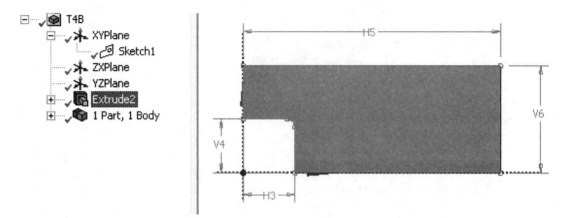

Figure 4-31 Updated DesignModeler geometry.

Now we create a new Simulation Model with the new geometry.

19. **With Copy of T4B selected, Click New simulation**

20. **Project Tab > Simulation Model**

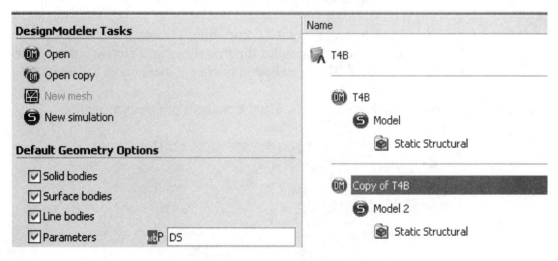

Figure 4-32 Update the model.

21. Now working in the **Simulation module**, **right click** and **Copy** the **Static Structural** object from the square corner model. **Right click** on **Model2** and **Paste**.

22. Do the same with the **Solution** object.

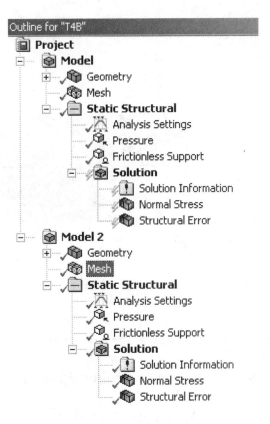

Figure 4-33 Outline tree with two models.

The project now has two models, one without a corner fillet and one with the fillet. Since the geometry is new, the application surfaces for the **Pressure** and **Frictionless Supports** have to be **defined** for the Model2. This is indicated by the '?' symbols in the tree.

Apply the pressure and frictionless supports, and the analysis proceeds as before.

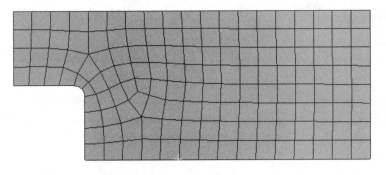

Figure 4-34 Default mesh for modified geometry.

23. Right click **Normal Stress > Solve** [Solve]

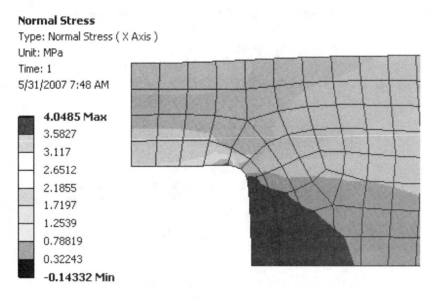

Figure 4-35 Normal stress plot.

The computed maximum stress associated with the 15 mm corner radius is about **4 MPa**. We can control the accuracy of the solution by requesting an iterative solution process to be employed that will use models with successively smaller element sizes and will monitor the change in the requested solution quantity.

24. Right click **Normal Stress > Insert >** Left click **Convergence**

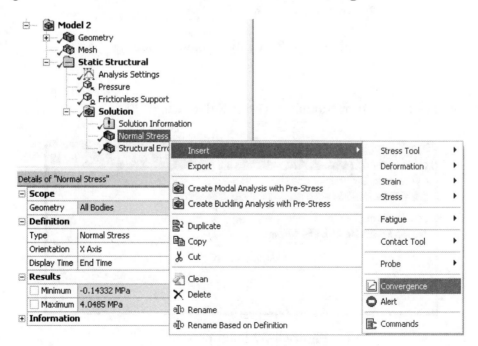

Figure 4-36 Insert convergence criterion.

Define monitoring of the Normal Stress as the iterative convergence condition.

25.   Details of "Convergence" > Allowable Change > 5 per cent

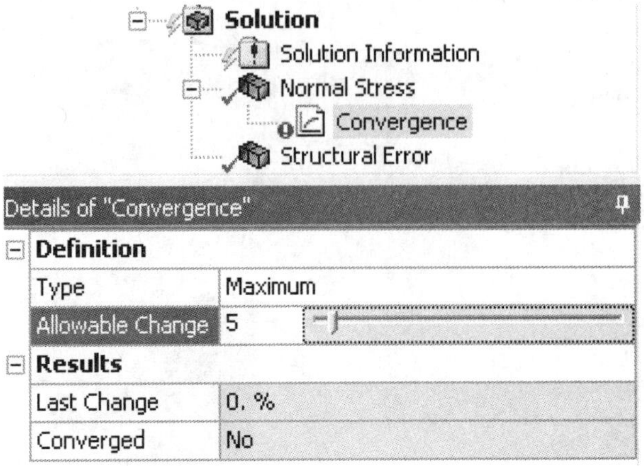

Figure 4-37 Allowable change in normal stress.

Use the default number of mesh refinements and depth (refinement gradations).

26.   Solution > Max Refinement Loops > 1; Refinement Depth > 2

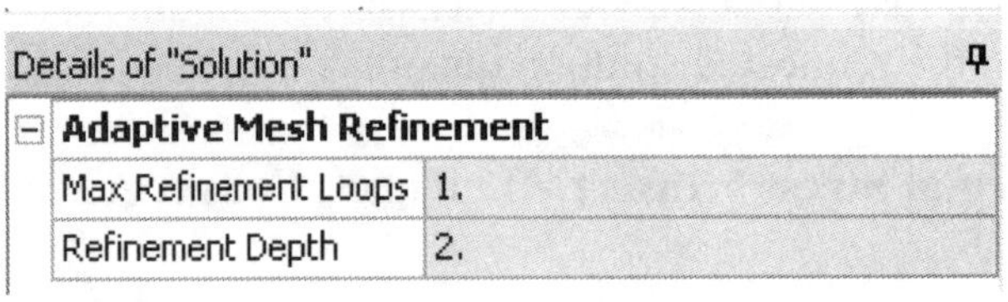

Figure 4-38 Adaptive convergence.

27.   Right click Solution or Normal Stress > Solve ⫶ Solve

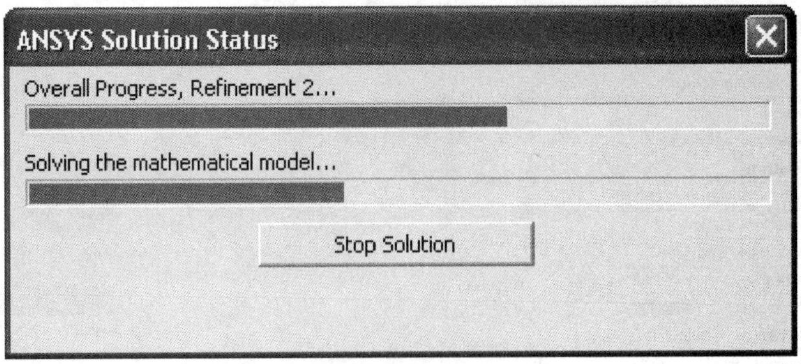

Figure 4-39 Solution status.

28. Once the solution process has finished, click on **Convergence**.

The convergence results shown in the next figure are displayed. The model is refined from 1144 nodes and 143 elements to one with 3992 nodes and 1960 elements. The maximum normal stress in the X-direction changes from 4 MPa to about 4.1 MPa, a difference of about **1.5 per cent** which meets the 5 per cent condition we set. See the next figure.

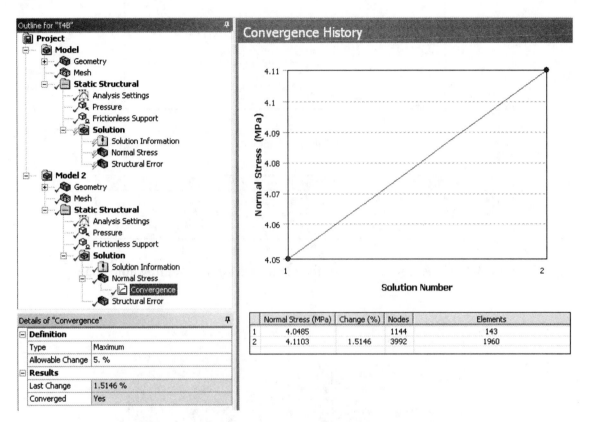

Figure 4-40 Convergence history.

Let's set the Allowable Change in the normal stress to 1 per cent.

29. Details of "Convergence" > Allowable Change > 1 per cent.

30. Solve ⅀ Solve

We obtain the convergence history and the refined mesh shown in the figures below and note that things got worse rather than better. Unfortunately the maximum stress value has now changed by more than **15 per cent**.

This obviously requires further investigation.

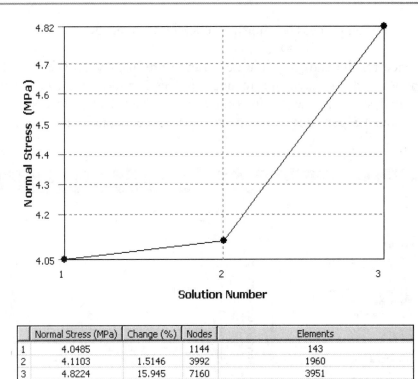

	Normal Stress (MPa)	Change (%)	Nodes	Elements
1	4.0485		1144	143
2	4.1103	1.5146	3992	1960
3	4.8224	15.945	7160	3951

Figure 4-41 Convergence history for requested 1 per cent allowable change.

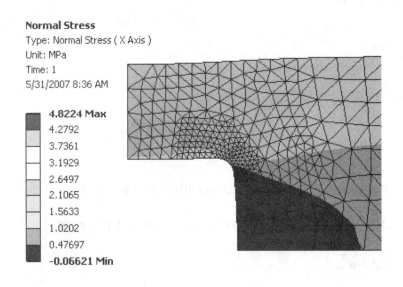

Figure 4-42 Mesh and X Axis normal stress for iteration 3.

Set the Allowable Change in the normal stress to **0.5 per cent**. Values less than 1.0 entered in the dialog box display as **0.0 per cent**. Solving the problem again gives the results shown in the next two figures.

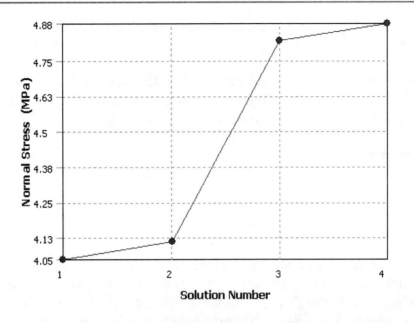

	Normal Stress (MPa)	Change (%)	Nodes	Elements
1	4.0485		1144	143
2	4.1103	1.5146	3992	1960
3	4.8224	15.945	7160	3951
4	4.8814	1.2154	20404	12742

Figure 4-43 Convergence history for requested 0.5 per cent allowable change.

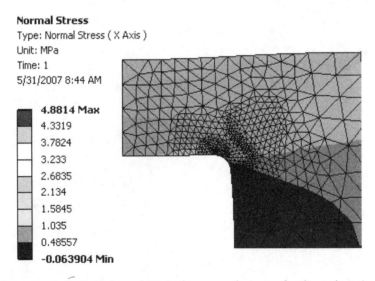

Figure 4-44 Mesh and X Axis normal stress for iteration 4.

The last convergence results give us confidence in the computed stress values for the case where the actual corner radius of curvature is included. The stress history plot is seen to converge nicely. The final value of 4.88 MPa found in iteration 4 is only about **1.2 per cent** different from the value calculated in iteration 3. It is, however, around 20 per cent different from the first value computed.

Note that the model of iteration 4 had 12,742 elements, almost 100 times as many as in the default mesh.

The convergence path could be altered by the choice of the mesh refinements. A uniform mesh refinement followed by a local refinement using this convergence object will likely produce different intermediate results. Experimentation and experience are important.

31.   Save your work.

4-5   SUMMARY

The tutorials in Chapter 4 illustrate basic concepts of stress computation with ANSYS Simulation coupled with DesignModeler. We note that computed values must be examined carefully to evaluate their accuracy and that convergence tools can and should be used to insure quality of results. In the next Chapter we will extend these ideas to more complex parts and introduce additional simulation modeling options.

4-6   PROBLEMS

4-1   Consider a thin plate such as the one shown below. Select your own dimensions and material; use the methods of this chapter to compute the maximum normal stress due to a tensile load. Compare your result with the value you compute using tabulated stress concentration factors for this geometry. Insert a convergence control to help access the accuracy of your solution.

Figure P4-1

4-2   Place a hole to left and to the right of the vertical centerline but on the horizontal centerline of the part in Problem 4-1. See if you can select a hole size and location that reduces the maximum stress in plate (as compared to the stress with original geometry).

4-3   Consider a long, thin plate as shown below. Select your own dimensions and material. Apply a pressure on the upper edge and compute the deflection at the free end. Compare your result with the result you can compute from beam theory.

Figure P4-3

4-4   Repeat the problem described in Problem 4-3 but make the beam short and wide. Slender beam theory no longer applies to this geometry. Compare results to verify that.

Figure P4-4

NOTES:

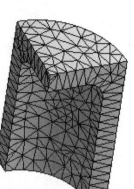

Chapter 5

Simulation II

5-1   OVERVIEW

This chapter covers stress and deflection simulation response of some three-dimensional solids representative of typical mechanical parts. We consider the simulation of the following objects

- ♦ Pressure Vessel

- ♦ Angle Bracket

- ♦ Clevis Yoke

5-2   INTRODUCTION

The close integration with DesignModeler and other solid modeling tools makes ANSYS Simulation particularly well suited to the analysis of solids. We consider a few typical examples in the tutorials that follow.

5-3   TUTORIAL 5A - CYLINDRICAL PRESSURE VESSEL

A steel pressure vessel with planar ends is subjected to an **internal pressure of 35 MPa**. The vessel has an **outer diameter of 200 mm**, an over-all **length of 400 mm** and a **wall thickness of 25 mm**. There is a **25 mm fillet radius** where the interior wall surface joins the end cap as shown in the figure below.

The vessel has a longitudinal axis of rotational symmetry and is also symmetric with respect to a plane passed through it at mid-height. Thus the analyst need consider only the top or bottom half of the vessel.

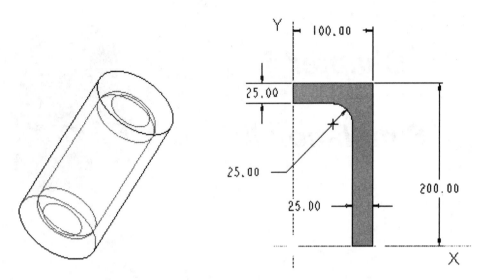

Figure 5-1 Cylindrical pressure vessel.

We will use a 90-degree segment of the solid model of the vessel for analysis. The symmetric nature of the geometry and loading means that displacements are zero in directions normal to the faces exposed by the vertical and horizontal cuts employed to create this one-eighth segment of the cylinder. Use ANSYS DesignModeler or other solid modeler to create a solid model of the upper portion of the vessel.

1.   **Start ANSYS Workbench Simulation** and **attach the quadrant geometry**.

We will use the **default values for steel. Check the units setting,** then

2.   **Mesh** > (right click) **Generate Mesh**

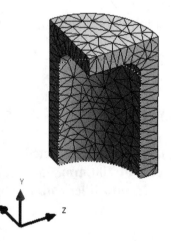

Figure 5-2 Quadrant of cylinder and initial mesh.

Apply Frictionless Support boundary conditions on the planes of symmetry.

3.   Environment > Supports > Frictionless Support

4.   Select the Three surfaces on the planes of symmetry > **Apply**

Details of "Frictionless Support"	⊉
⊟ **Scope**	
Scoping Method	Geometry Selection
Geometry	3 Faces
⊟ **Definition**	
Type	Frictionless Support
Suppressed	No

■ Frictionless Support

Figure 5-3 Displacement boundary conditions.

5.   Environment > Loads > Pressure > Ctrl Select all interior surfaces > **Details of "Pressure" > Apply**

6.   Details of "Pressure" > Magnitude > 35 MPa

Details of "Pressure"	⊉
⊟ **Scope**	
Scoping Method	Geometry Selection
Geometry	3 Faces
⊟ **Definition**	
Define By	Normal To
Type	Pressure
☐ Magnitude	35. MPa (ramped)
Suppressed	No

■ Pressure: 35. MPa

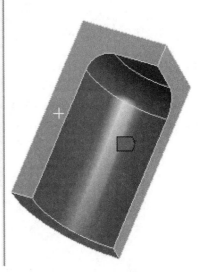

Figure 5-4 Apply pressure loading.

7.   **Solution > Stress > Equivalent (von Mises) Stress**

8.   **Solution** > (Right click) **Solve**

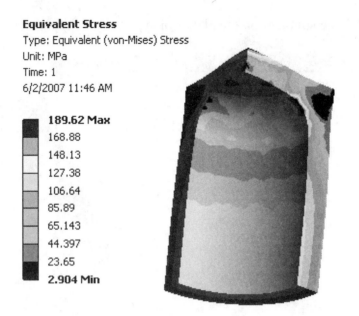

Equivalent Stress
Type: Equivalent (von-Mises) Stress
Unit: MPa
Time: 1
6/2/2007 11:46 AM

189.62 Max
168.88
148.13
127.38
106.64
85.89
65.143
44.397
23.65
2.904 Min

Figure 5-5 Computed von Mises stress using the default mesh.

We note in the figure above that the stress distribution is not smooth and uniform particularly on the inside corner fillet where the maximum values occur. The problem is symmetric in geometry, material properties, loading, and boundary conditions about the Y axis, so we would expect the solution to be also. We will manually adjust the mesh density to improve the solution.

9.   **Mesh > Details of "Mesh" > Advanced > Element Size > 10 mm**

Now solve the problem again.

10.   **Solution** > (right click) **Solve**

The new mesh and von Mises stress distribution is shown below. Note that the mesh in most locations has a least two elements through the 25 mm wall thickness.

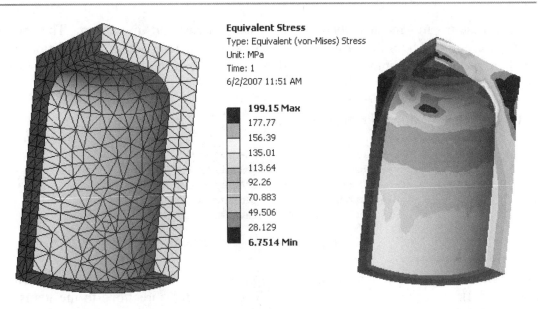

Figure 5-6 Mesh and von Mises stresses for 10 mm element size specification.

Since we still have a non-uniform stress distribution, we will reduce the mesh size to **4 mm** to seek a better computed result.

11.   Mesh > Details of "Mesh" > Advanced > Element Size > 4 mm

12.   Solution > (Right click) **Solve**

The mesh and solution are shown next.

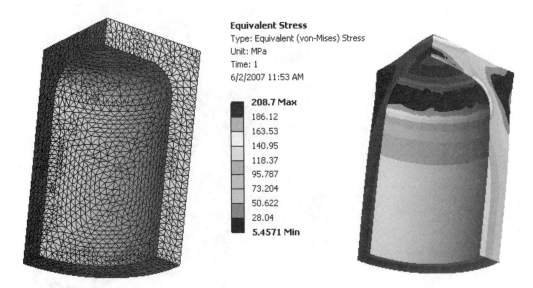

Figure 5-7 Mesh and von Mises stresses for 4 mm element size specification.

These results are much better; we'll accept them and move on. The **Solution Information** object in the project tree displays many items about the solution process including the mesh parameters. Click the solution object and scroll down to view the mesh statistics.

13. **Solution > Solution Information**

```
--- Number of total nodes = 30786
--- Number of contact elements = 1768
--- Number of spring elements = 0
--- Number of solid elements = 18657
--- Number of total elements = 20425
```

Figure 5-8 Mesh statistics.

Let's find the stress components at the mid-plane of the complete cylinder (the bottom of our model). Add the normal stresses in the X, Y, and Z directions to the items in the solution object.

14. **Solution > Stress > Normal > Details of "Normal Stress" > Type > Normal Stress > Direction > X Axis**

15. **Repeat for Y and Z axis normal stresses**

16. **Solution >** (right click) **Evaluate All Results**

17. **Solution > Normal Stress** (X axis) The Sx distribution is shown below.

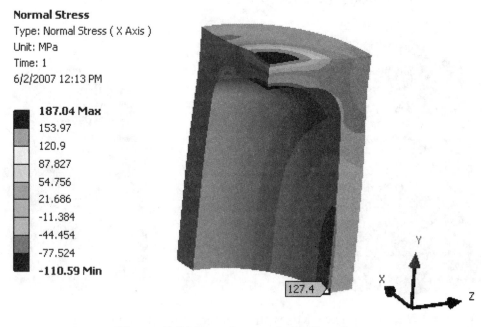

Normal Stress
Type: Normal Stress (X Axis)
Unit: MPa
Time: 1
6/2/2007 12:13 PM

187.04 Max
153.97
120.9
87.827
54.756
21.686
-11.384
-44.454
-77.524
-110.59 Min

127.4

Figure 5-9 Normal stress in X direction.

For the orientation shown, the normal stress in the X direction is the cylinder **hoop stress**. Use the "123 Probe" tool to display the X stress at the inside of the cylinder on the face normal to the X axis. [123] Probe The value shown is 127.4 MPa. Similarly we find the normal stresses in the Y and Z directions at this point to be 46.5 MPa and -34.9 MPa. These correspond to the **axial stress** and the **radial stress** in the cylinder.

Compute the radial deflection also.

18.   Solution > Deformation > Directional > Details of "Directional Deformation" > Type > Directional Deformation > Orientation > Z Axis > Evaluate All Results

The result as shown in the next figure is 0.0465 mm.

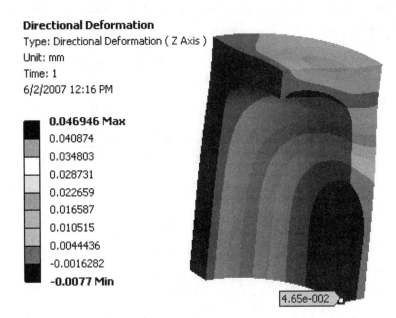

Figure 5-10 Deflection in the Z direction.

Theoretical Solution

The stresses at points removed from the stress concentration associated with the end caps can be predicted reasonably well using thick walled cylinder equations from solid mechanics or elasticity theory. For the geometry and loading of this example, theory predicts the following stress components at the **inner surface** of the cylinder. The results are summarized in the table below.

	Theoretical	Workbench	Error, per cent
Hoop Stress (Sx), MPa	125	127.4	1.9
Axial Stress (Sy), MPa	45	46.5	3.3
Radial Stress (Sz), MPa	-35	-34.9	0.3
Radial Deflection, mm	0.0458	0.0465	1.5

Thus the Workbench model arrives at a solution within a few per cent of the theoretical values, and, since the theoretical solution assumes a uniform distribution for the axial stress, the Workbench solution may give a better picture of the actual stress state in that instance. Before we quit, let's examine an **alternative meshing**.

In ANSYS Workbench we can manage the mesh in a number of different ways in addition to those already discussed. We illustrate by continuing with an alternate analysis of the pressure vessel.

First clear the results already calculated and return to the basic mesh.

19.   **File > Clean > Yes**

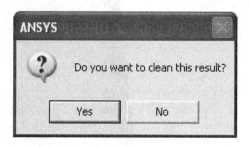

Figure 5-11 Clean results dialog.

20.   **Mesh > Details of "Mesh" > Advanced > Element Size > (enter 0, return) Default**

21.   **Mesh >** (right click) **Generate Mesh** (Gives us the mesh we started with.)

Since the interior fillet is the source of stress concentration we will use this geometry to refine the mesh.

22.   **Mesh >** (right click) **Insert > Refinement** (Select the interior fillet; see next figure.)

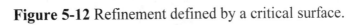

Figure 5-12 Refinement defined by a critical surface.

23.   **Details of Refinement > Geometry > Apply; Refinement 1**

24.   **Mesh > Generate Mesh** (Gives us the following mesh, dense in the high stress area.)

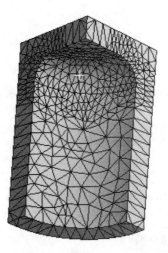

Figure 5-13 Locally refined mesh.

Let's solve this problem and examine the computed results.

25. Solution > Solve

The von Mises stress distribution is shown next, and we see reasonably smooth contours and computed magnitudes only slightly different from values for the most dense mesh obtained by manual manipulation of the element size specification in the meshing parameters details dialog box.

The **Solution Information** object or Mesh > Statistics shows this model to have around **6,000 nodes** and **3,500 elements**.

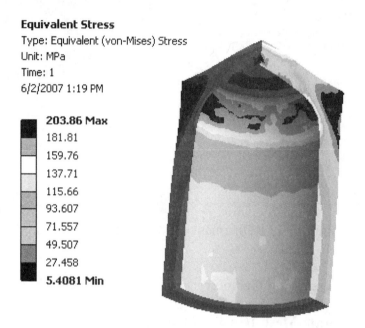

Figure 5-14 Equivalent (von-Mises) Stress.

We can take this a step further by performing an additional refinement. Change the refinement parameter from 1 to 3.

26. Mesh > Refinement > Details of "Refinement" > Refinement > 3

Details of "Refinement" - Refinement

Scope	
Scoping Method	Geometry Selection
Geometry	1 Face
Definition	
Suppressed	No
Refinement	3

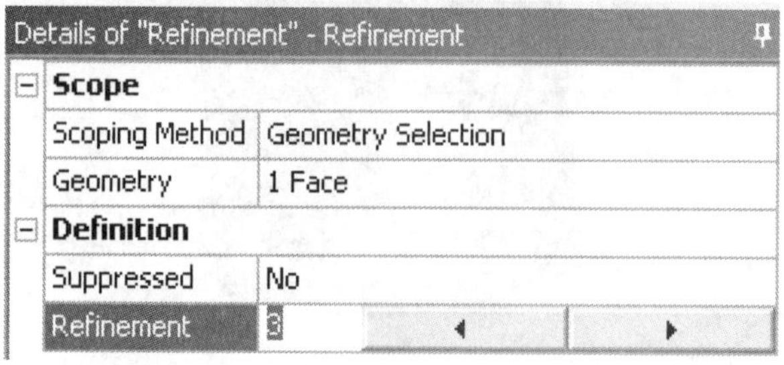

Figure 5-15 Refinement settings.

The resulting mesh with around 31,000 nodes and 20,000 elements is shown b
even though the mesh is not pretty considering the abrupt transition from low
density to high density, the computed maximum von Mises stress result seem
good.

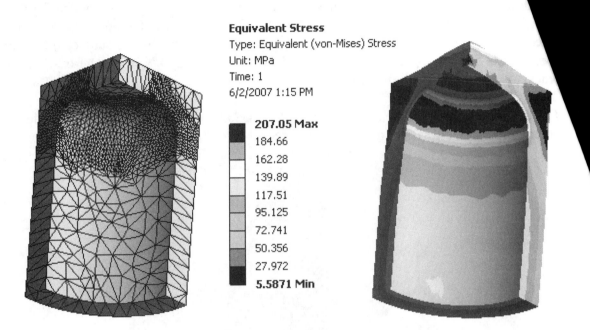

Figure 5-16 Mesh and results after second refinement.

Another meshing option we have is to insert a convergence object and perform adaptive
mesh solutions as discussed in the previous chapter. We leave this as a problem at the end
of the chapter.

elow, and
element
is quite

ET

compute the **stress** and **deflection** response of the
gure below. The bracket is 10 mm thick, 100 mm tall, 50
n. It has a 30 mm diameter bearing hole located 70 mm
let radii are 10 and 20 mm, and the 10 mm mounting bolt
from the front and side edges. The bearing is subjected to load
the X direction, 3500 N in Y, and 1700 N in Z. The base of the
st all motion.

to create the solid model of the bracket. Open ANSYS DesignModeler or
odeling system and create the bracket model using the given dimensions.

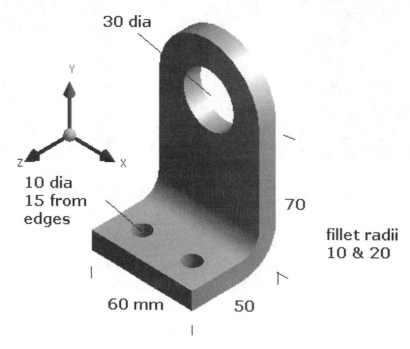

Figure 5-17 Bracket.

1.   Start **ANSYS Workbench Simulation** and **attach the bracket geometry**.

We will **import** the aluminum properties from the ANSYS library for the analysis, and.
apply a fixed support displacement constraint on the bottom of the bracket.

2.   **Model > Geometry > Solid** Right Click and **Rename** the solid **Lbrack**

3.   **Lbrack > Material >** Click the box to get the menu > **Import ...**

Figure 5-18 Import materials.

4. **Aluminum Alloy > OK**

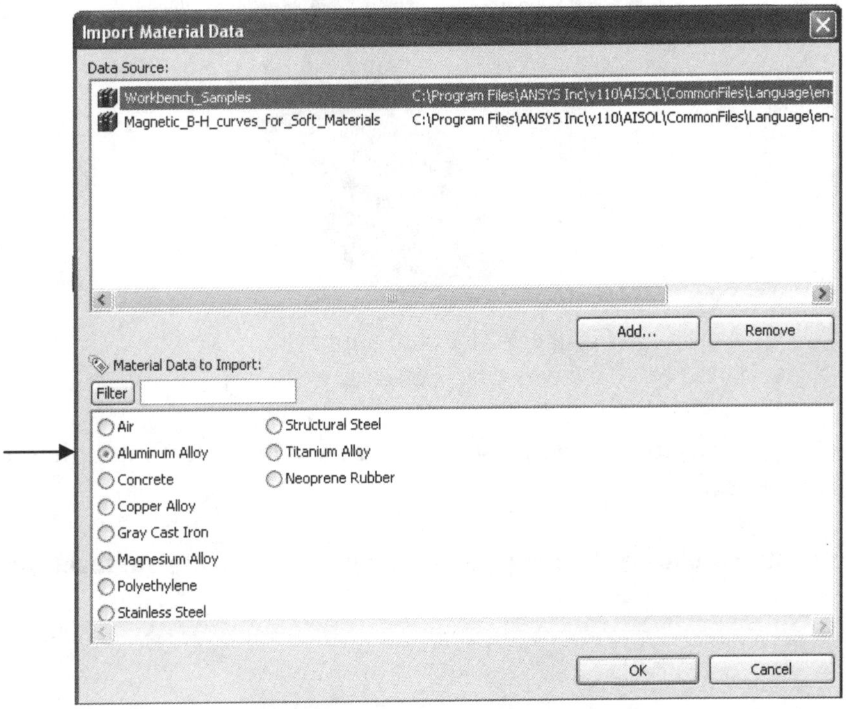

Figure 5-19 Import aluminum alloy.

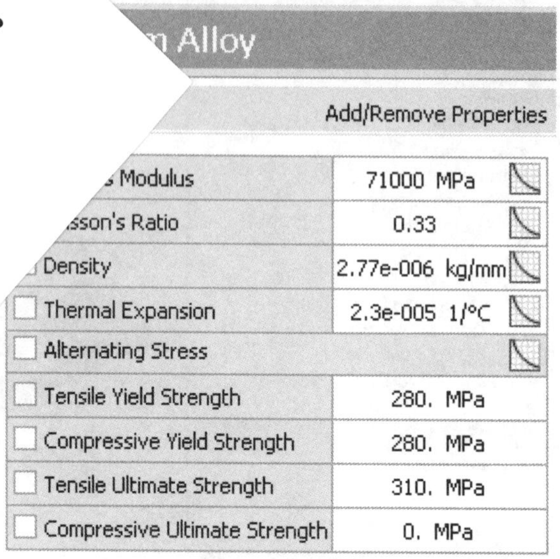

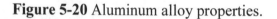

Alloy	Add/Remove Properties
Modulus	71000 MPa
sson's Ratio	0.33
Density	2.77e-006 kg/mm
☐ Thermal Expansion	2.3e-005 1/°C
☐ Alternating Stress	
☐ Tensile Yield Strength	280. MPa
☐ Compressive Yield Strength	280. MPa
☐ Tensile Ultimate Strength	310. MPa
☐ Compressive Ultimate Strength	0. MPa

Figure 5-20 Aluminum alloy properties.

5. **Environment > Supports > Fixed Support >** Select the **bottom > Apply**

Fixed Support
Time: 1. s
6/3/2007 10:55 AM

■ Fixed Support

Figure 5-21 Fixed support.

Apply the load conditions to the bearing surface. Use **Ctrl** to select multiple segments of the bore surface if need be.

6. **Environment > Loads > Bearing Load >** Select the **bearing surface(s) > Apply**

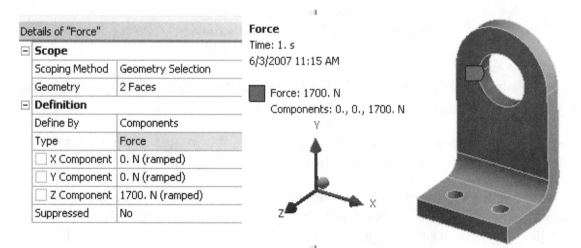

Details of "Bearing Load"	
Scope	
Scoping Method	Geometry Selection
Geometry	2 Faces
Definition	
Define By	Components
Type	Bearing Load
X Component	5500. N
Y Component	3500. N
Z Component	0. N
Suppressed	No

Bearing Load
Time: 1. s
6/3/2007 11:08 AM

Bearing Load: 6519.2 N
Components: 5500., 3500., 0. N

Figure 5-22 Bearing loading.

The bearing load object does not allow an axial component, so the axial component has to be added as a separate Force load.

7. **Environment > Loads > Force >** Select the **bearing surface(s) > Apply > 1700 N**

Details of "Force"	
Scope	
Scoping Method	Geometry Selection
Geometry	2 Faces
Definition	
Define By	Components
Type	Force
X Component	0. N (ramped)
Y Component	0. N (ramped)
Z Component	1700. N (ramped)
Suppressed	No

Force
Time: 1. s
6/3/2007 11:15 AM

Force: 1700. N
Components: 0., 0., 1700. N

Figure 5-23 Force loading.

Add **Equivalent Stress**, **Total Deformation**, and **Structural Error** to the items to be computed.

8. **Solution > Stress > Equivalent (von Mises)**

9. **Solution > Deformation > Total**

10. **Solution > Stress > Error**

...out **291 MPa** and occurs on the **bottom** side of the ...gent to the flat bottom. Call this location point "A". ...lay the default mesh along with the stress contours.

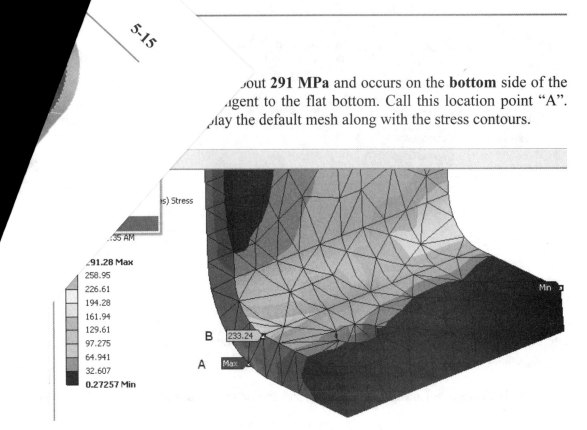

Figure 5-24 von Mises stress distribution.

The maximum von Mises stress on the **top surface** of the bracket is about 233 MPa and is located at point "B" as shown.

The total **deformation** (vector sum of components) is shown next, and it's no surprise that the maximum value is at the top of the bracket. Its value is about 1.3 mm.

Next we plot the **estimated error** and find that the maximum value is on the bottom of the bracket where the fixed support surface ends at the tangent point of the fillet radius with the fixed bottom surface. The estimated error ranges from around 2e-3 to 19.7 mJ and indicates a singularity where the fixed support surface abruptly ends much like a zero radius interior corner.

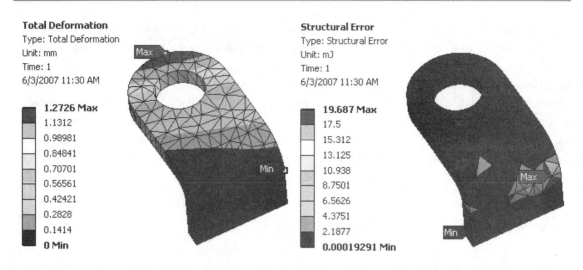

Figure 5-25 Total deformation and error estimate.

If we set the element size to 2.5 mm under Details of "Mesh" (around 15,000 elements) and solve the problem again, the computed total deflection increases to about 1.4 mm. The von Mises stress at point B increases to 271 MPa and stress on the bottom at the singular point A increases to 740 MPa.

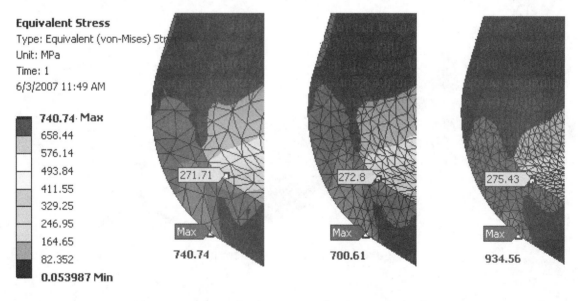

Figure 5-26 Equivalent stress for three mesh sizes.

If we reduce the characteristic element size further (1.5 mm, 45,000 elements), the deflection remains the same but the singular stress continues to change (700 MPa). The stress at point A remains essentially constant. (Your ability to solve problems with a large number of elements will depend upon the capability of the computer hardware you are using.)

Reduce the characteristic element size further (1.0 mm, 65,000 elements); the singular stress increases to change to 934 MPa but the stress at point A is about 275 MPa.

Interpretation of the stress at point A depends, among other things, upon support details, characteristic of the load (static or dynamic), material (brittle or ductile; this example assumes a ductile aluminum). In the actual part, the contact area between the bottom and its support may increase or decrease as bending of the bracket occurs. We see that determination of loadings and boundary conditions can be much more difficult than modeling the geometry.

5-5   TUTORIAL 5C – CLEVIS ASSEMBLY

In the final tutorial of this chapter we examine the stress and deformations in the clevis component of the yoke-stem-pin assembly discussed at the end of Chapter 2. The objective is to determine the yoke stresses caused by a tensile load carried by the yoke and stem.

1.   Start **ANSYS Workbench Simulation** and **attach the yoke assembly**. The assembly can be developed in ANSYS DesignModeler or in another solid modeler of your choice. The assembly shown below is similar to the DesignModeler tutorial T2C.

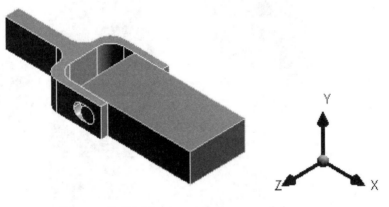

Figure 5-27 Clevis, pin, stem model.

2.   **Check the units settings** to be sure you're using **in-lbf-sec**.

3.   **Expand** the **Geometry** object in the simulation outline tree.

There are **three solids** in the geometry item: the **Yoke**, the **Stem**, and the **Pin**. If need be, **right click on the label "Solid"** and **rename** the items yoke, stem or pin. We accept the default **structural steel material** for all the parts.

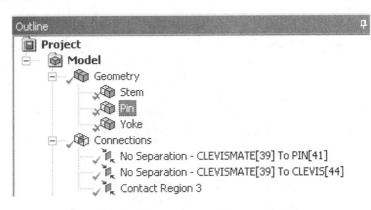

Figure 5-28 Geometry and contact objects.

4.   Expand the **Contact** object in the simulation outline tree.

There are **three regions of contact** in the assembly: the **insides of the yoke fingers contacting the sides of the stem**, the **pin contacting the hole in the stem**, and the **pin contacting the slots in the yoke fingers**.

5.   Click on each of the three contact items in turn. We see the three different contact surfaces as shown below. The order of your contact surfaces may be different depending upon how you built your assembly model.

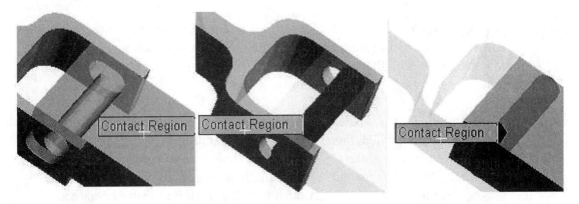

Figure 5-29 Three contact surfaces.

There are a number of different contact models available to us to represent different kinds of contacting surfaces. Click on the first contact item and examine the options.

6.   Contact > Contact Region > Details of "Contact Region" > Definition > Type

The options for the type of contact are: **Bonded, No Separation, Frictionless, Rough,** and **Frictional**. The **default** selection is **Bonded**.

Details of "Contact Region"	⊓
Scope	
Scoping Method	Geometry Selection
Contact	2 Faces
Target	2 Faces
Contact Bodies	Yoke
Target Bodies	Stem
Definition	
Type	Bonded ▼
Scope Mode	Bonded
Behavior	No Separation / Frictionless
Suppressed	Rough / Frictional
Advanced	
Formulation	Pure Penalty
Normal Stiffness	Program Controlled
Update Stiffness	Never
Thermal Conductance	Program Controlled
Pinball Region	Program Controlled

Figure 5-30 Types of contact modeling available.

These contact types are defined as follows (from the **ANSYS Simulation Help** files. Search on 'Contact' then select information on the 'Type' of contact):

- **Type**: The differences in the contact settings determine how the contacting bodies can move relative to one another. This is the most common setting and has the most impact on what other settings are available. Most of these types only apply to contact regions made up of faces only.

    - **Bonded**: This is the default configuration for contact regions. If contact regions are bonded, then no sliding or separation between faces or edges is allowed. Think of the region as *glued*. This type of contact allows for a linear solution since the contact length/area will not change during the application of the load. If contact is determined on the mathematical model, any gaps will be closed and any initial penetration will be ignored.
    - **No Separation**: This contact setting is similar to the bonded case. It only applies to regions of faces. Separation of faces in contact is not allowed, but small amounts of frictionless sliding can occur along contact faces.
    - **Frictionless**: This setting models standard unilateral contact; that is, normal pressure equals zero if separation occurs. It only applies to regions of faces. Thus gaps can form in the model between bodies depending on the loading. This solution is nonlinear because the area of contact may change as the load is applied. A zero coefficient of friction is assumed, thus allowing free sliding. The model should be well constrained when using this contact setting. Weak springs are added to the assembly to help stabilize the model in order to achieve a reasonable solution.

- **Rough**: Similar to the frictionless setting, this setting models perfectly rough frictional contact where there is no sliding. It only applies to regions of faces. By default, no automatic closing of gaps is performed. This case corresponds to an infinite friction coefficient between the contacting bodies.
- **Frictional**: In this setting, two contacting faces can carry shear stresses up to a certain magnitude across their interface before they start sliding relative to each other. It only applies to regions of faces. This state is known as "sticking." The model defines an equivalent shear stress at which sliding on the face begins as a fraction of the contact pressure. Once the shear stress is exceeded, the two faces will slide relative to each other. The coefficient of friction can be any non-negative value.

Choosing the appropriate contact type depends on the type of problem you are trying to solve. If modeling the ability of bodies to separate or open slightly is important and/or obtaining the stresses very near a contact interface is important, consider using one of the nonlinear contact types (**Frictionless**, **Rough**, **Frictional**), which can model gaps and more accurately model the true area of contact. However, using these contact types usually results in longer solution times and can have possible convergence problems due to the contact nonlinearity. If convergence problems arise or if determining the exact area of contact is critical, consider using a finer mesh (using the Sizing control) on the contact faces or edges."

We will focus in our example on the **pin contacting the slots in the yoke fingers** and the **stress in the yoke**. Since the tensile loading can be assumed to maintain contact between these two surfaces, the **No Separation** model seems most appropriate.

And since **No Separation** allows for small amounts of sliding along the contacting surfaces, we will use that model for the fingers contacting the sides of the stem as well.

If we assume that the pin is tightly fit into the hole in the stem, **Bonded** is an appropriate choice for this contacting pair.

These choices result in linear models that solve rather quickly. If more detail is desired at the pin-yoke contact surface, one of the nonlinear contact models can be used.

7. **Set the contact types to No Separation, No Separation, Bonded**. (Your order may be different.)

8. **Restrict the Yoke** from motion in the **X Direction** and **Apply a -1000 psi pressure** to the **Stem** also in the **X Direction**. The stem cross sectional area is 2 sq. inches, so this corresponds to a **tensile load of 2,000 lbf**.

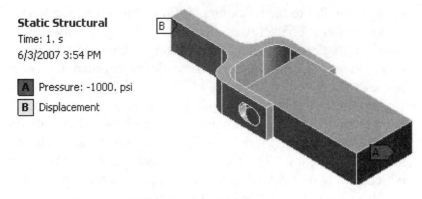

Figure 5-31 Structural environment conditions.

9.   **Select X Direction Displacement**, **X Direction Normal Stress** and **Equivalent Stress** as solution items.

10.   **Mesh > Generate Mesh** The default mesh is shown below.

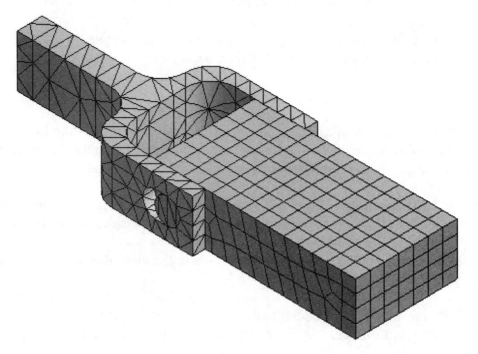

Figure 5-32 Default mesh.

We will **refine the default mesh** at the pin-yoke contact surfaces in order to increase the accuracy of the modeling in this region.

To isolate the yoke so we can see the contact surface, hide the other objects.

11. Geometry > Right Click Yoke > Hide All Other Bodies

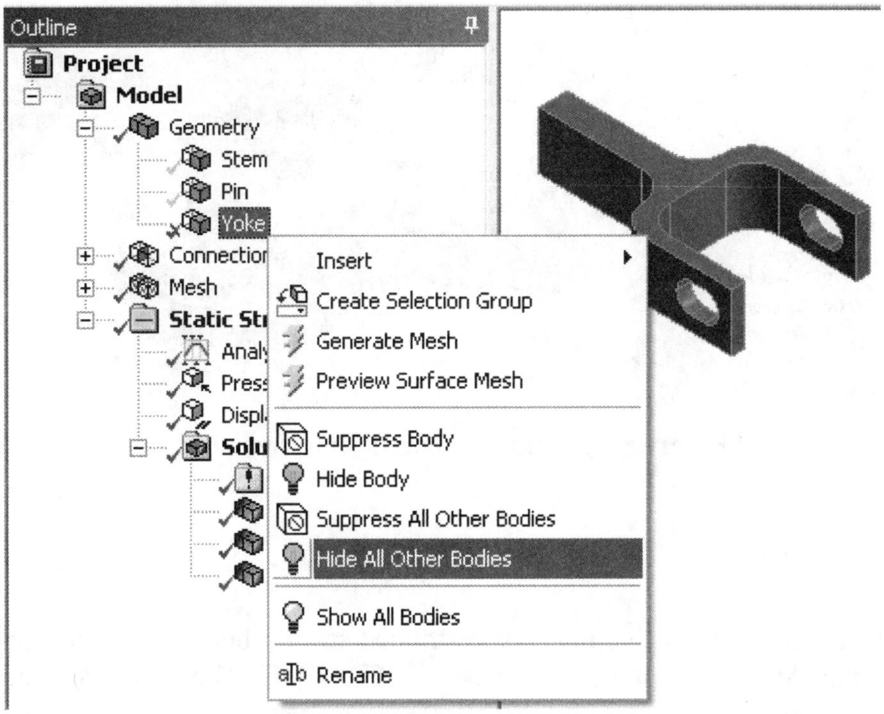

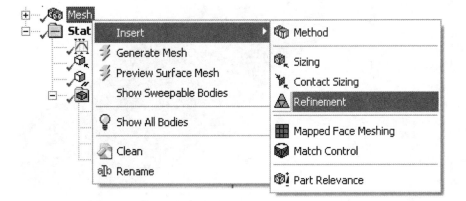

Figure 5-33 Isolate the yoke.

12. Right Click Mesh > Insert > Refinement

Figure 5-34 Insert refinement.

13. Use Ctrl Select to select the yoke slot surfaces.

The refined meshes are shown below.

14. Repeat this process to isolate the pin and refine its surface.

Show all the bodies and then solve the simulation model.

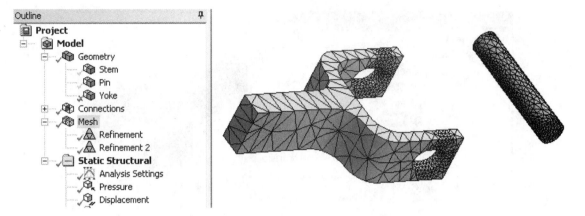

Figure 5-35 Yoke and pin mesh refinements.

15. Solve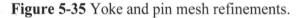

Rigid body motions are not completely restrained by the boundary conditions, so the **Weak Springs Added Warning** may be issued. **Click OK**. The following figure shows the computed von Mises stresses with a maximum just over 32 kpsi.

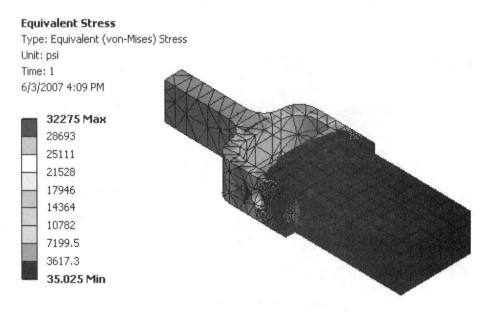

Figure 5-36 Computed von Mises stress.

Hide all bodies except the yoke and display the computed stresses in the yoke.

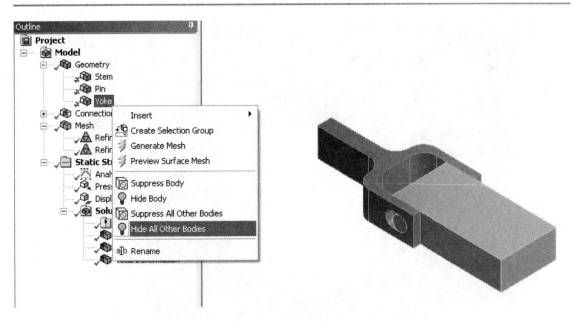

Figure 5-37 Isolate the yoke for evaluation.

The figure below shows the yoke von Mises and X Direction normal stress distributions in the yoke. The maximum values occur in the thin region of the yoke slots.

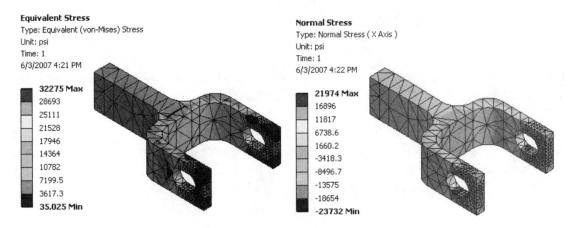

Figure 5-38 Stresses in the yoke.

Zoom in on the bearing surface where the pin and yoke are in contact and examine the stress in the X Direction.

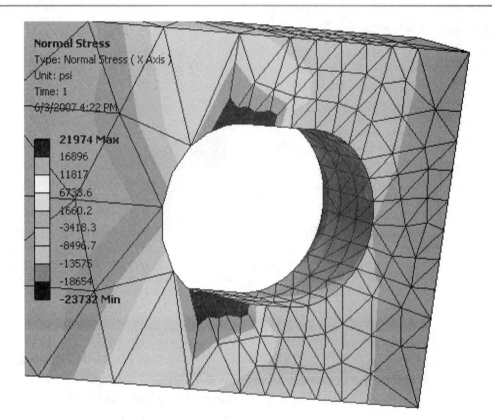

Figure 5-39 Normal stress in the X Direction.

The minimum value (maximum compressive stress) is around –24 kpsi, and the maximum tensile X Direction stress is about 22 kpsi.

Symmetry can be used to eliminate all rigid body motions and avoid the automatic addition of weak springs to stabilize the model. To enforce symmetric behavior, open the clevis assembly in the solid modeler and remove three quarters of the solid model, say the bottom and right portions as shown in the figure below.

Figure 5-40 Quadrant of clevis assembly

Apply displacement boundary conditions that prevent motion of the exposed plane of symmetry surface in directions perpendicular to those surfaces.

5-6 SUMMARY

The tutorials of Chapter 5 illustrate the use of ANSYS Simulation for calculation of stress and deflection response of typical three-dimensional solids. Included is an example of analysis of an assembly with contacting parts. In the next chapter we examine the many wizards and tools provided by ANSYS Simulation to assist with simulations of the type described in this book.

5-7 PROBLEMS

5-1   Determine the magnitude and location of the **maximum von Mises** stress for the cylinder of Tutorial 5A if the 35 MPa pressure is an **external pressure**.

5-2   The flat head of the cylinder of Tutorial 5A is replaced with a head that is hemispherical. Find the magnitude and location of the **maximum principal tensile stress** due the 35 MPa internal pressure if the cylinder is made of gray cast iron. Report your computed stress results in MPa and in psi. Also find the maximum outward deflection of a point on the inner surface.

5-3   Select your own dimensions and material, create a solid model of a foot control lever such as the one shown in the figure below, and determine the magnitude and location of the maximum von Mises stress and the maximum total deflection if a load equal to your weight is applied to the foot plate while the inside of the cylindrical bore is held fixed in all directions.

Figure P5-3

NOTES:

Chapter 6

Wizards & Tools

6-1   OVERVIEW

ANSYS Simulation provides a number of Tools and Wizards to assist with successful simulation projects. This Chapter illustrates the use of these typical applications. In particular we discuss the use of

♦ Wizards for simulation problem setup

♦ Tools for simulation assessment

6-2   INTRODUCTION

ANSYS Simulation provides a large number of aids and help file information to assist the user with problem setup and interpretation of computed results. In this chapter we discuss their use for problems involving static loading and fatigue loading. Wizards and tools for other problem types are covered in later discussions.

6-3   TUTORIAL 6A – STATIC LOADINGS - DUCTILE MATERIALS

In this tutorial we compute the stress state and deflection response of the plate with a central hole that was considered at the beginning of Chapter 4 but use an ANSYS Simulation Wizard to assist with the solution. The **1000 x 400 x 10 mm** plate is shown in the illustration below. It has a central circular hole **200 mm** in **diamete**r and supports an axial **tensile load** of **120 kN** which we apply as a uniformly distributed pressure of **-30 MPa**.

The first step is to create the **solid model** of the bracket. Open ANSYS DesignModeler or other parametric modeling system and develop the model of the **complete plate** and save it for use later.

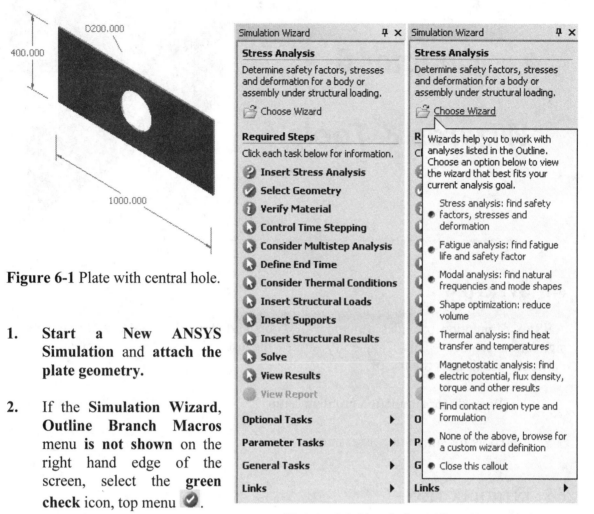

Figure 6-1 Plate with central hole.

1.   **Start a New ANSYS Simulation** and **attach the plate geometry.**

2.   If the **Simulation Wizard, Outline Branch Macros** menu **is not shown** on the right hand edge of the screen, select the **green check** icon, top menu ✅.

Figure 6-2 Simulation Wizard menus.

The Simulation Wizard Menus outline the steps to be taken in a Simulation.

3.   Select **Choose Wizard** to view the **seven predefined wizards** available to you. **Stress Analysis is the default.** Then **Close this callout**.

4.   Choose **Insert Stress Analysis**.

5.   Select **New Analysis > Static Structural**.

The **Static Structural object** is inserted in the **outline tree** as shown below.

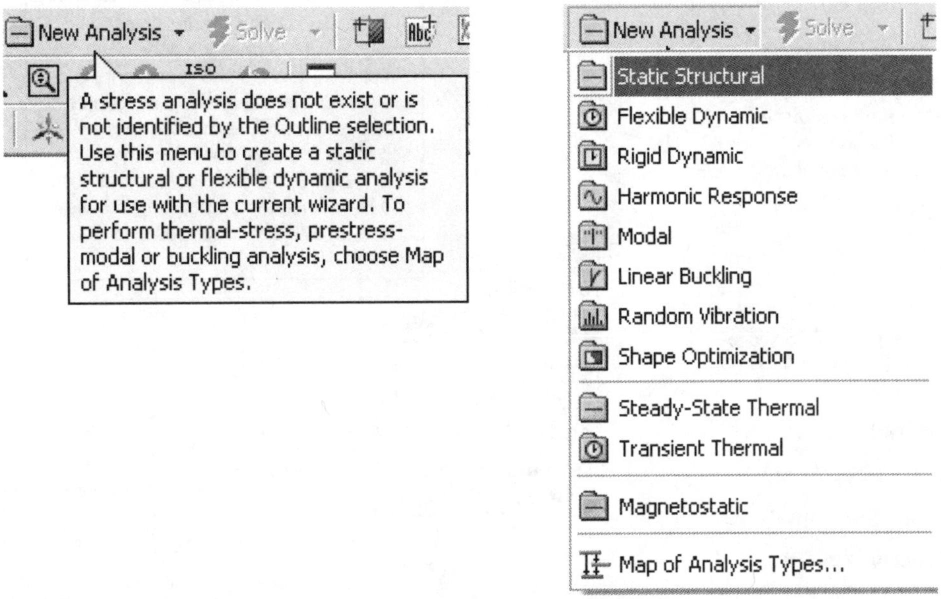

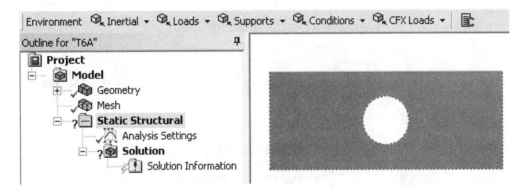

Figure 6-3 New analysis.

The **Solution Object has been** inserted in the **Project Tree** as shown in the figure below.

Figure 6-4 Structural static solution added to outline.

In the Stress Analysis Simulation Wizard (shown below) an 'X' ✗ indicates a step that has not been completed while a Check ✓ marks a completed step. Additional information is indicated with an ⓘ.

Note that because we have already attached the plate geometry, the **Select Geometry** for this simulation is checked as complete.

Read the **Environment** information note and select **Static Structural** in the Details of Static Structural box.

6.   Details of Static Structural > Static Structural

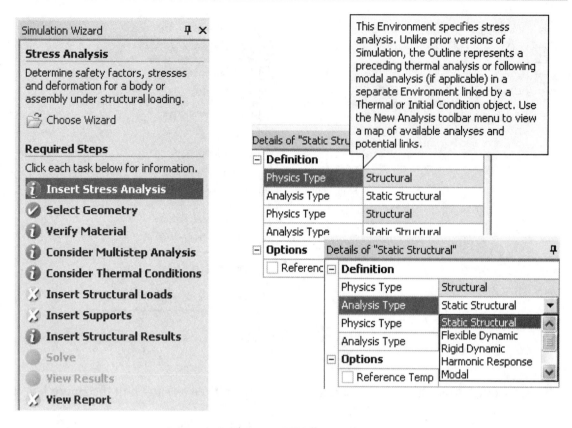

Figure 6-5 Details of Static Structural.

The link to the geometry step is now checked off and we will **Verify** the **Material** next.

7.   **Verify Material**

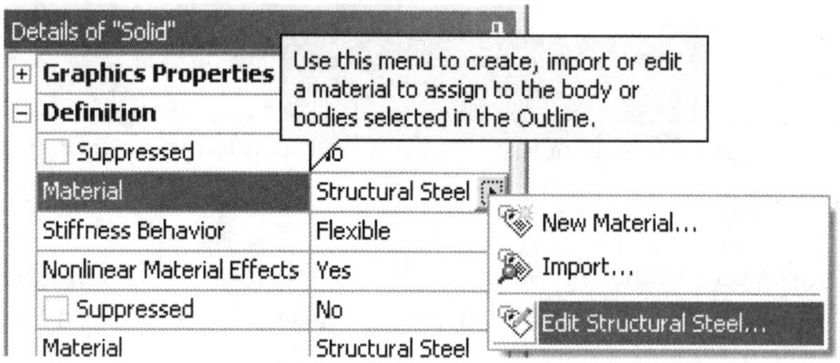

Figure 6-6 Verify the material assigned to this part.

8.   Select **Edit Structural Steel**.

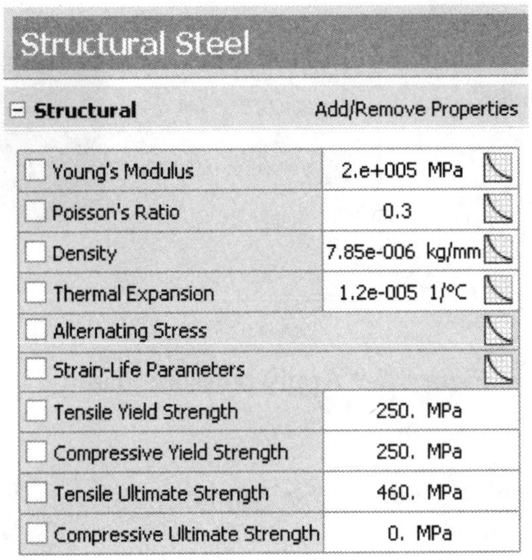

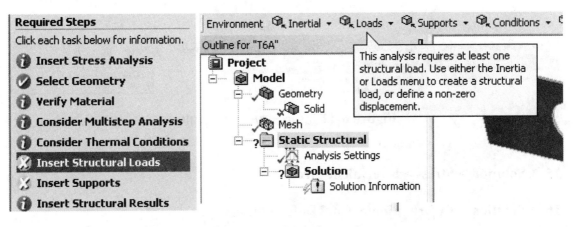

Figure 6-7 Edit the material properties.

We will not change any of these quantities but note the values of the **Yield** and **Ultimate Strengths** for the default structural steel.

9.   Close the Engineering Data Tab. 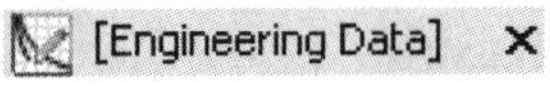   [Engineering Data]   ✕

The next item on the list of **Required Steps** is **Insert Loads**.

10.   Insert Structural Loads.   Insert Structural Loads

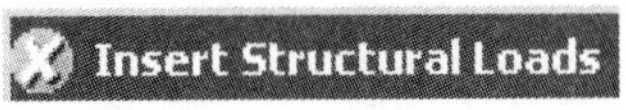

Figure 6-8 'Insert Loads' information message.

Apply a -30.0 MPa pressure to each end face of the plate. (We're using the whole plate this time.)

11.   Environment > Loads > Pressure > Ctrl Left Click to select both end planes.

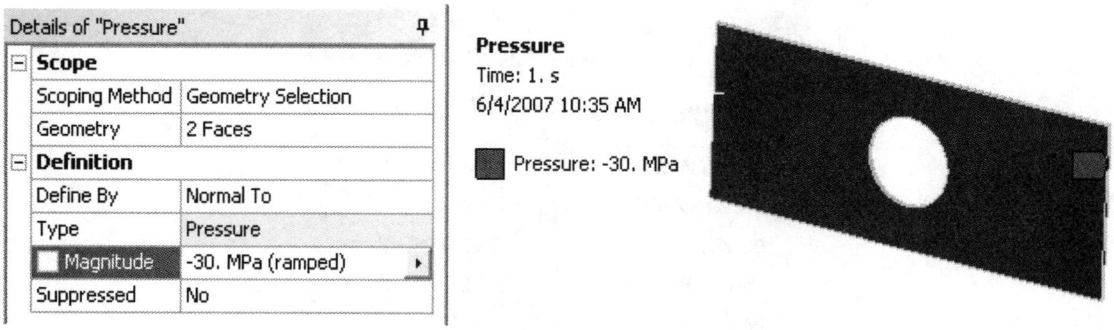

Figure 6-9 Apply pressure loading.

12. **Details of "Pressure" > Geometry > Apply**

13. **Details of "Pressure" > Magnitude > -30.0**

Insert Loads is now checked off, and the next item is **Insert Supports**. We are not going to supply any supports and see if the **Weak Springs** feature will take care of the rigid body motions well enough.

14. **Insert Structural Results** is the next item in the wizard.

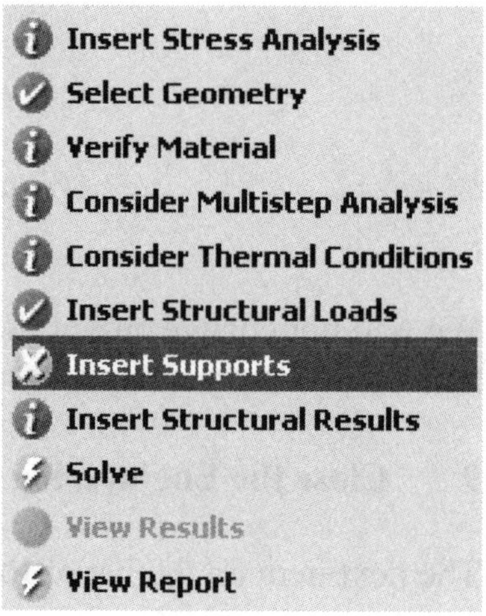

Figure 6-10 Wizard status.

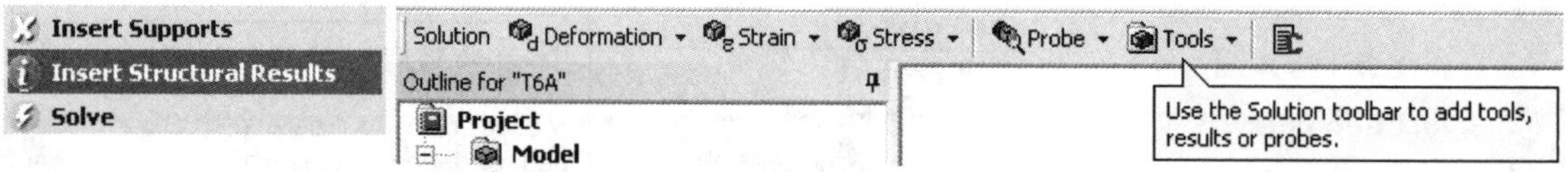

Figure 6-11 Insert structural results.

15. **Solution > Stress > Equivalent Stress**

16. **Solution > Deformation > Total Deformation**

17. **Solution > Tools > Stress Tool**

18. **Solution > Tools > Stress Tool > Safety Margin**

19. Solve

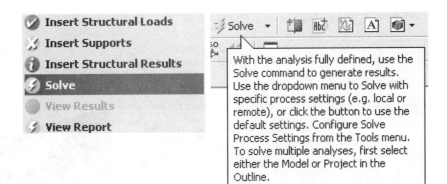

Figure 6-12 'Solve' information message.

We get the solution status message and the rigid-body warning message as shown below.

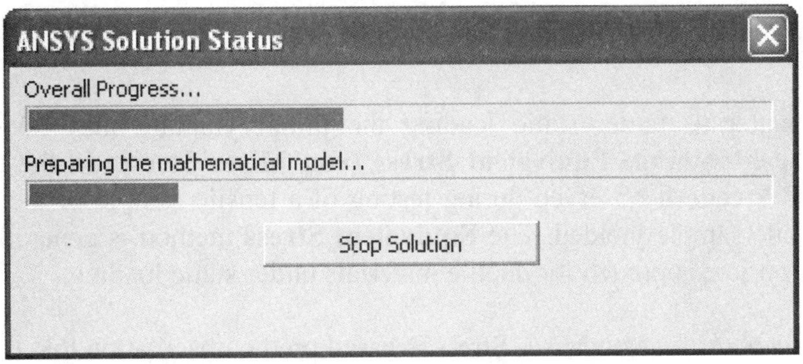

Figure 6-13 Solution status.

This model has no displacement constraints to prevent rigid body motion from occurring. To suppress rigid body motion, ANSYS Workbench automatically adds weak spring supports and issues a warning in the message box at the bottom of the screen.

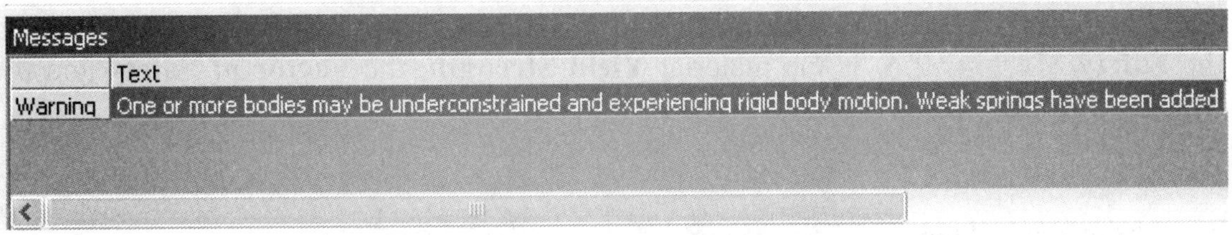

Figure 6-14 Rigid body motion warning.

The Wizard menu is complete and we are ready to **View Results**.

20.   Solution > Equivalent Stress

21.   Edges > Show Elements

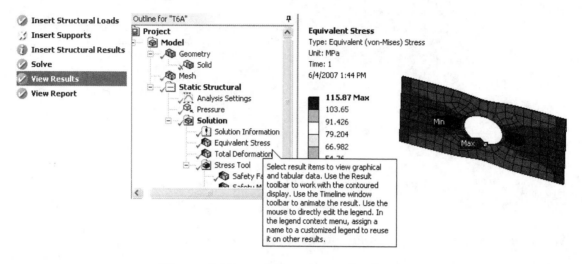

Figure 6-15 von Mises stress distribution.

For ductile materials under static loading the initial yielding may be predicted by comparing the **Maximum Equivalent Stress (von Mises Stress)** in the part with the **Tensile Yield Strength** observed during testing of a tensile sample of the part material when the tensile sample yielded. The **Equivalent Stress** method is generally considered the most appropriate approach for ductile materials under static loading.

The Equivalent Stress or von Mises Stress is based on the observation that the hydrostatic component of a general stress state does not influence yielding in a ductile material and it combines the various stresses in a generally complex stress situation into a single quantity as follows:

$$\sigma_e = \sqrt{\frac{(\sigma_1 - \sigma_2)^2 + (\sigma_2 - \sigma_3)^2 + (\sigma_3 - \sigma_1)^2}{2}}$$

The stress tool wizard automatically inserts the **Safety Factor** computation and we added the **Safety Margin**. If S_y is the material **Yield Strength**, the **Factor of Safety** and the **Margin of Safety** are defined as:

$$F_s = \frac{S_y}{\sigma_e} \qquad\qquad M_s = F_s - 1$$

22.   Click Stress Tool, then **Safety Factor**, then **Safety Margin**. We see the following in the details boxes. Minimum values of these are the significant quantities.

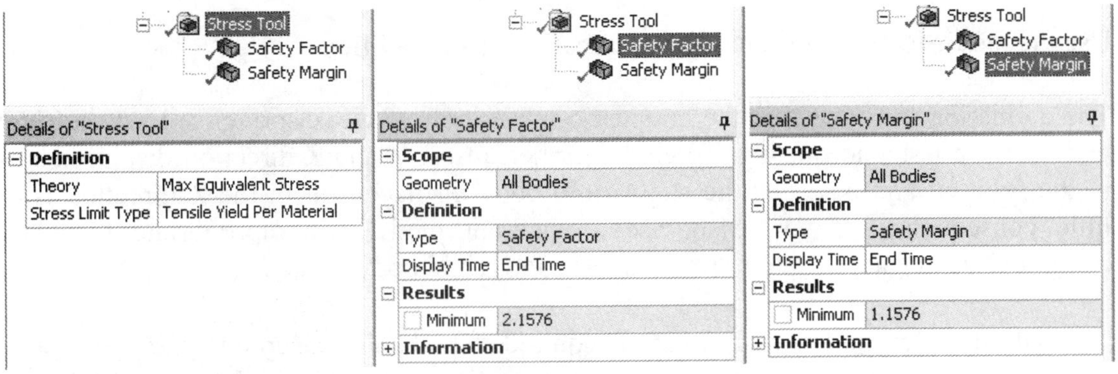

Figure 6-16 Stress tool results.

Check to see if the lack of constraints caused any undesirable rigid body motion.

23.   **Solution > Total Deformation > Animation > Play**

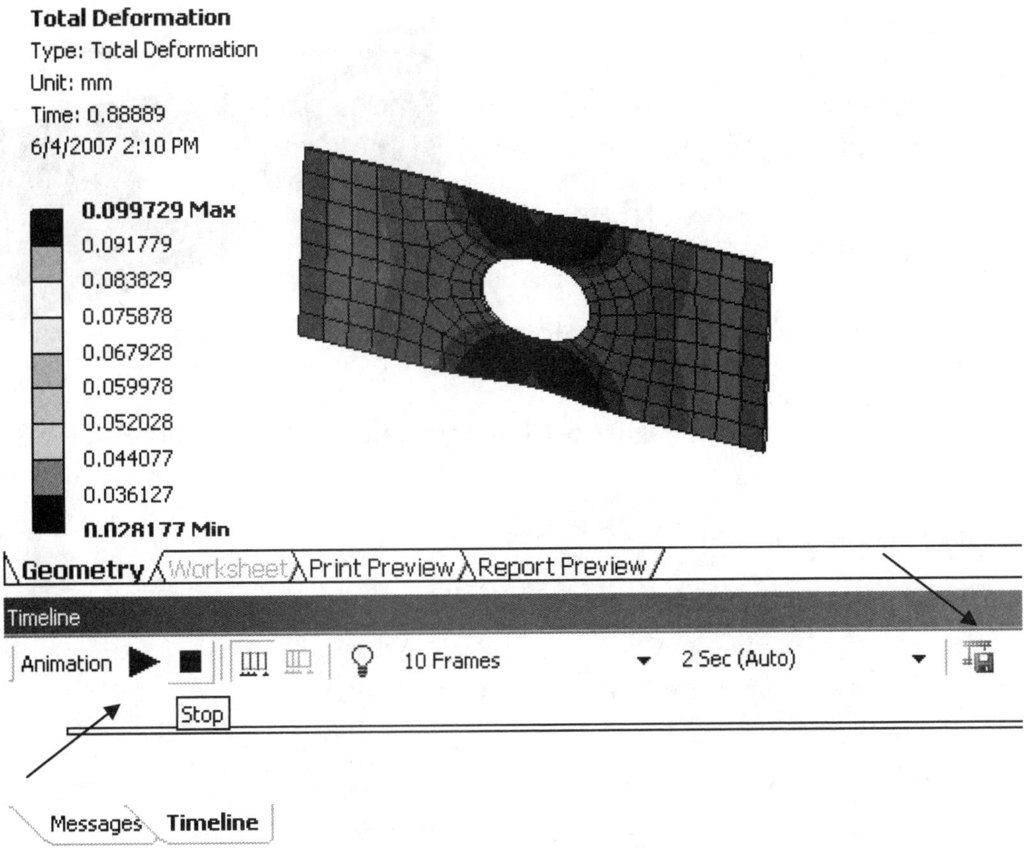

Total Deformation
Type: Total Deformation
Unit: mm
Time: 0.88889
6/4/2007 2:10 PM

0.099729 Max
0.091779
0.083829
0.075878
0.067928
0.059978
0.052028
0.044077
0.036127
0.028177 Min

Figure 6-17 Deformation plot.

Use the movie icon 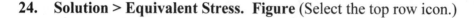 to capture the animation in an **AVI file**.

The animation indicates that the automatic imposition of weak springs solved the rigid body motion issue adequately. To check further, insert Y and Z direction displacements in the solution and note that the slight rigid body displacement in the Z direction is of little consequence. If you wish, use a quadrant model with appropriate boundary conditions as in Chapter 4 to prevent any spurious rigid body motion.

The only item left on the wizard list of required steps is **View Report**.   🖉 **View Report**
Before viewing the report, **insert a figure** of the **Equivalent Stress Distribution** in the solution. This figure will appear in the report.

24.   Solution > Equivalent Stress. Figure (Select the top row icon.)

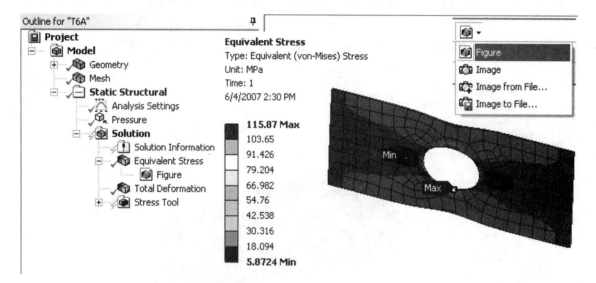

Figure 6-18 Insert a figure.

Now select view report.

25.   Simulation Wizard > View Report

The result is shown in the figure on the next page.

Project

Author	*Kent L Lawrence*
Subject	*Tutorial T6A*
Prepared for	*ANSYS WorkBench 11.0 Tutorial*
First Saved	*Wednesday, February 22, 2006*
Last Saved	*Wednesday, February 22, 2006*
Product Version	*11.0 Release*

Contents

- **Model**
  - Geometry
    - Solid
  - Mesh
  - **Static Structural**
    - Analysis Settings
    - Pressure
    - Solution
      - Solution Information
      - Results
      - Stress Tool
        - Results
- **Material Data**
  - Structural Steel

Figure 6-19 Report first page and contents.

The details of the project are included in this report including any figures that were inserted in the solution. Once the report has been generated, it can be printed, published, sent as an email, imported into Word or Power Point, or refreshed as project tree items change by selecting from the icon menu below.

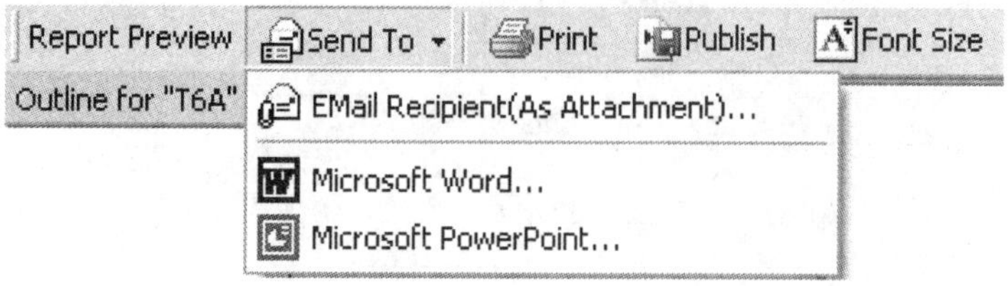

Figure 6-20 Report options.

26.   Save your work as T6A.

The results of this tutorial show that the maximum equivalent or von Mises stress computed for this loading and geometry is around **116 MPa**, and based upon the **equivalent stress method** and a material **tensile yield strength** of **250 MPa**, the predicted **factor of safety** for the part is around **2.2**. We may wish to insert an error estimate, refine the mesh, and evaluate these measures again, but will leave that for a problem. In the next tutorial we will solve the same problem but assume that the part is made of a brittle material.

6-4   TUTORIAL 6B – STATIC LOADINGS – BRITTLE MATERIALS

Two changes to the analysis are required to consider the plate with a central hole to be made of a brittle material. We need to change the material specification as well as the solution quantities and the details of the factor and margin of safety. Use the same geometry and loading for this tutorial as in Tutorial 6A.

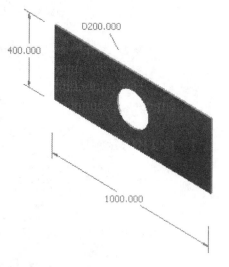

1.   Verify Material

2.   Geometry > Solid > Details of "Solid" > Material > Structural Steel > New Material

Figure 6-21 Plate with central hole.

We will use a **cast iron** with **E = 1.0E5 MPa, Poisson's ratio = 0.28, Ultimate Tensile Strength = 152 MPa** and an **Ultimate Compressive Strength = 572 MPa**.

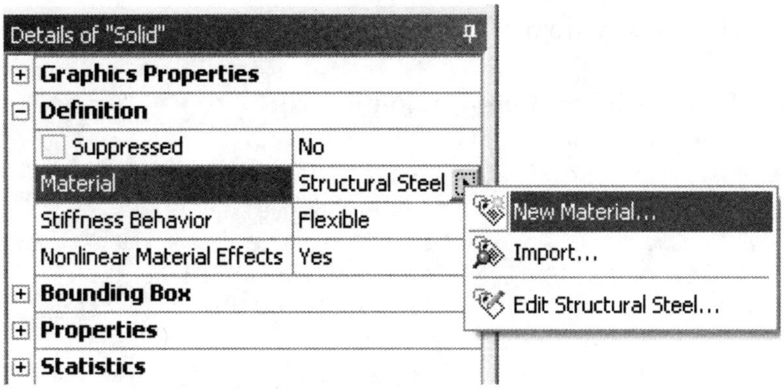

Figure 6-22 Select a new material.

3. **New Material > Add/Remove Properties** (Remove **Density** and **Thermal Expansion**; add **Tensile** and **Compressive Ultimate Strength**.) **> OK > OK**

We will assume that the yield strength and ultimate strength are the same since there is little or no material ductility.

4. **Right click** on **New Material** in the materials tree and **change the name to Cast Iron**. See the illustration that follows.

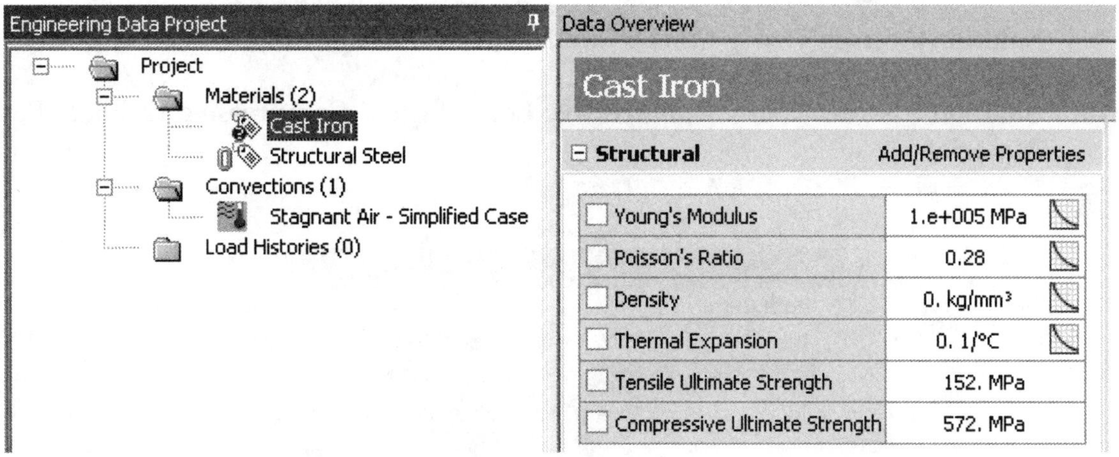

Figure 6-23 Material properties for cast iron.

5. **Delete the Equivalent Stress object from the outline tree.**

Add the maximum and minimum principal stress objects to the outline.

6. **Solution > Stress > Maximum Principal**

7. **Solution > Stress > Minimum Principal**

Change the stress tool theory from Max Equivalent to Mohr-Coulomb Stress.

8.   Solution > Stress Tool > Mohr-Coulomb Stress

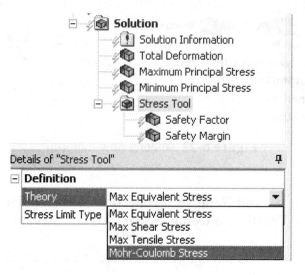

Figure 6-24 Project tree.

Make sure the Limit Types are the material Ultimate Strengths.

9.   Solution > Stress Tool > Tensile Limit Type > Tensile Ultimate Per Material

10.   Solution > Stress Tool > Compressive Limit Type > Compressive Ultimate Per Material

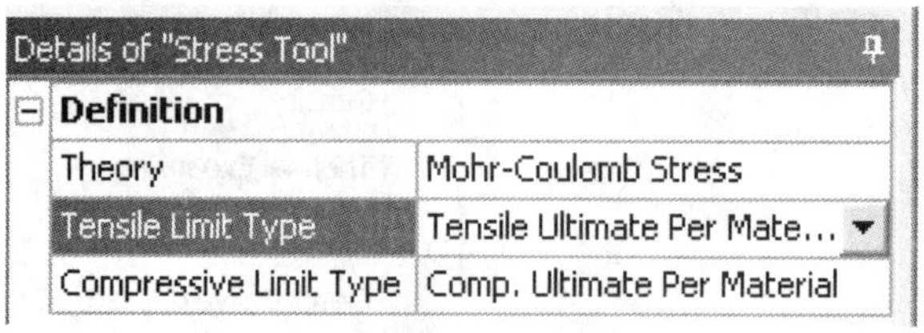

Figure 6-25 Details of Stress Tool.

The Mohr-Coulomb method may be used to predict failure of parts made from brittle materials. The Mohr-Coulomb method takes into account the differences between tensile ultimate strength and compressive ultimate strength that are common in brittle materials. The method compares the maximum principal tensile stress σ_1 to the material ultimate tensile strength S_{ut} and the minimum principal stress σ_3 with the material ultimate compressive strength S_{uc}. No fracture is predicted if

$$\frac{\sigma_1}{S_{ut}} + \frac{\sigma_3}{S_{uc}} < 1$$

The factor of safety and margin of safety are defined as

$$\frac{1}{F_s} = \frac{\sigma_1}{S_{ut}} + \frac{\sigma_3}{S_{uc}} \qquad\qquad M_s = F_s - 1$$

All of the required steps in the simulation wizard are now complete and we can solve for the response.

11.   Solve $\not\!\!\!\! \not{\,} $ Solve

The minimum **factor of safety** based upon the **Mohr-Coulomb** (or Coulomb-Mohr) method is found to be **1.28** giving a 0.28 or **28 per cent margin of safety**.

The figure below shows the distribution of the computed results for safety factor.

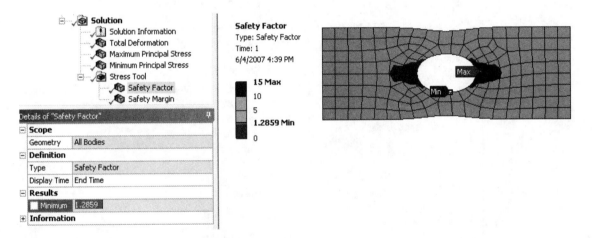

Figure 6-26 Computed safety factor.

12.   Save your work as T6B.

In the next section we consider the use of simulation wizard for **fatigue analysis**.

6-5   TUTORIAL 6C – FATIGUE LOADINGS – DUCTILE MATERIALS

Return to the problem of Tutorial 6A but now consider a fatigue environment for the ductile steel plate.

1.   **Start ANSYS Simulation, Open T6A,** and turn on **Simulation Wizard** if necessary.

2.   **From Choose Wizard select Fatigue** (see the figure below).

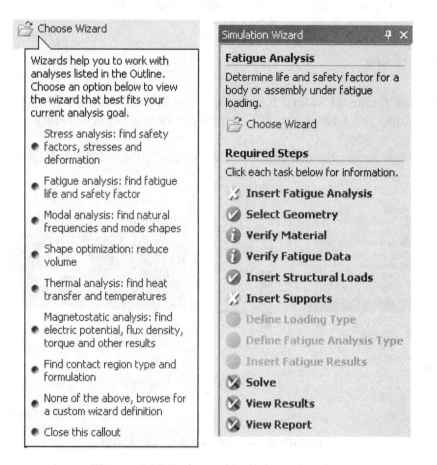

Figure 6-27 Fatigue simulation wizard.

3.   **Insert Fatigue Analysis**

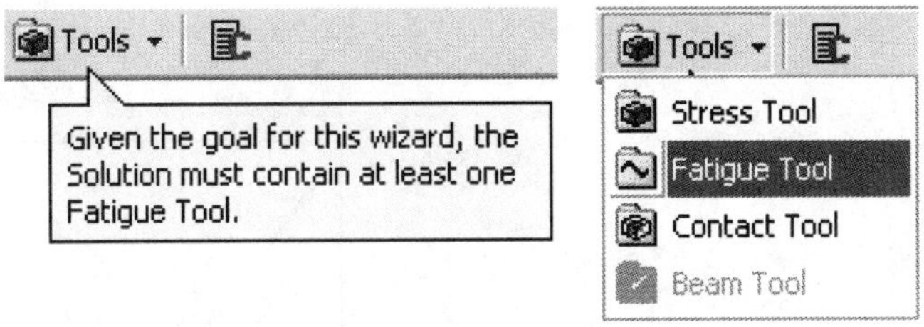

Figure 6-28 Fatigue simulation wizard.

Details of "Fatigue Tool"	
Materials	
Fatigue Strength Factor (Kf)	1.
Loading	
Type	Fully Reversed
Scale Factor	1.
Definition	
Display Time	End Time
Options	
Analysis Type	Stress Life
Mean Stress Theory	None
Stress Component	Equivalent (Von Mises)
Life Units	
Units Name	cycles
1 cycle is equal to	1. cycles

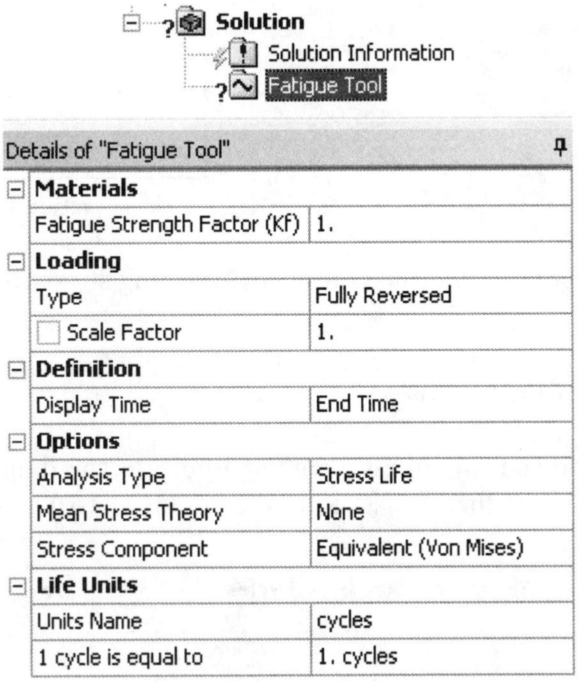

Figure 6-29 Fatigue simulation wizard.

Select the default options to consider the case of a **completely reversed loading** based on a **stress S-N curve** using the **von Mises equivalent stress** method to combine stress with no surface, size, etc. corrections applied to the material properties ($K_f = 1$).

4.   Solution > Stress > Equivalent Stress

We will use the **default structural steel** for the material.

5.   Verify Material (Select structural steel.)

6.   Verify Fatigue Data   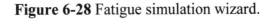 **Verify Fatigue Data**

Verify that the material has an **Alternating Stress vs. Cycles curve**.

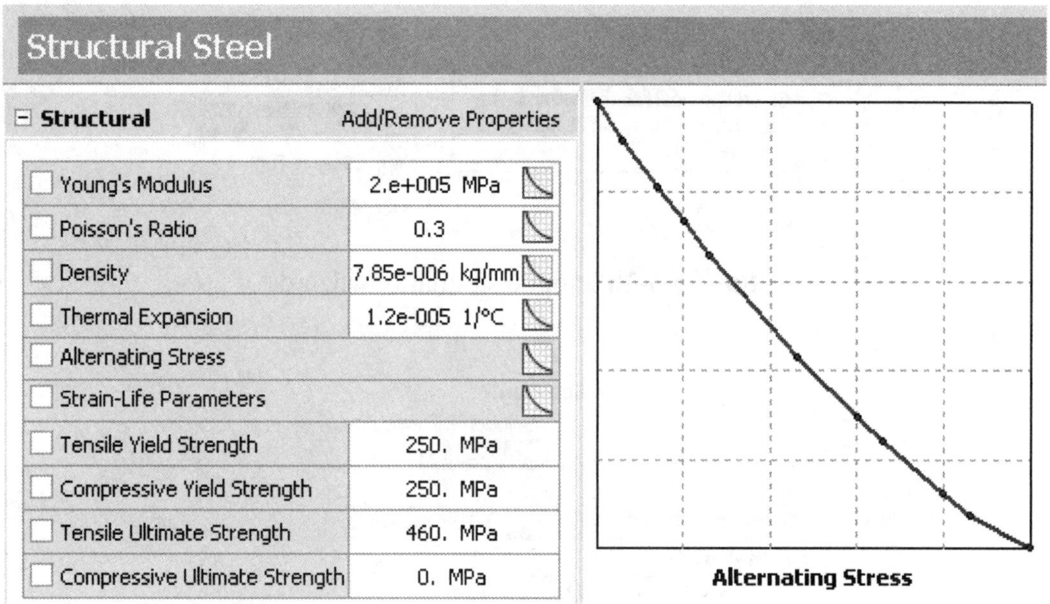

Figure 6-30 Structural steel alternating stress curve.

The alternating stress data is present.

7.   **Click on the Alternating Stress graph symbol.** The figure below displays the **S-N curve** data. Note that the last entry is **86.2 MPa** at **10^6 cycles**.

Alternating Stress vs. Cycles

	Cycles	Alternating Stress MPa
1	10.	3999.
2	20.	2827.
3	50.	1896.
4	100.	1413.
5	200.	1069.
6	2000.	441.
7	10000	262.
8	20000	214.
9	1.e+005	138.
10	2.e+005	114.
11	1.e+006	86.2
*		

Figure 6-31 Alternating stress curve data.

Insert Life and Safety Factor in Fatigue Tool.

8.   **Fatigue Tool > Contour Results > Life**

9.   Fatigue Tool > Contour Results > Safety Factor

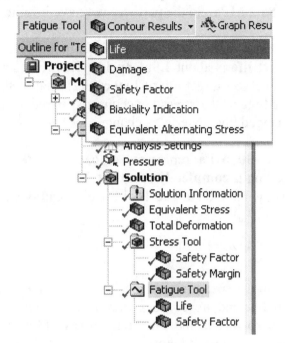

Figure 6-32 Insert Life object in Fatigue Tool.

Initiating solve will compute the stress state in the part and evaluate the fatigue state using the material properties given.

10.   Solve   ⚡ Solve

Results for the **Equivalent Stress**, **Safety Factor** and **Safety Margin** are the same as in Tutorial 6A.

New in this exercise is the response to the completely reversed loading as interpreted by the **Fatigue Tool**. See the figure below.

Details of "Life"	⊕		Details of "Safety Factor"	⊕
Scope			**Scope**	
Geometry	All Bodies		Geometry	All Bodies
Definition			**Definition**	
Type	Life		Design Life	1.e+009
Results			Type	Safety Factor
Minimum	1.8854e+005		**Results**	
Information			Minimum	0.74394

Figure 6-33 Completely reversed loading fatigue tool results.

The maximum von Mises stress for the part is almost **116 MPa** (115.87). The lowest point on the S-N data is **86.2 MPa**. So the part will not have infinite life.

These results indicate that for the stress level and completely reversed nature of the loading the estimated **part life** is about **1.9e5 cycles**. This represents a **safety factor** of **0.74** (86.2/116) with respect to a target life of 1.e9 cycles. That is, this design won't make the target life unless it's bigger, the stress concentration is reduced, the load is reduced, its characteristics are changed, the material is changed, or some combination of these.

The applied pressure of **-30 MPa** represents a load of **120 kN** magnitude. In the simulation above the loading is **completely reversed**. That is, it varies from +120 kN to 0 to -120 kN to 0, etc as shown in the Fatigue Tool Loading Options figure above.

Repeated Loading

Suppose instead of the above scenario that the load is repeated; that is, it varies from +120 kN to 0 to +120 kN and never goes negative. We can consider that case by changing the **Type** to **Zero-Based** and the **Mean Stress Theory** to **Goodman** in the **Details of "Fatigue Tool"** as depicted below.

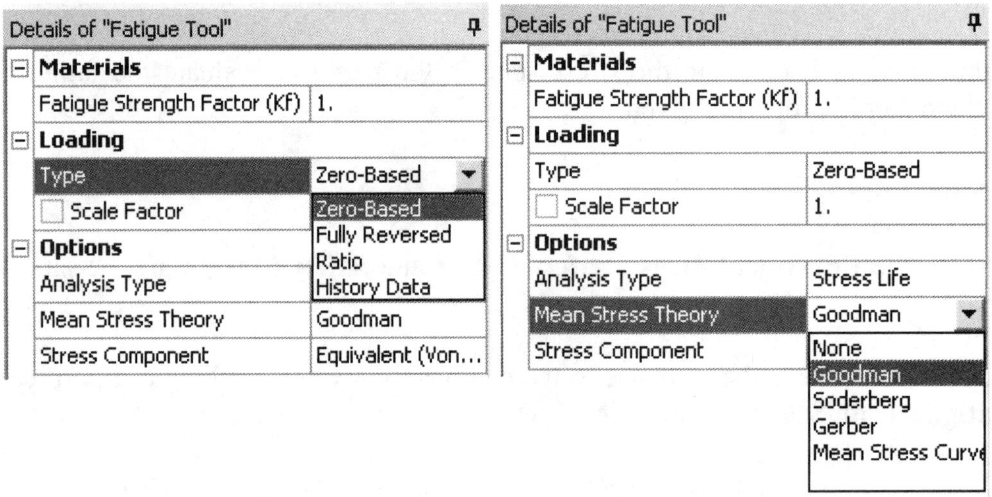

Figure 6-34 Repeated loading.

The Goodman method relates the mean value of the stress to the ultimate strength of the material and the oscillatory component to the fatigue strength of the material. See a good discussion on fatigue design.

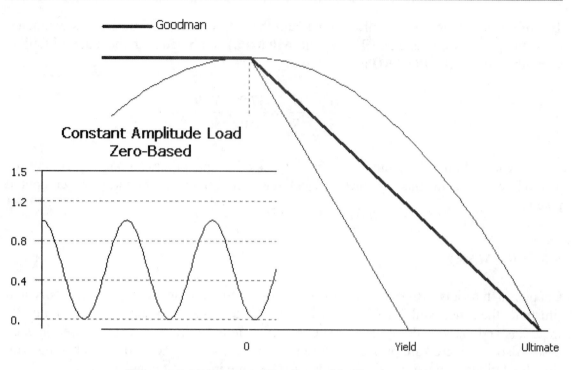

Figure 6-35 Repeated loading with Goodman line.

We now want to reevaluate the results.

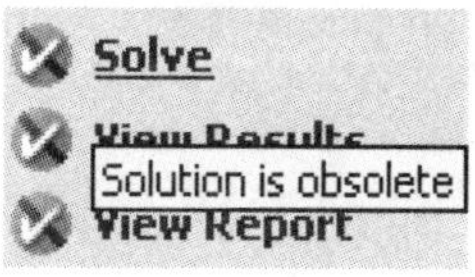

The simulation wizard warns that the current solution is obsolete.

11. Solve Solve

The fatigue tool results are shown in the figure that follows.

Details of "Life"	
Scope	
Geometry	All Bodies
Definition	
Type	Life
Results	
Minimum	1.e+006
Information	

Details of "Safety Factor"	
Scope	
Geometry	All Bodies
Definition	
Design Life	1.e+009
Type	Safety Factor
Results	
Minimum	1.2531

Figure 6-36 Repeated loading fatigue tool results.

The repeated loading is not as severe as the completely reversed loading on the same part. The mean stress and the stress amplitude are both 115.87/2 = **57.9 MPa** for this condition.

The life is 10^6 cycles, essentially infinite, and the safety factor, *SF*, is 1.25 as computed using the material ultimate tensile strength (**450 MPa**) combined with the material fatigue strength at 10^6 cycles (**86.2 MPa**).

$$\frac{1}{SF} = \frac{\sigma_m}{S_y} + \frac{\sigma_a}{S_e} = \frac{57.9}{450} + \frac{57.9}{86.2}$$

The fatigue tool provides a number of other types of fatigue process modeling. Again, see a good reference on this complex subject for a complete interpretation of computed results.

6-6   SUMMARY

Chapter 6 tutorials introduce the use of ANSYS Simulation Wizards and Tools and illustrate their use with problems involving static loads with parts made of ductile materials and parts made of brittle materials. A different failure criterion is used in each case. Also considered are problems of a fatigue nature where the load is fluctuating with time the fatigue characteristics of the material become important considerations.

6-7 PROBLEMS

6-1 Find the minimum factor of safety for the modified plate with the square hole of Tutorial 4B (include the 15 mm radius) if it is made of the default structural steel and carries a static axial load of 100 kN.

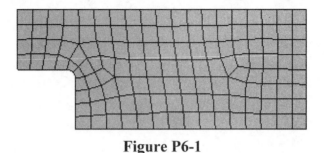

Figure P6-1

6-2 Repeat Problem 6-1 but let the material be the gray cast iron used in Tutorial 6B of this chapter.

6-3 Consider the Problem 6-1 with the part made of steel and find its life if the applied load is completely reversed.

6-4 Consider the Problem 6-1 with the part made of steel and find its life if the applied load is repeated, i.e., varies from zero to its maximum positive value back to zero then to its maximum positive value again without becoming negative.

6-5 Find the minimum factor of safety for the pressure vessel of Tutorial 5A under static loading conditions if it is made of the default structural steel.

6-6 Find the minimum factor of safety for the pressure vessel of Tutorial 5A under static loading conditions if it is made of the gray cast iron used in Tutorial 6B of this chapter.

NOTES:

Chapter 7

Heat Transfer &

Thermal Stress

7-1 OVERVIEW

In previous chapters we have considered problems in structural and continuum mechanics; however ANSYS Workbench capabilities also include modeling of problems involving the behavior of thermal systems and electromagnetic systems. In this chapter we demonstrate

♦ Determining temperature distributions for conduction/convection problems

♦ Using temperature distributions to find thermal stresses

7-2 INTRODUCTON

Linear thermal conduction/convection problems are formulated using the finite element approach with temperature as the single degree-of-freedom variable at each node in the mesh and with the material conduction properties used to form the thermal 'stiffness matrix' to be solved.

ANSYS Workbench includes capability for modeling many types of thermal and thermal stress problems of interest to practicing engineers. The temperature distributions found at each thermal analysis node can be used with the equivalent structural model as inputs for finding stresses caused by temperature changes.

7-3 HEAT TRANSFER

We start by solving a simple heat transfer problem involving conduction as well as convection and select a problem that we have a theoretical solution available for comparison.

7-4   TUTORIAL 7A – TEMPERATURE DISTRIBUTION IN A CYLINDER

Objective: We wish to compute the temperature distribution in a long steel cylinder with inner radius 5 inches and outer radius 10 inches. The **interior surface** of the cylinder is kept at **75 deg F**, and heat is lost on the **exterior** by **convection** to a fluid whose temperature is **40 deg F**. The **convection coefficient is 2.0e-4 BTU/sec-sq.in-F** and the **thermal conductivity** for steel is taken to be **8.09e-4 BTU/sec-in-F** (the default value for structural steel).

1.   **First create the geometry associated with this tutorial problem. That can be done in ANSYS DesignModeler or your favorite solid modeling system.** For analysis of the long cylinder, the length of the model we create is arbitrary since every section along the length behaves like every other section. For this tutorial we'll use a segment that is 1.0 inch long. Save your geometry file using the name **T7A.**

2.   **Start ANSYS Workbench**

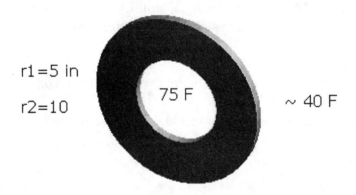

Figure 7-1 Segment of cylinder one inch in length.

3.   **New > Simulation**

4.   **Geometry > From File** (Locate the T7A file you created.)

5.   **Units > U. S. Customary (in, lbm, lbf, °F, s, V, A)** Verify the units.

6.   **Geometry > Solid > Details of "Solid" > Material > Structural Steel > Edit Structural Steel** (Check the material properties.)

Insert Steady-State Thermal Analysis.

7.   **New Analysis > Steady-State** (Top row menu)

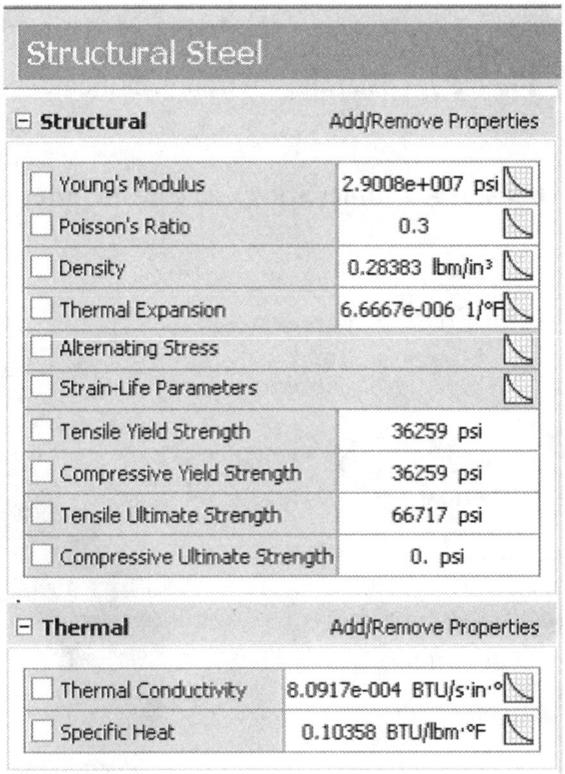

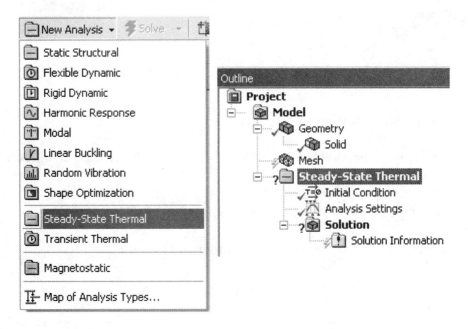

Figure 7-2 Material properties.

Figure 7-3 Thermal analysis.

Apply the **temperature boundary condition** to the interior surface.

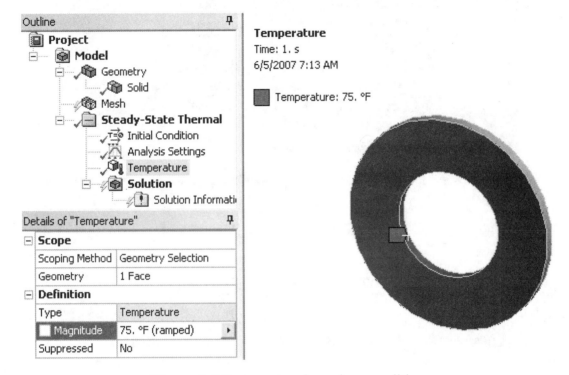

Figure 7-4 Thermal environment menu.

8.   **Environment > Thermal > Temperature; Select the inner surface > Apply; Magnitude 75 F**

Figure 7-5 Temperature boundary condition.

Apply the **convection condition** on the exterior surface.

9.   **Environment > Thermal > Convection;** Select the outer surface **Geometry Selection > Apply**

10.   **Details of "Convection" > Film Coefficient > 2.e-4 BTU/s in² F**

11.   **Details of "Convection" > Ambient Temperature > 40 F**

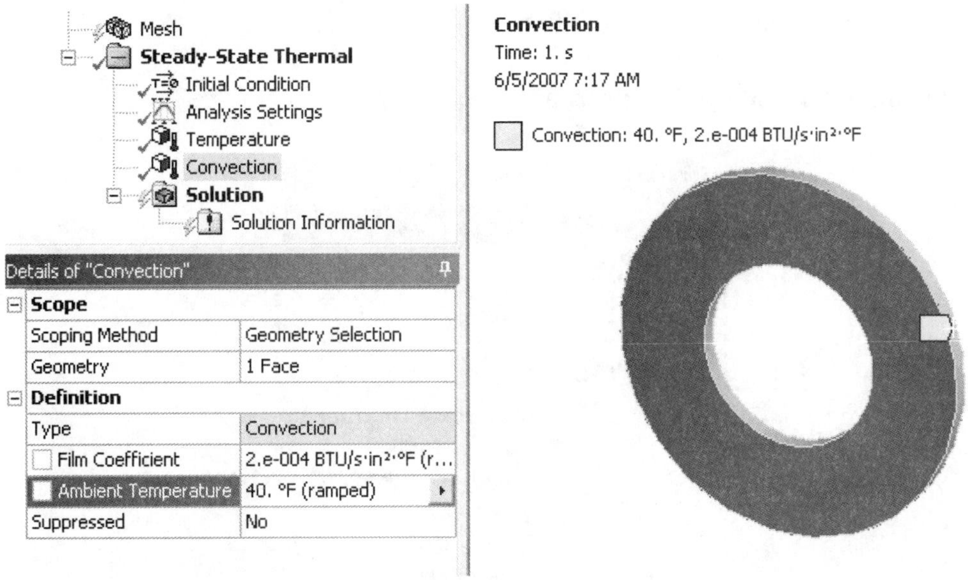

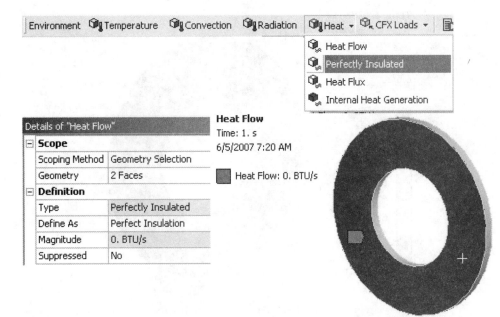

Figure 7-6 Convection boundary conditions.

Since each cross section along the length of the cylinder behaves in the same way, the front and back surfaces of the washer model are given **perfect insulation** boundary conditions to prevent any heat transfer in our model in the direction along the length of the cylinder.

12.   **Environment > Heat > Perfectly Insulated** (Select the front face; Ctrl Select the back face.)

Figure 7-7 Temperature distribution.

Add Temperature as the solution quantity to be determined.

13.   Solution > Thermal > Temperature

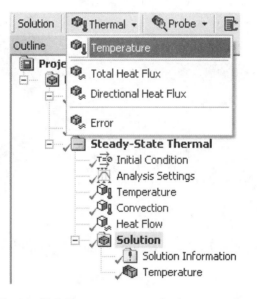

Figure 7-8 Temperature solution quantity.

14.   Solution > Solve (Solve the problem)   ⚡ Solve

The computed temperature distribution is shown in the next figure.

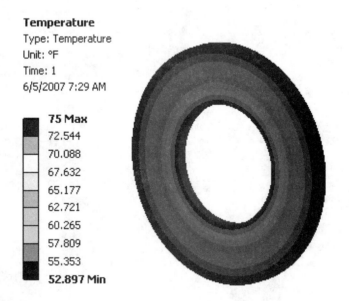

Figure 7-9 Temperature distribution.

The maximum temperature is on the interior and is the specified 75 F as expected, and on the outside wall the minimum temperature is found to be almost 53 F.

Insert the thermal error object.

15. Solution > Thermal > Error

The default mesh for this problem together with the thermal error distribution is displayed in the figure that follows. The estimated energy of the error in the solution ranges from around 3e-9 to 1.2e-6 BTU. These small error estimates give us confidence in the results of this simulation.

The results for this sample problem can be verified using closed form solutions from heat transfer theory, and we find that the computed surface temperature is very accurate.

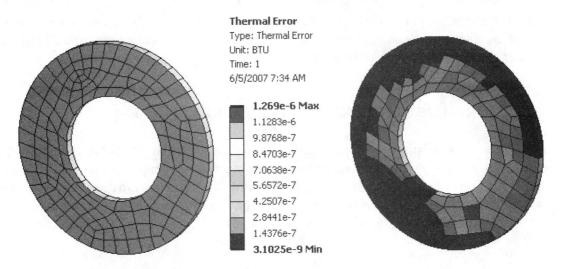

Thermal Error
Type: Thermal Error
Unit: BTU
Time: 1
6/5/2007 7:34 AM

1.269e-6 Max
1.1283e-6
9.8768e-7
8.4703e-7
7.0638e-7
5.6572e-7
4.2507e-7
2.8441e-7
1.4376e-7
3.1025e-9 Min

Figure 7-10 Problem mesh and thermal error distribution.

Because of its symmetry, this problem could have been solved with a much smaller model, say a small wedge with the cut faces perfectly insulated.

Figure 7-11 Wedge model.

7-5   THERMAL STRESS I

The **objective** of the second tutorial of this chapter is to **determine the stresses** in an object caused by a uniform temperature change.

When a temperature change occurs in an object, its coefficient of thermal expansion causes an expansion or contraction of the object depending upon whether the temperature increases or decreases. If the object is uniform and unrestrained, there is no stress associated with this free motion. On the other hand, if the object is subject to restraint against the thermally induced movement, a stress will occur.

ANSYS Workbench provides tools for the solution of thermal stress problems of various types. The temperature changes can be uniform throughout the body or distributed due to thermal conditions such as the temperature distribution in the previous tutorial. First we consider a uniform temperature change.

7-6   TUTORIAL 7B – UNIFORM TEMPERATURE CHANGE

Consider a block of material surrounded by a second material as shown in the figure below. The composite object is subjected to a temperature change so that both regions attain a uniform final temperature throughout. **Find the deformations and stresses** that result if the initial state is stress free. We're missing a couple of components here, but this is similar to the situation that occurs during the **epoxy** encapsulation of **silicon** computer chips.

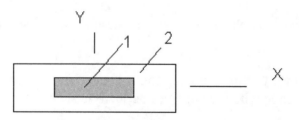

Figure 7-12 Encapsulation model.

For our model we assume a representative geometry of about **15 x 10 x 2 mm** for the silicon item being encapsulated. After encapsulation the **package size** is **25 x 15 x 6 mm**. The properties for the materials are given in the table below.

Figure 7-13 15 x 10 x 2 mm silicon chip and 25 x 15 x 6 mm epoxy encapsulation.

	Elastic Modulus	**Poisson's Ratio**	**CTE**
Silicon	27.6 E 6 psi	0.28	1.3 E –6 /F
Epoxy	1.89 E 6 psi	0.30	9.4 E –6/F

We consider the case in which the epoxy and silicon experience a temperature change of **-150 deg C** during cool down of the molding process.

The package was modeled as an **assembly in Pro/ENGINEER** and is shown below.

Figure 7-14 The complete chip/epoxy package.

Before importing into ANSYS Simulation however we will isolate an **octant of the package** and make use of **symmetry** in the geometry and loading. The next figure shows the Pro/E model of an octant of the package after the rest of the solid has been trimmed away.

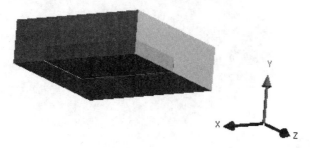

Figure 7-15 Octant of the package.

The portion selected for analysis lies in the octant defined by the positive X, Y and Z axes. Symmetric deformation requires that no movement across the planes of symmetry be allowed.

1.   **Start ANSYS Workbench > New Simulation**

2.   **Geometry > From File**   ⬛Geometry ▾   Load the geometry file for the package octant.

The interfacial boundary between silicon and epoxy is defined in ANSYS Simulation by a **contact region**. A number of different contact models are provided for use, and in our case we accept the default of **bonded contact**. This means that the surfaces are bonded together and do not separate or slide upon one another. This behavior best describes the case for the encapsulation model we are building. The component parts of our Pro/E model were named **OUTSIDEPART** and **CHIP**.

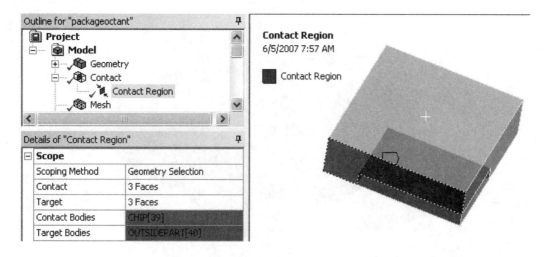

Figure 7-16 Contact surfaces of model.

Next we need to define the structural properties for silicon and epoxy materials. We'll do that by duplicating the properties of the default material structural steel and editing them.

3. **Engineering Data** > right click **Structural Steel** > **Duplicate**

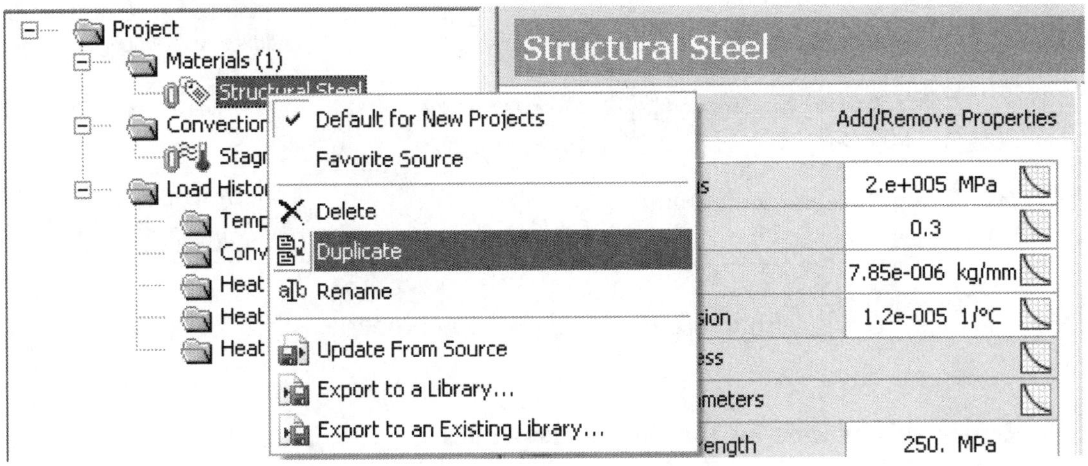

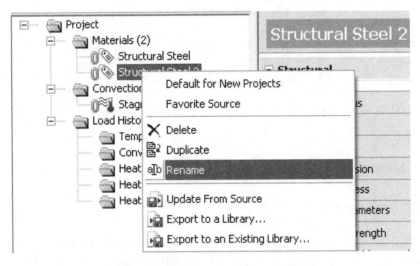

Figure 7-17 Duplicate the material data.

4. Right Click **Structural Steel2** > **Rename**

Figure 7-18 Rename the material.

5. **Rename Structural Steel2 > Silicon**

Since the given property values are in US Customary units, change the current units.

6. **Units > U. S. Customary (in, lbm, lbf, °F, s, V, A)**

Edit the values of the structural properties Young's Modulus, Poisson's Ratio, and Thermal Expansion entering the values for silicon.

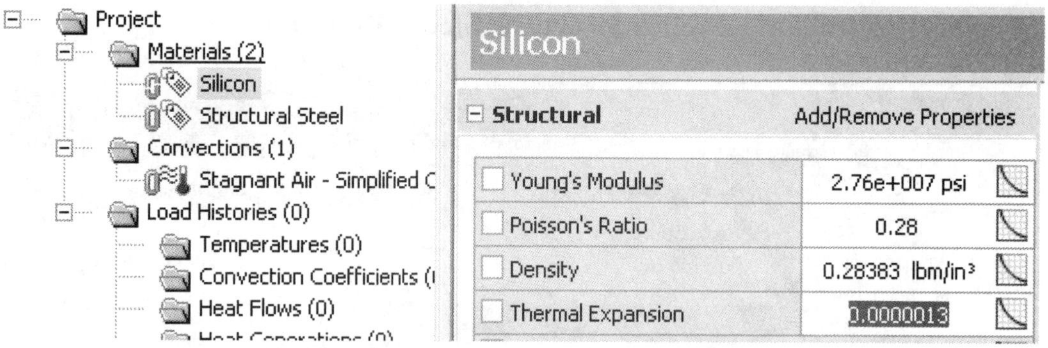

Figure 7-19 Edit the silicon properties.

7.   Repeat this process for the Epoxy properties

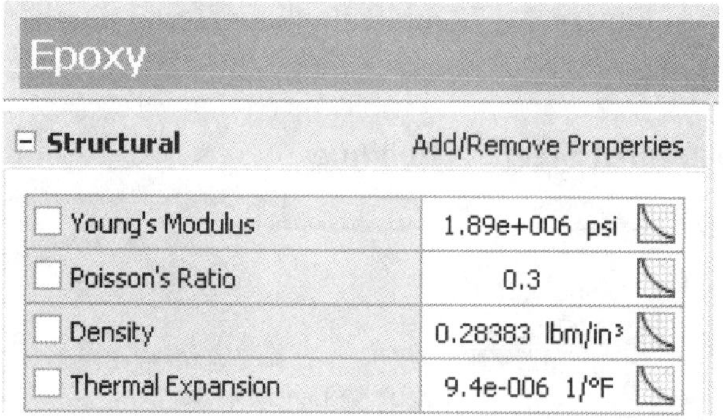

Figure 7-20 Edit the epoxy properties.

Click on the **Simulation Tab** and Reset the units to Metric.

8.   Units > Metric (mm, kg, N, °C, s, mV, mA)

In this tutorial we have a structural model subjected to a thermal environment. The package is stress free when the temperature is 150 deg C. It then cools down to room temperature 22 deg C. The **whole package** gets the same temperature change.

9.   New Analysis > Static Structural

Change the stress free reference temperature to 150 deg C.

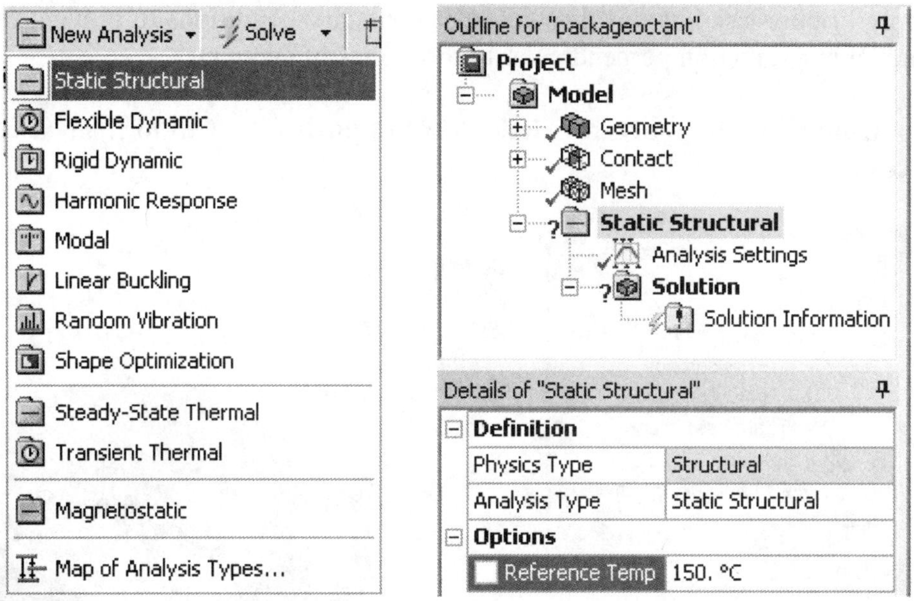

Figure 7-21 Structural static analysis.

Apply the final uniform temperature.

10.   Environment > Conditions >Thermal Condition = 22 deg C

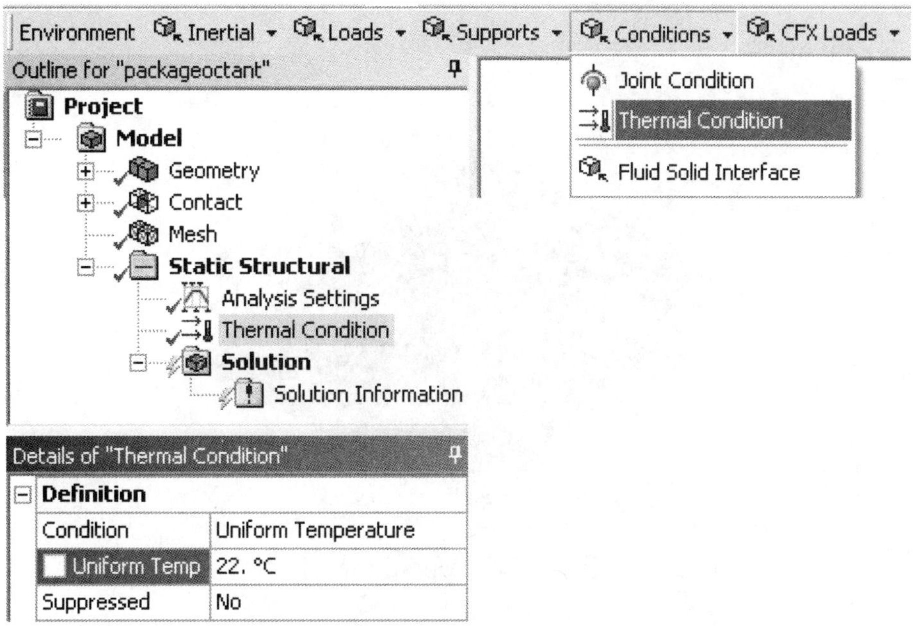

Figure 7-22 Thermal condition.

Now apply Frictionless Support displacement boundary conditions to prevent movement of the model in a direction perpendicular to the planes of symmetry.

11.   Environment > Supports > Frictionless Supports (Use Ctrl to chain select six faces.)

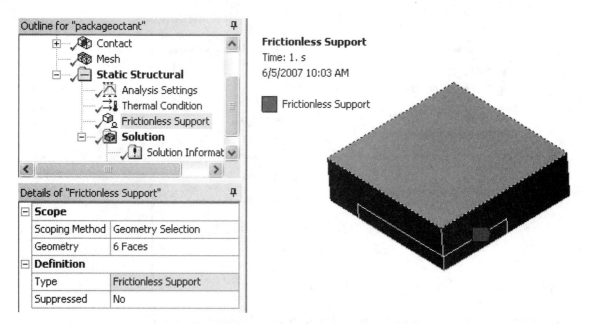

Figure 7-23 Displacement boundary condition.

Use the default mesh.

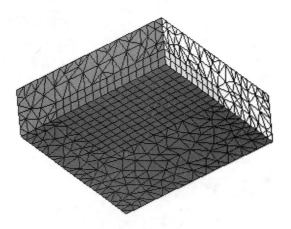

Figure 7-24 Default mesh.

Add the **maximum principal stress**, the **total deformation**, and the **stress error** to the solution items.

12. **Solution > Stress > Maximum Principal**

13. **Solution > Deformation > Total**

14. **Solution > Stress > Error**

15. **Solve**   ⌁ Solve

View the maximum principal stress distribution from the bottom side of the octant.

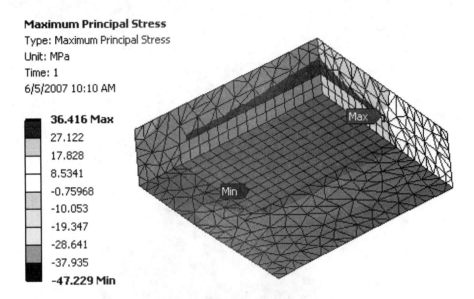

Maximum Principal Stress
Type: Maximum Principal Stress
Unit: MPa
Time: 1
6/5/2007 10:10 AM

36.416 Max
27.122
17.828
8.5341
-0.75968
-10.053
-19.347
-28.641
-37.935
-47.229 Min

Figure 7-25 Maximum principal stress.

The coefficient of thermal expansion of the epoxy is seven times greater than that of silicon, so the epoxy shrinks at a greater rate than the silicon during the process of cooling. That puts the silicon in compression and the epoxy in tension and is reflected in the stress distributions shown above.

To better see what's going on we will **hide the chip** component and view the stresses in the epoxy.

16.   Right click **Chip > Hide Body**.

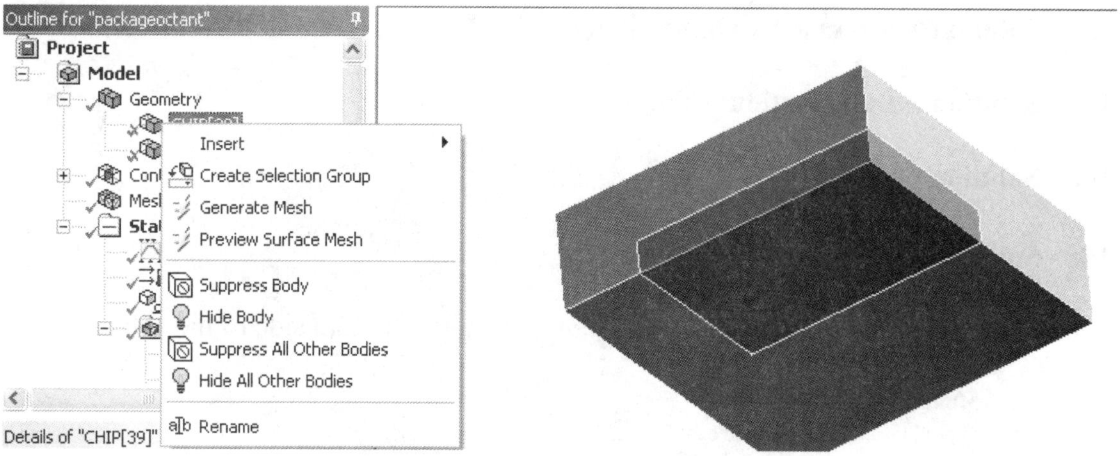

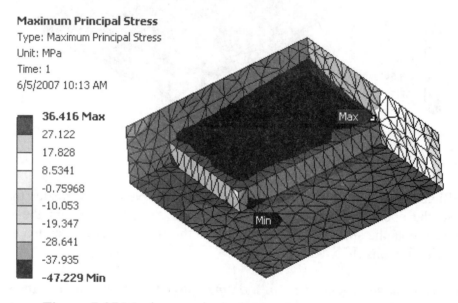

Figure 7-26 Hide the chip component.

Then display the **maximum principal stress**.

17.   Solution > Maximum Principal Stress

Figure 7-27 Maximum principal stress in epoxy component.

Next display the **structural error**.

18.   Solution > Structural Error

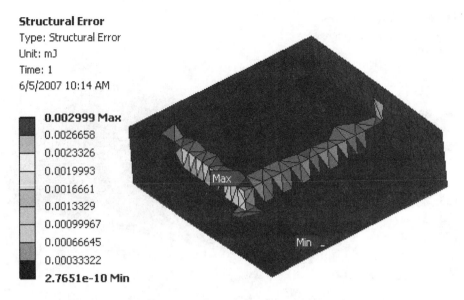

Figure 7-28 Structural error in the epoxy component.

Note that the errors are large along the interior edge and highest at the corner where the two edges meet. These are regions of singularity because of the zero radius geometry. If we want good stress estimates for this component, we will need to include the actual corner radius at these locations.

Unhide the chip and **hide the epoxy portion**.

19.   Right click **CHIP > Show Body**.

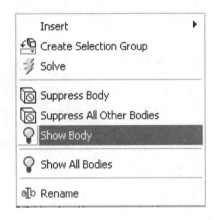

Figure 7-29 Show body option.

20.   Right click **OUTSIDEPART > Hide Body**.

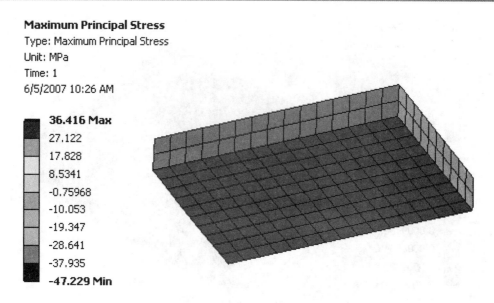

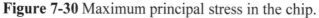

Figure 7-30 Maximum principal stress in the chip.

21.   Right click in the model display area > **Isometric View**.

This shows the chip from the top, and the corner region of maximum compressive stress is evident.

22.   Display Total Deformation (Show Undeformed Wireframe) **Save your work**.

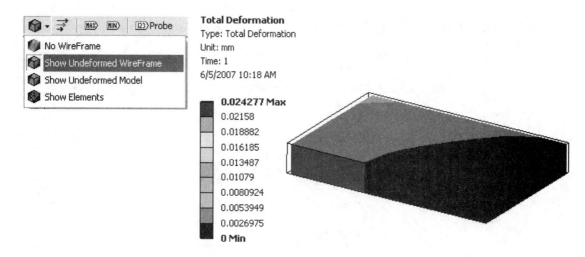

Figure 7-31 Total deformation in the chip.

Stresses and deformations computed for the chip with this mesh should be reasonably accurate as are the deformations computed for the epoxy portion and stresses in the epoxy portion at locations removed from the singularities.

7-7 THERMAL STRESS II

In tutorial **T7C** we will determine the stresses that are produced in a cylinder by an internal pressure acting together with a temperature variation through the wall thickness similar to the one we calculated in tutorial T7A.

Consider the same 5 inch interior radius, 10 inch exterior radius steel cylinder as considered in tutorial T7A. The cylinder is subjected to an internal **pressure of 300 psi**. The **internal surface temperature is 480 deg F** and the **external surface temperature is 75 deg F**. The **objective** is to find stress distribution and the magnitude and location of the maximum von Mises stress.

7-8 TUTORIAL 7C – THERMAL STRESS IN A CYLINDER

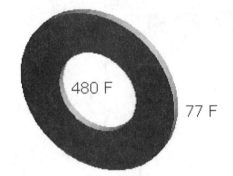

Figure 7-32 Temperature boundary conditions.

1. **Start ANSYS Workbench > New Simulation**

2. **Geometry > From File** 🗍Geometry ▾ Load the geometry file for the cylinder.

Apply the internal pressure.

3. **Units > U. S. Customary (in, lbm, lbf, °F, s, V, A)** (Check the units.)

Use the default structural steel material.

4. **Geometry > Solid > Details of "Solid" > Material > Structural Steel**

Refer to the Map of Analysis Types under New Analysis.

5. **New Analysis > Map of Analysis Types.**

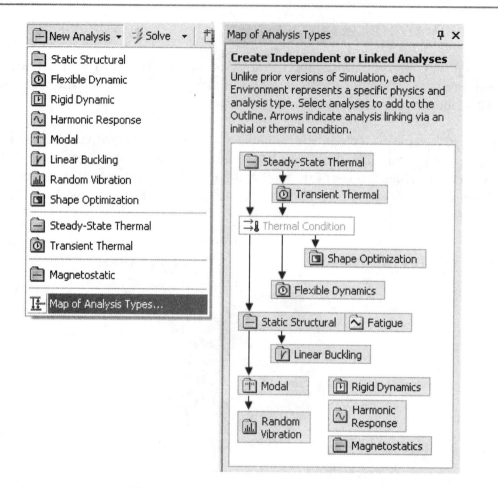

Figure 7-33 Map of analysis types.

We apply the **thermal conditions** first and calculate the temperature distribution.

6.   **New Analysis > Steady-State Thermal**

7.   **Steady-State Thermal > Initial Condition > 71.6 deg F** (default ambient)

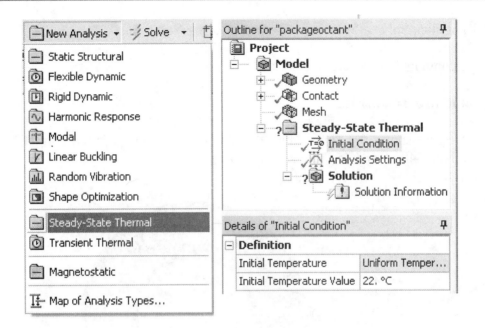

Figure 7-34 Steady state thermal analysis.

8. **Environment > Temperature** Select the inside surface of the cylinder.

9. **Details of "Temperature" > Geometry > Apply**

10. **Details of "Temperature" > Magnitude > 480 F**

11. **Apply the 75 F condition to the exterior surface.**

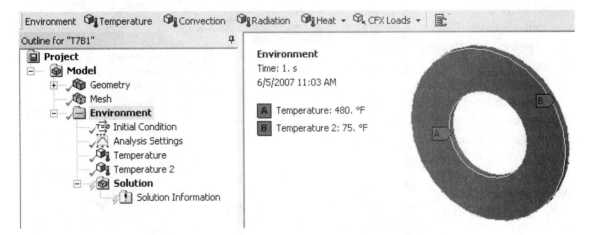

Figure 7-35 Temperature boundary conditions.

Find the temperature distribution.

12. **Solution > Thermal > Temperature**

13.   Right click **Solve** > **Solution** > **Temperature** > **Solve**   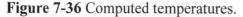 Solve

View the computed temperature distribution.

14.   Solution > Temperature

The next figure shows the temperature distribution, and note that the correct boundary temperatures of 480 F and 75 F are displayed as expected.

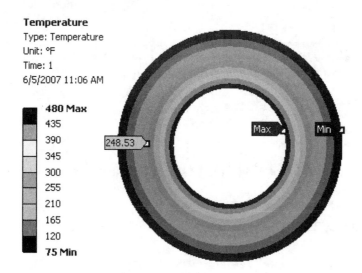

Figure 7-36 Computed temperatures.

Use the probe option 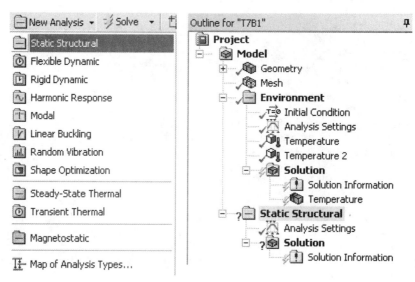 123 Probe to determine the temperature near the point midway through the wall of the cylinder. The computed temperature here agrees well with the analytical solution to this problem.

Add the Static Structural Analysis to the model.

15.   New Analysis > Static Structural

Figure 7-37 Static structural analysis.

Accept the default reference temperature of 71.6 deg F. Apply the structural loads.

16. **Environment > Structural > Pressure** Select the inside surface of the cylinder.

17. **Details of "Pressure" > Geometry > Apply**

18. **Details of "Pressure" > Magnitude > 300 psi**

Right click and rename **Environment** as **Disk Thermal Prob**.

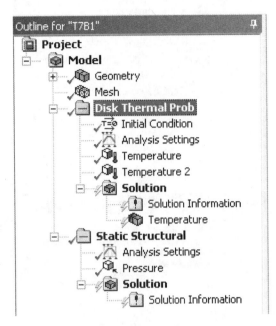

Figure 7-38 Disk Thermal Prob.

Add a Temperature Condition to the Static Structural object.

19. **Environment > Conditions > Thermal Condition**

Reference the temperature distribution found in **Disk Thermal Prob**.

Step	Condition	Uniform Temp (°F)	Thermal Environment
1	Non-Uniform Temperature	N/A	Disk Thermal Prob

Details of "Thermal Condition"

Definition	
Condition	Uniform Temperature
Uniform Temp	Uniform Temperature
	Non-Uniform Temperature
Suppressed	

Details of "Thermal Condition"

Definition	
Condition	Non-Uniform Temperature
Thermal Environment	Disk Thermal Prob
Time	End Time
Suppressed	No

Figure 7-39 Thermal Condition.

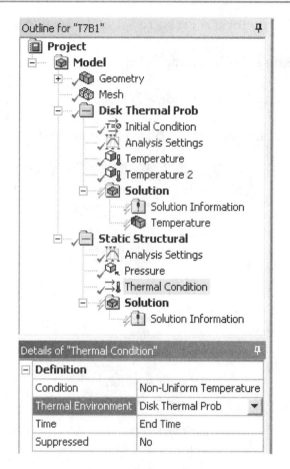

Figure 7-40 Outline.

Add the von Mises stress quantity to the computed solution quantities.

20.   Solution > Stress > Equivalent (von-Mises)

21.   Right click Solution > Solve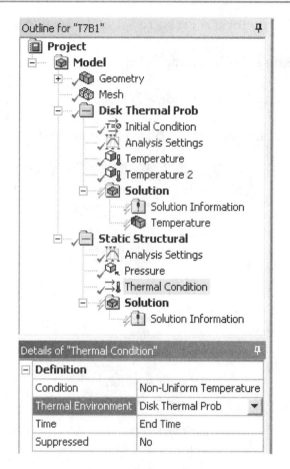

The response of structural systems to **static** loads requires the displacement boundary constraints be applied to restrain the motion of the object as a rigid body otherwise the applied loads cause motion to occur and the problem becomes a problem in **dynamics**. Normally these restraints are obvious from the problem setting (a building is fixed to the ground, a part is restrained by the parts to which it is joined, etc.).

We applied no constraints in the current tutorial; the simulation software recognized the possibility of rigid body motion and applied some weak springs to restrain the rigid body motion. The warning shown below is issued so the user can make adjustments if necessary. In our case the weak springs work just fine, so we continue with the evaluation of the computed results.

Messages	
	Text
Warning	One or more bodies may be underconstrained and experiencing rigid body motion. Weak springs have been added

Figure 7-41 Weak spring warning.

22.   Solution > Equivalent Stress to display the von Mises stress distribution.

The next figure shows that the maximum von Mises stress occurs at the interior surface of the cylinder and has a value of **47,730 psi**. The value on the outer surface is **30,939 psi**.

The stress contours are a little ragged indicating that a refined mesh would be expected to give slightly more accurate answers.

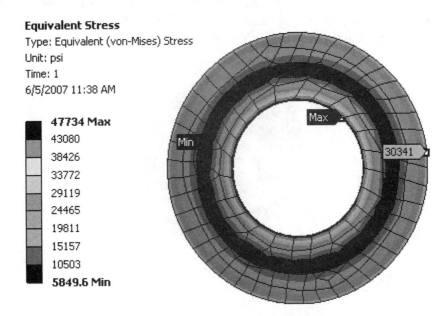

Figure 7-42 von Mises stress distribution.

It is interesting to note the computed temperature distribution contours (Figure 7-12) are quite smooth while the stress contours are not. This is because in general a finer mesh is required for an accurate solution to the stress problem than is required for an accurate solution to the temperature problem, something to keep in mind when constructing the initial mesh for problems of this type. We could go back and refine the mesh and re-evaluate the results, but we'll leave that for one of the problems at the end of the chapter.

23.   Save your work.

7-9 SUMMARY

The tutorials in this chapter illustrate the solution of thermal conduction/convection problems as well as the determination of thermal stresses arising from uniform or non-uniform temperature distributions.

7-10 PROBLEMS

7-1 An 8 in diameter steel disk 0.25 inches in thickness has a 2 in diameter hole located 2 inches radially from its center. The surface of the hole is maintained at 75 F, and the exterior surface is kept at 32 F. The front and back surfaces are perfectly insulated.

Find the magnitude and location of the maximum von Mises stress, the maximum principal stress, and the maximum principal strain if the disk is initially in a stress-free state before the thermal conditions are applied.

Figure P7-1

7-2 Solve problem 7-1 using the exterior convection conditions of Tutorial T7A.

7-3 Refine the mesh for Tutorial T7C so as to compute smooth von Mises stress contours. Compare the maximum and minimum von Mises stress values you compute with those found in the tutorial.

Chapter 8

Surface & Line Models

8-1 OVERVIEW

This chapter discusses structural and thermal simulation response of problems that can be analyzed with surface or line models. These include:

♦ Plane stress, plane strain or axisymmetric problems

♦ Plate (shell) problems

♦ Line-body (beam element) problems

8-2 INTRODUCTION

Surface models are often easier to develop and easier to solve than solid models and can be employed in many practical situations **if** they can accurately represent the behavior of the object under consideration. We are interested in **two-dimensional surface models** for plane stress, plane strain, or axisymmetric analysis and **three-dimensional surface models** for plate analysis.

A state of **plane stress** exists in a thin object loaded in the plane of its largest dimensions. Let the X-Y plane be the plane of analysis. The non-zero stresses σ_x, σ_y and τ_{xy} lie in the X-Y plane and do not vary in the Z direction. Further, the other stresses (σ_z, τ_{yz} and τ_{zx}) are all zero for this kind of geometry and loading. A thin beam loaded in its plane and a thin spur gear tooth are good examples of plane stress problems.

Problems in **plane strain** are typically objects with large dimensions in the Z direction relative to its dimensions in the X-Y plane that have loadings uniformly distributed in the Z direction and restrained from Z motion at its ends. A retaining wall is a common example.

A problem in which the geometry, loadings, boundary conditions and material properties are symmetric with respect to an axis is one that can be solved with an **axisymmetric** finite element model.

Plate or **shell** structural components are surfaces that resist loads applied normal and parallel to their surfaces and provide resistance to bending and in-plane deformation similar to beam components. The plate surface of the deck of a ship is a typical example.

8-3   TUTORIAL 8A – SHEET WITH CIRCLUAR HOLE – PLANE STRESS

In this tutorial we will use ANSYS Simulation to compute the maximum stress in the thin steel sheet with a central hole considered in **Tutorial T4A**. The object is loaded in the long direction by pressures at each end. Its dimensions are 1000 mm long, 400 mm high and 10 mm thick. The central circular hole is 200 mm in diameter as shown below.

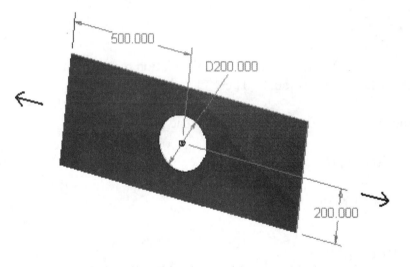

Figure 8-1 Thin sheet with central hole.

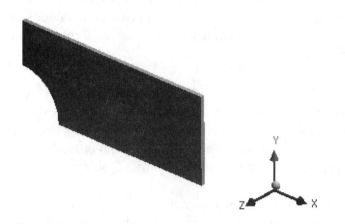

Figure 8-2 Quadrant of sheet.

We need a surface model of the plate, and this can be created with DesignModeler.

1. **Start ANSYS Workbench DesignModeler.**

2. **Open the file for the quadrant of the sheet and click on the sketch used to extrude the model.**

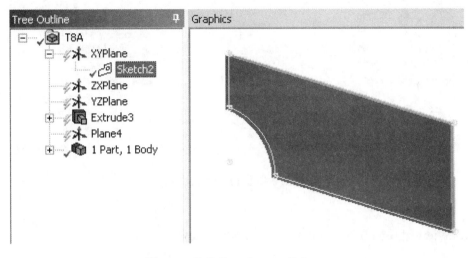

Figure 8-3 Quadrant of sheet.

3. **Concept > Surfaces From Sketches**

Enter the sheet thickness.

4. **Details of SurfaceSk1 > 10 mm**

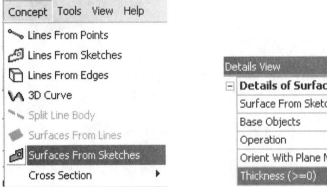

Figure 8-4 Surface creation.

5. **Generate** ⟶ Generate to create the surface.

We no longer need the extrusion, so highlight 'Extrude' and delete it.

6.   **Extrude3 > Delete** (The 3 is the sequence number assigned to my model during creation of the solid. Yours may be different.)

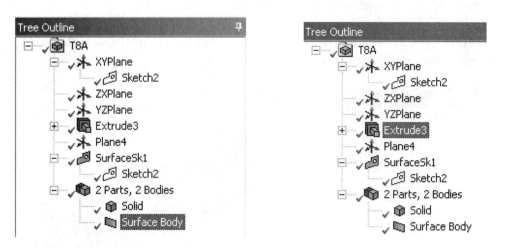

Figure 8-5 Tree outline.

We get the view shown below. Object has no thickness.

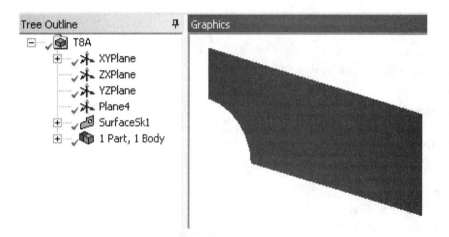

Figure 8-6 Surface model outline.

Now indicate that you're going to use a 2D model for the simulation.

7.   **Click the Project Tab**

In the left portion of the Project screen select Advanced Geometry Defaults.

8.   **Advanced Geometry Defaults > Analysis Type > 2-D** (See the next figure.)

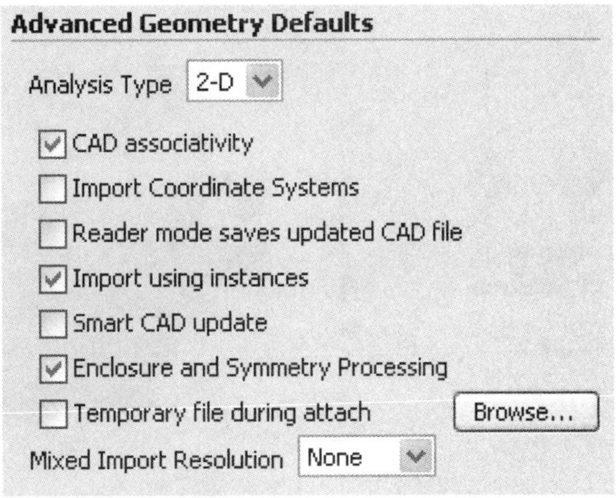

Figure 8-7 Advanced geometry defaults.

9.   **New Simulation**   ⑤ New simulation   (Set Units to mm, etc. if need be.)

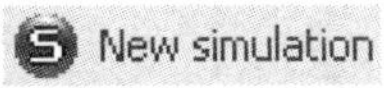

10.   Select **Geometry > Details of "Geometry" > 2D Behavior**.

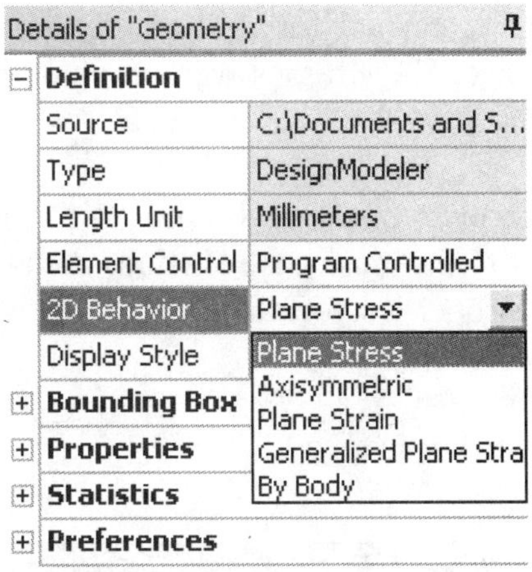

Figure 8-8 Plane stress default.

Observe the **2D Behavior** options and note that **Plane Stress** is the default.

11.   Select **Surface Body > Details of "Surface Body"**.

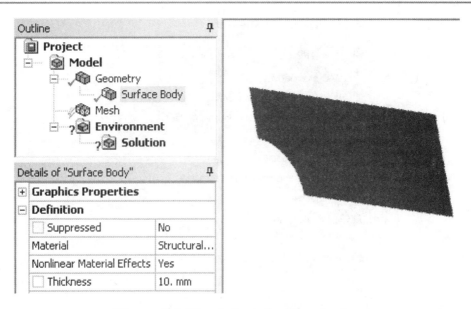

Figure 8-9 Simulation of surface body.

Note that the geometry in the simulation is a surface (has no geometric thickness), but the 10 mm thickness for the part is carried forward to the simulation and shows up in the **Details of "Surface Body"** box. The stresses we compute will be inversely proportional to the thickness of the part.

The structural simulation proceeds much as before. We need to first create the **Mesh**, then define the **Environment**, the desired **Solution** items to be computed, and then **Solve**. The default material properties for structural steel will be used. We outline the steps in what follows.

12.   **Mesh > Generate Mesh**

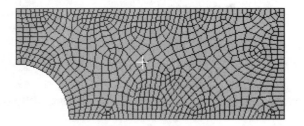

Figure 8-10 Default mesh.

13.   **New Analysis > Static Structural**

14.   **Environment > Supports > Displacement**

15.   Click on the **Edge Selection Filter** .

16. Select the **Left Edge > Apply**.

17. X Component > 0 mm (Notice that only X and Y displacements are available.)

Details of "Displacement"	⊣
⊟ **Scope**	
Scoping Method	Geometry Selection
Geometry	Apply Cancel
⊟ **Definition**	
Define By	Components
Type	Displacement
X Component	Free
Y Component	Free
Suppressed	No

Figure 8-11 Applying boundary conditions.

18. Repeat to **Set the Y Component to zero** for the **bottom edge**.

Now apply the loading.

19. Environment > Loads > Pressure

20. Select the **Right Edge > Apply**.

21. Magnitude > -1 MPa

Static Structural
Time: 1. s
6/5/2007 4:55 PM

A Displacement
B Displacement 2
C Pressure: -1. MPa

Figure 8-12 All environment conditions.

Now indicate that we want to compute the Normal Stress in the X Direction.

22. Solution > Stress > Normal > Orientation > X Axis

23. Solution > Solve Solve

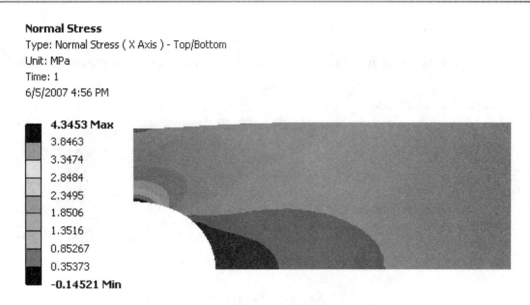

Normal Stress
Type: Normal Stress (X Axis) - Top/Bottom
Unit: MPa
Time: 1
6/5/2007 4:56 PM

4.3453 Max
3.8463
3.3474
2.8484
2.3495
1.8506
1.3516
0.85267
0.35373
-0.14521 Min

Figure 8-13 Normal stress along X Axis.

The maximum value of the normal stress in the X direction is around **4.3 MPa**, which agrees with our previously computed and theoretical estimates in Chapter 4. **Save your work.**

8-4   TUTORIAL 8B – PRESSURE VESSEL

Problems that are axisymmetric in nature can be solved with two-dimensional models using ANSYS built-in analysis methods that automatically incorporate the 'hoop' direction stress in the analysis of the 2D model. This tutorial revisits the pressure vessel problem we solved in Chapter 5. The process is very similar to that employed in T8A.

1.   **Start ANSYS Workbench DesignModeler.**

2.   **Open the file for the pressure vessel from Chapter 5** and **select the sketch used to create the solid model by revolving.**

3.   **Concept > Surfaces From Sketches**

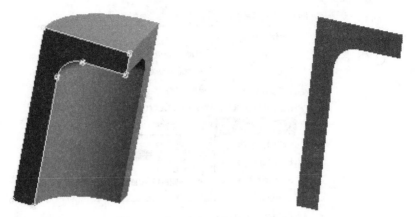

Figure 8-14 Surface model.

4.   **Click the Project Tab** 📕 [Project] ✕ .

5.   **Advanced Geometry Defaults > Analysis Type > 2-D** (See the next figure.)

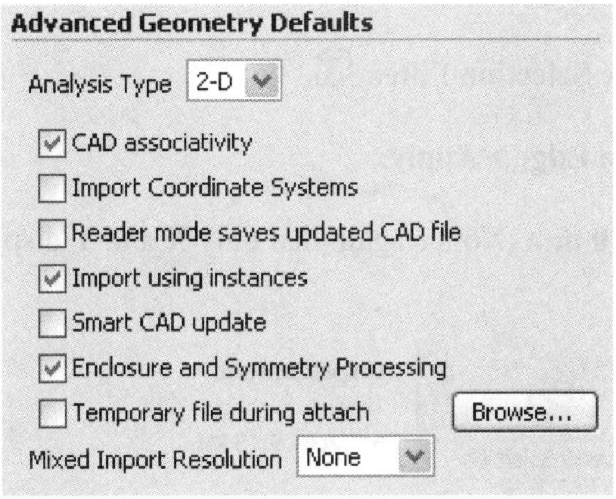

Advanced Geometry Defaults

Analysis Type 2-D ▼

☑ CAD associativity
☐ Import Coordinate Systems
☐ Reader mode saves updated CAD file
☑ Import using instances
☐ Smart CAD update
☑ Enclosure and Symmetry Processing
☐ Temporary file during attach   [Browse...]
Mixed Import Resolution None ▼

Figure 8-15 Advanced geometry defaults.

6.   **New Simulation** Ⓢ New simulation

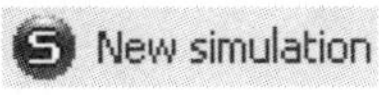

7.   Select **Geometry > Details of "Geometry" > 2D Behavior > Axisymmetric**

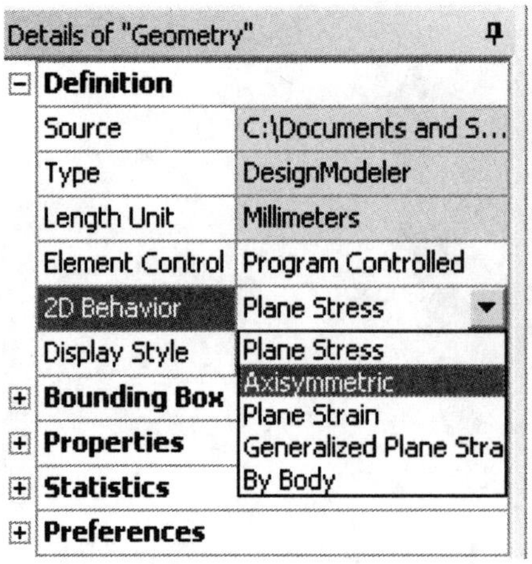

Figure 8-16 Select an axisymmetric model.

8.   **New Analysis > Static Structural**

9.   **Environment > Supports > Displacement**

10.   Click on the **Edge Selection Filter** .

11.   Select the **Bottom Edge > Apply**.

12.   **Y Component > 0 mm** (Notice again that only X and Y displacements are available.)

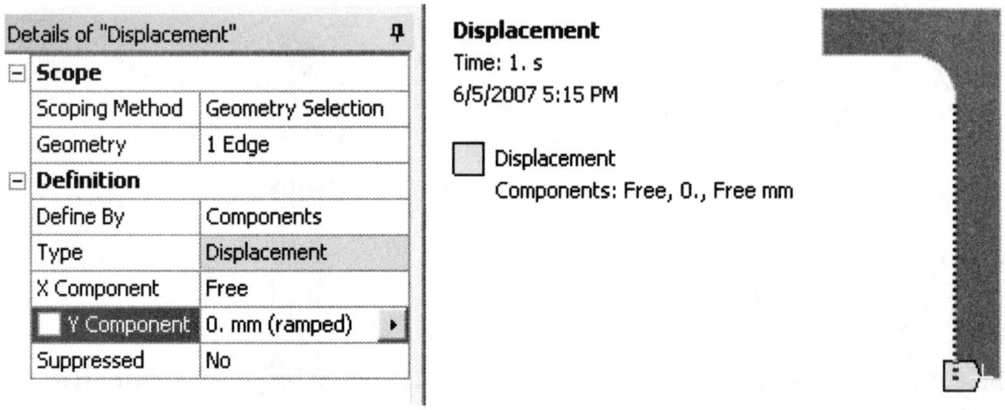

Figure 8-17 Displacement boundary condition.

The upper left edge of the sketch is on the axis of symmetry and requires no displacement constraint. Apply the internal pressure next.

13.   **Environment > Loads > Pressure > Cntl select the inside edge segments > Apply > Pressure Magnitude > 35 MPa**

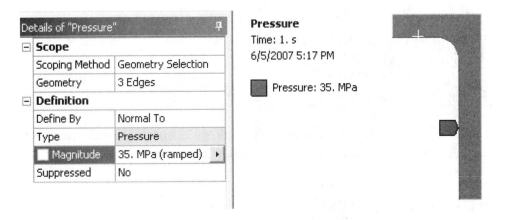

Figure 8-18 Pressure loading.

14. Add solution item **Stress > Equivalent Stress (von Mises) > Solve**

The following figure shows the von Mises stress distribution; the maximum computed value compares well with the results calculated in Chapter 5. If anything, the contour curves for this simpler model are smoother at the maximum stress region, and we would expect the computed maximum equivalent stress (201 MPa) to be more accurate than that of Chapter 5 (207 MPa) where the coarseness of the mesh produced more jagged contour plots. But you see that the two values are only about 3 per cent different.

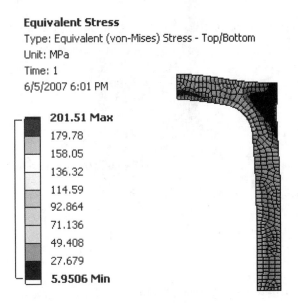

Figure 8-19 von Mises stress distribution.

If we add **Normal Stress** and **Directional Displacement** solution items we can make a complete comparison of this model with the theoretical solution at the base as before. See the table below. These results are virtually identical with those shown in Chapter 5.

	Theoretical	Workbench	Error, per cent
Hoop Stress (Sx), MPa	125	127.4	1.9
Axial Stress (Sy), MPa	45	46.5	3.3
Radial Stress (Sz), MPa	-35	-34.9	0.3
Radial Deflection, mm	0.0458	0.0465	1.5

Tutorial T8B has 2D axisymmetric modeling as its focus while the next tutorial is concerned with 3D surface modeling using plates (shells). **Save your work.**

8-5   TUTORIAL 8C – BRACKET

The **objective** of this tutorial is to compute the **stress** and **deflection** response of the steel bracket that was analyzed in Chapter 5. See the figure below. The bracket is 100 mm high, 50 mm deep, 60 mm in width, and has a 10 mm thickness. It has a 30 mm diameter hole located 70 mm from its base plane. The fillet radii are 10 and 20 mm, and the 10 mm mounting bolt holes are located 15 mm from the front and side edges. The bearing is subjected to load components 5500 N in the X direction, 3500 N in Y, and 1700 N in Z. The base of the bracket is fixed against all motion.

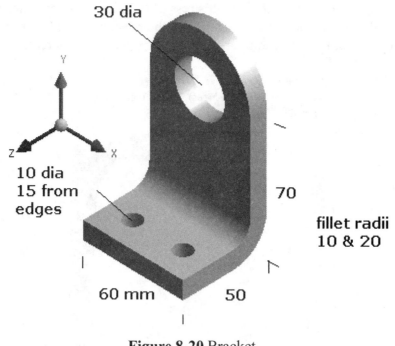

Figure 8-20 Bracket.

We will start with the solid model of the bracket and create an equivalent **surface model**.

1.   Start **ANSYS Workbench DesignModeler** and **attach the bracket geometry**.

We want to capture the middle surface of the bracket.

2.   **Tools > Midsurface**

Figure 8-21 Mid-Surface tool.

3.   **Details of MidSurf1 > Face Pairs**

4.   Use **Cntl Select** to sequentially pick **all** the front and corresponding back face pairs on the bracket model > **Apply**.

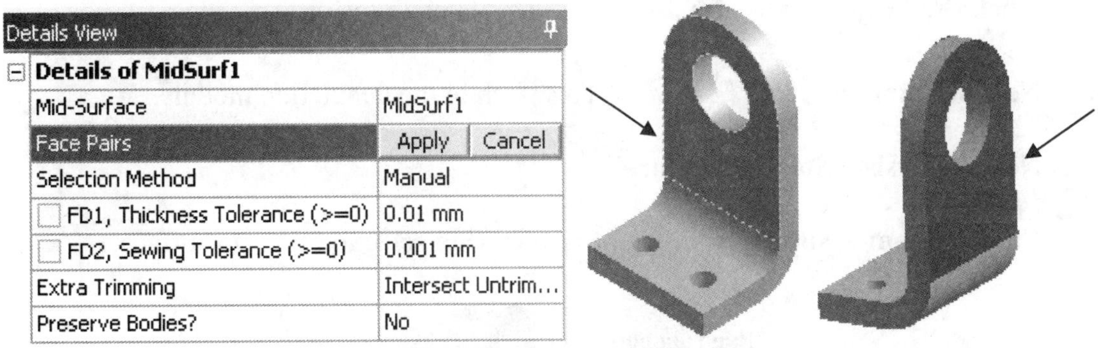

Figure 8-22 Mid-Surface face pairs.

5.   **Generate**   ⫶ᵍ Generate   To create the surface.

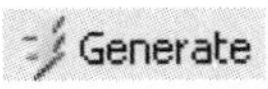

Notice that this is a **three-dimensional surface model**.

6.   **Enter the thickness = 10 mm**

Tree Outline

- ✓ 🗔 T8C3D
  - ✓ ✱ XYPlane
  - ✓ ✱ ZXPlane
  - ✓ ✱ YZPlane
  - ✓ 🗔 Import1
  - ✓ 🗔 MidSurf1
  - ✓ 🗔 1 Part, 1 Body
    - ✓ 🗔 LBRACK

Sketching   Modeling

Details View

Details of Body	
Body	LBRACK
Thickness (>=0)	10 mm
Surface Area	4.3635e+006 mm²
Faces	3
Edges	13
Vertices	11

Figure 8-23 3D surface model of bracket.

7.   **Click the Project Tab** 🅰 [Project] ✕ To switch to the project view.

8.   **New Simulation** ⑤ New simulation To switch to the simulation module.

9.   **New Analysis > Static Structural**

10.   **Environment > Supports > Fixed Support** (Set selection filter to surface.)

Fixed Support
Time: 1. s
6/5/2007 6:18 PM

■ Fixed Support

Figure 8-24 Fixed support.

11.   **Environment > Loads > Force**

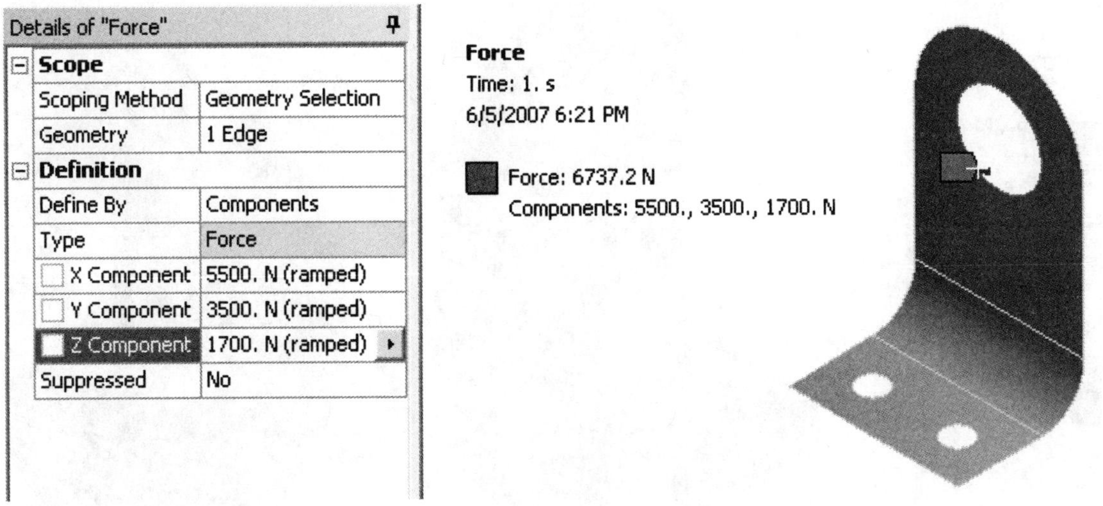

Figure 8-25 Bearing load.

12.   **Solution > Stress > Equivalent Stress (von Mises)**

13.   **Solution > Stress > Error**

14.   **Solution > Deformation > Total**

15.   **Solution > Solve**

The computed von Mises stress is shown in the next figure.

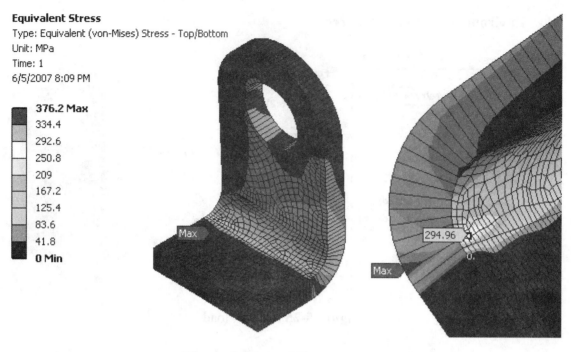

Equivalent Stress
Type: Equivalent (von-Mises) Stress - Top/Bottom
Unit: MPa
Time: 1
6/5/2007 8:09 PM

376.2 Max
334.4
292.6
250.8
209
167.2
125.4
83.6
41.8
0 Min

Figure 8-26 von Mises stresses.

The von Mises stress value on the inside of the fillet (295 MPa) compares well with the result we calculated in Chapter 5 even though this part is a little thick in relation to its 'length' to be typical of plate geometry. The mesh is displayed as a three-dimensional mesh even though the model is really a surface model. Bending stresses vary linearly from the neutral surface in a plate model, so the surface mesh is extended as a prism on both sides of the mid-surface for display purposes.

The **Total Deformation** is displayed next.

The maximum total displacement is computed to be 1.15 mm which is about 16 per cent smaller than the 1.37 we calculated with the solid model in Chapter 5. This may be due in part to the difference in the solid and plate modeling as well as differences in the load modeling. The solid model bearing loads are applied only as pressures to the cylindrical bearing surface, while the surface model loads are distributed around the entire circumference of the hole (see below).

Total Deformation 2
Type: Total Deformation
Unit: mm
Time: 1
6/5/2007 8:15 PM

1.1515 Max
1.0235
0.89559
0.76765
0.63971
0.51176
0.38382
0.25588
0.12794
0 Min

Figure 8-27 Total deformation.

Save your work.

16.   Simulation > File > Save (or Save As) > T8C

ANSYS Workbench Simulation prepares an input batch file that is run by the **ANSYS Classic finite element code**. To examine the modeling a little more closely let's look at the model in ANSYS Classic module.

17.   Click the Project Tab [Project] ✕

18.   Open analysis in ANSYS > **Ⅱ** Static Structural (Click Static Structural.)

19.   Fit model to display. Click 🔍 (right-hand column icons).

20.   PlotCtrls > Symbols (Top line of icons.)

All Applied BCs

Surface Load Symbols > Pressures
Show pres and convect as > Arrows > OK

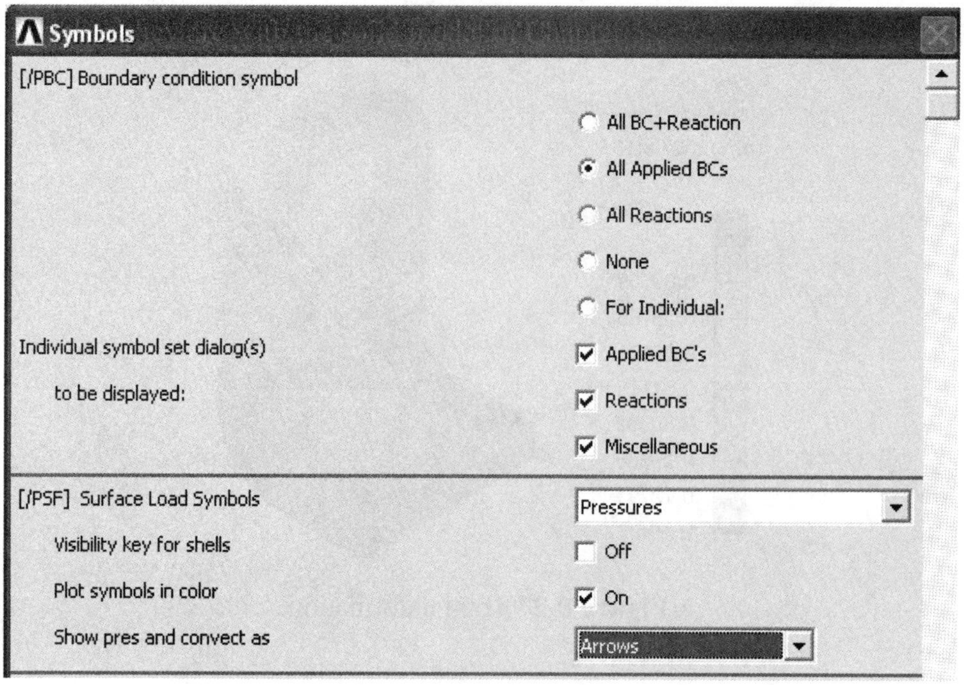

Symbols

[/PBC] Boundary condition symbol

- ◯ All BC+Reaction
- ⦿ All Applied BCs
- ◯ All Reactions
- ◯ None
- ◯ For Individual:

Individual symbol set dialog(s)   ☑ Applied BC's
   to be displayed: ☑ Reactions
                        ☑ Miscellaneous

[/PSF] Surface Load Symbols   Pressures ▾
   Visibility key for shells   ☐ Off
   Plot symbols in color   ☑ On
   Show pres and convect as   Arrows ▾

Figure 8-28 Symbols display options.

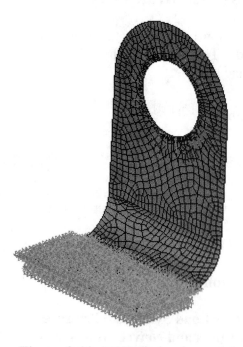

Figure 8-29 ANSYS classic model.

The model in ANSYS classic is shown to be a surface model; the loads boundary conditions are displayed as well. Note that the bearing surface loads are distributed differently than they are with the solid model of Chapter 5.

21.   **File > Exit**

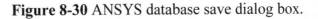

The operations that have been performed in the ANSYS Interface are not automatically recorded in the ANSYS Workbench Interface. Do you wish to save a copy of your database and command log?

Yes   No

Figure 8-30 ANSYS database save dialog box.

22.   **No** (To exit the classic FEM module and return to Workbench.)

This concludes the three-dimensional surface modeling exercise with plate (shell) elements. There are many objects where plate modeling is an appropriate choice for analysis.

8-6   TUTORIAL 8D – LINE-BODY MODEL

In the final tutorial of this chapter we attach the line-body model of Chapter 3 Tutorial 3D and perform structural analysis using ANSYS beam elements. The object is to determine the displacement and stress response to horizontal loads applied to the structure.

1.   **Start ANSYS Workbench DesignModeler** and **attach the T3D tutorial geometry**.

2.   **Project > New Simulation**

3.   **Check the units** and make sure you are working in **inch-lbf-sec units**.

4.   **Right Click Mesh > Generate Mesh**

If the channel leg orientation of any edge is incorrect as shown in the figure on the left below, return to DesignModeler and fix it. (See Chapter 3.)

5.   **DesignModeler > Edge Selection Filter > Select Edge > Change the Reverse Orientation Flag** (**Yes** to **No** or **No** to **Yes**)

6.   **Project >** Update **Model** using parameter values and geometry from **Tutorial3D**.

7.   **Simulation > Right Click Mesh > Preview Mesh**

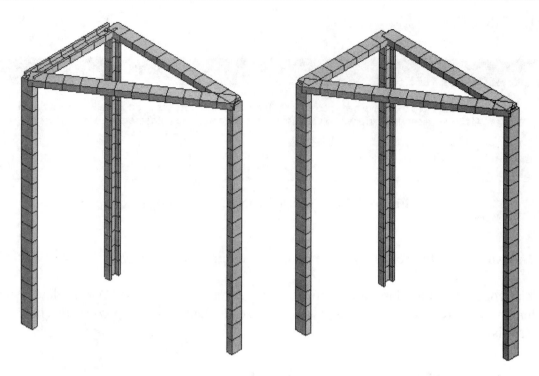

Figure 8-31 Default mesh and reversed section orientation.

8.   **New Analysis > Static Structural**

9.   **Environment > Supports > Fixed Support**

10.   **Ctrl Select the three column base points > Details of "Fixed Support" > Geometry > Apply** (Set selection filter to point.)

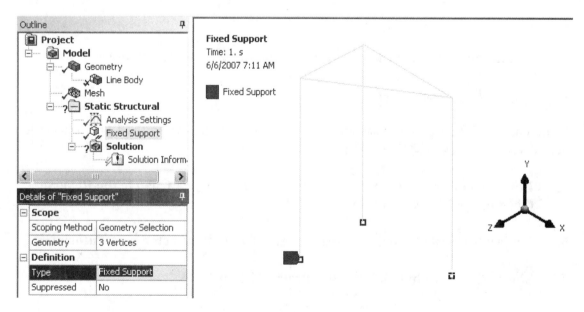

Figure 8-32 Fixed supports.

Also apply horizontal loadings of **5,000 lbf** in the Z Direction to the two upper vertices that lie in the XY Plane.

11. Environment > Loads > Force

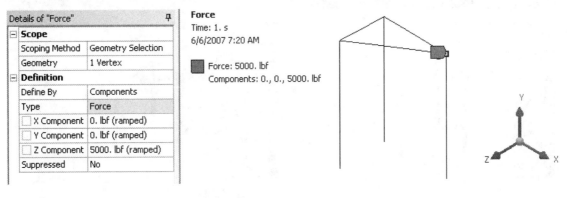

Figure 8-33 Applied loading.

12. Solution > Deformation Directional > Z Axis

13. Solution > Tools > Beam Tool > Solve

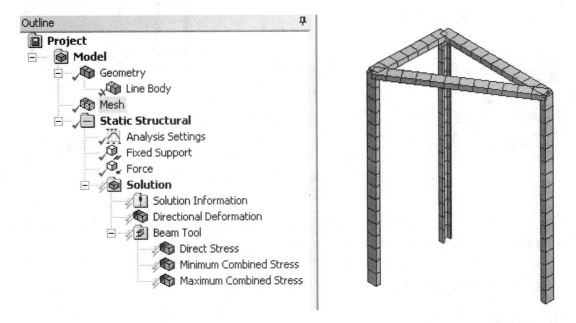

Figure 8-34 Project tree.

The beam tool uses the cross section properties and orientation to compute the **direct (axial) stress** as well as the **minimum and maximum stresses** over the cross section that result when the **direct stress is combined with the bending stress**.

We can display all four of these results at once by selecting multiple viewports. Select the four viewports option using the icon on the second line of icons. Select a viewport then select an item to display.

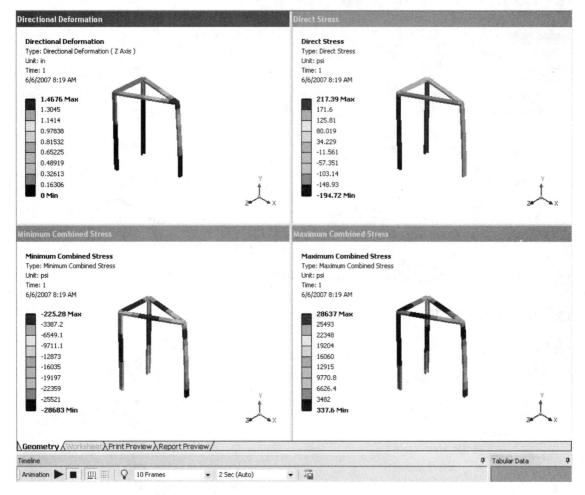

Figure 8-35 Outputs shown in four viewports.

Visualize the deformation and stress progression during loading by selecting the **animation option** at the bottom of the screen.

Control the animation using the icons   Animation ▶ ■ .

14. **Save your work.**

8-7 SUMMARY

The tutorials of Chapter 8 introduce the use of surface models in ANSYS Workbench Simulation and present results that agree with those we calculated previously using three-dimensional solid models. There are many engineering situations in which surface model development proves to be a cost effective and convenient analysis method when compared with comparable three-dimensional, solid modeling analysis approaches. For example, Tutorials T7A and T7C could be solved using 2D models. This chapter concludes by illustrating the use of line body models for those situations where beam elements are an appropriate option for analysis.

8-8 PROBLEMS

8-1 Formulate and solve Tutorial T4B as a surface model problem; be sure to include the interior corner fillet radius. Compare your results with those calculated in Chapter 4.

8-2 Compute the results shown in the table at the end of Tutorial T8B in this chapter.

8-3 Formulate and solve Tutorial T7C as a surface model problem.

8-4 Formulate and solve Tutorial T8D as solid model problem instead of a beam element model.

NOTES:

Chapter 9

Natural Frequencies & Buckling Loads

9-1 OVERVIEW

In this Chapter we discuss use of ANSYS Simulation to determine the natural frequencies and normal modes of structural parts and systems. The determination of buckling load estimates for such objects is also covered. In particular we illustrate the determination of

- ♦ Natural frequencies
- ♦ Corresponding mode shapes
- ♦ Buckling load estimates

9-2 INTRODUCTION

Natural frequencies of systems are those frequencies at which resonant response occurs under the right excitation conditions. Knowledge of these critical dynamic frequencies is an essential step in the design or evaluation of a system subjected to dynamic loadings.

Static loads too can produce instabilities given the particular combination of geometry and loading. Buckling of a long slender bar in axial compression is a common example.

This chapter presents tutorials that illustrate the use of the ANSYS Simulation software suite to address both of these problems.

9-3 TUTORIAL 9A – SIMPLY SUPPORTED BEAM FREQUENCIES

In this first tutorial we compute the natural frequencies of vibration of a long slender bar that has pinned supports at both ends.

Consider a steel bar **0.5 inch in thickness, 1.0 inch high,** and **25 inches in length** between **0.5 inch diameter pins.** See the figure below. Calculate the first **four bending frequencies** of this beam.

The first step is to create the solid model of the beam. Open ANSYS DesignModeler or other parametric modeling system and develop the beam model using the dimensions indicated. We will follow the Simulation Wizard outline.

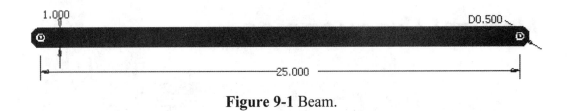

Figure 9-1 Beam.

1. **Start ANSYS Simulation; attach the beam geometry.** Check the units in Simulation.

2. **Simulation Wizard > Modal Analysis** (Required steps are shown below.)

Figure 9-2 Modal analysis requirements.

3. **New Analysis > Modal**

4. **Verify Material** (Use the default material properties for steel.)

5. **Analysis Settings > Max Modes to Find > 4**

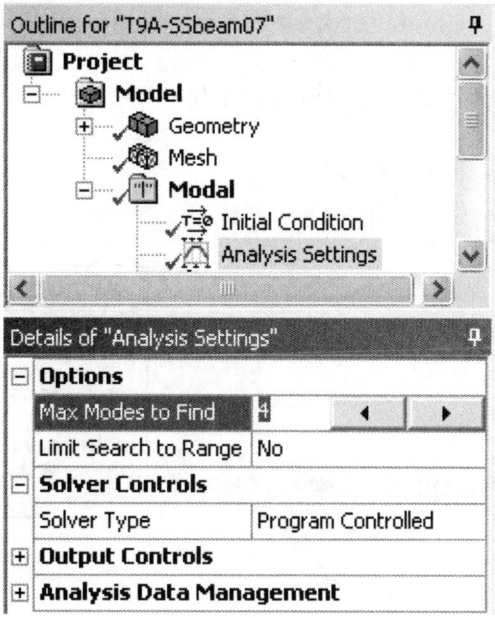

Figure 9-3 Max modes to find.

6. **Insert Supports** ✔ **Insert Supports**

7. **Environment > Supports > Cylindrical Support**

8. **Ctrl Select the Inside surfaces of the cylindrical holes at each end of the beam.**

9. **Radial > Fixed**

10. **Axial > Fixed**

11. **Tangential > Free** (See the next figure.)

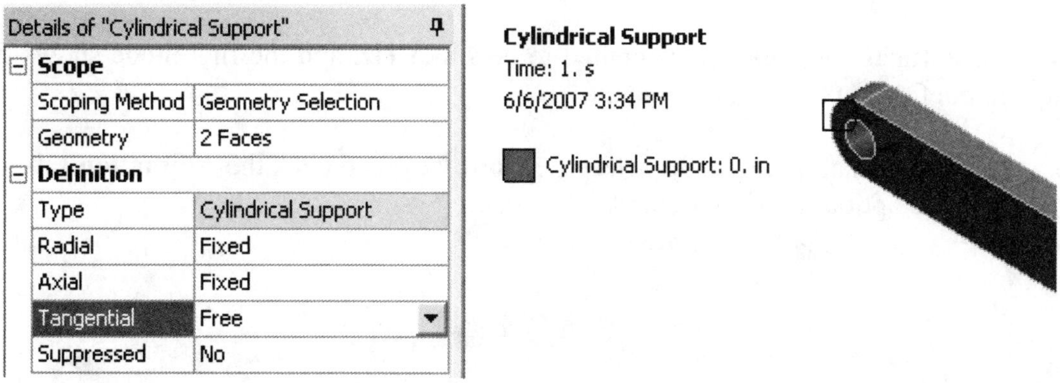

Figure 9-4 Cylindrical support conditions.

Set the mesh density by specifying an **element size** of **0.5 inch**.

12.   Mesh > Advanced > Element Size > 0.5 in >Generate Mesh

Insert a deformation object in the Solution branch.

13.   Solution > Deformation > Total

14.   Solve ⚡ **Solve**

Select frequencies in the Timeline chart or Tabular Data grid to view corresponding mode shapes. Use the Result toolbar to work with the contoured display. Use the mouse to directly edit the legend. In the legend context menu, assign a name to a customized legend to reuse it on other results.

15.   View Results ✓ **View Modal Results**

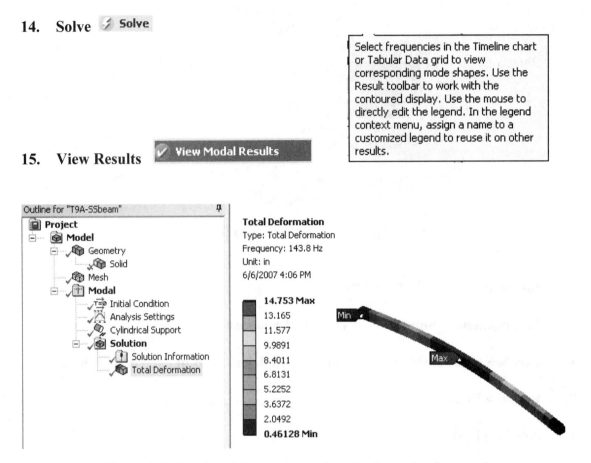

Figure 9-5 Computed frequency and mode shape for first mode.

The **first natural frequency** is computed to be **143.8 Hz**, and the first mode shows the mid point deflecting the greatest amount.

16.   To better visualize the mode, select the **front view** and click the **Animation tab** from the options at the bottom of the screen.

Figure 9-6 First mode.

17. **Rename the Total Deformation object 'Mode 1'**

Insert a second deformation object in the Solution branch and name it **'Mode 2'**.

18. **Solution > Deformation > Total; Rename 'Mode 2'**

In 'Details', change from mode 1 to mode 2 then evaluate the results.

19. **Details of 'Mode 2'** > Use the arrows to change **Mode** from **1** to **2**

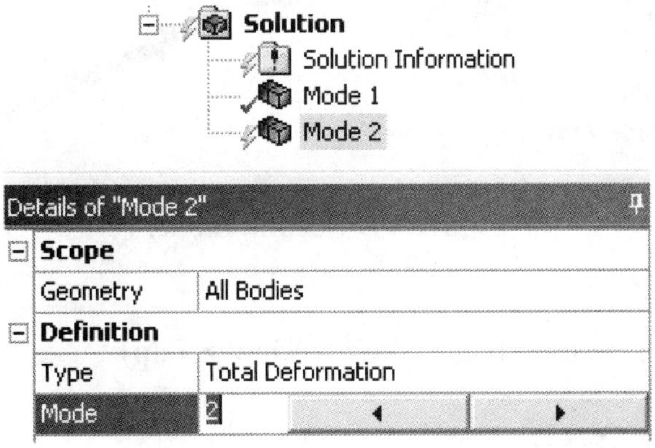

Figure 9-7 Change to second mode.

20. **Solution > Mode 2 > Right click > Evaluate All Results** (Retrieve This Result.)

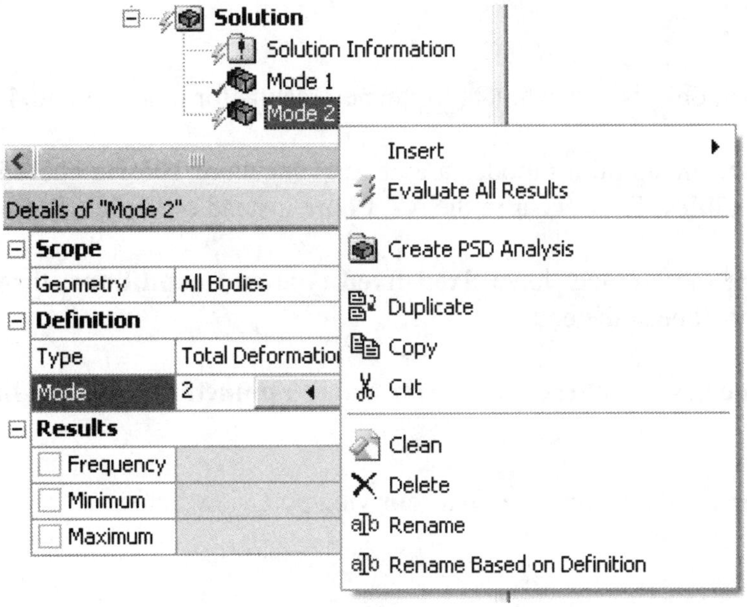

Figure 9-8 Evaluate second mode.

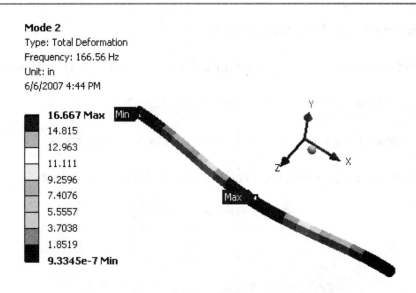

Figure 9-9 Second mode.

Examine Mode 2 from the top. (**Right click > View > Top**)

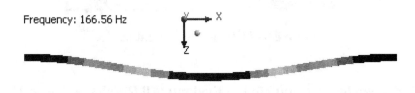

Figure 9-10 Second mode.

Add deformation objects and evaluate frequency results for modes 3 and 4.

Note that the second and third modes are at frequencies of **166 Hz** and **458 Hz** and both are **out-plane modes**. They occur in the **XZ Plane** instead of the **XY Plane**.

Notice also that these modes have **fixed-fixed** type **end conditions**; that is, there is no displacement or slope at the ends.

The fourth mode has a frequency of **571 Hz** and is a **pinned-pinned bending** mode in the **XY Plane**.

The four modes are shown together in a four viewport view below.

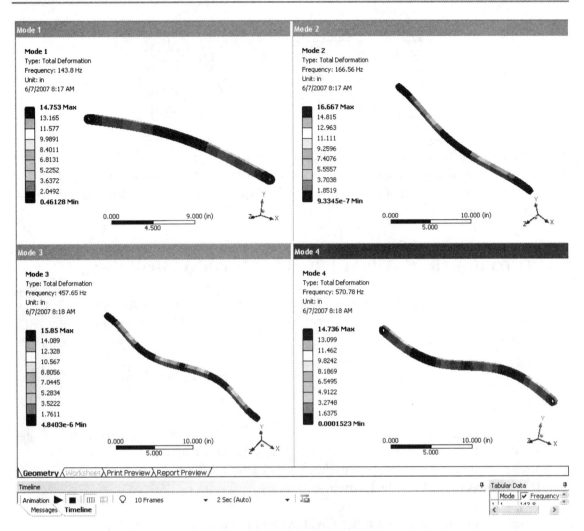

Figure 9-11 First four modes.

Although the modeling here is with three-dimensional solid elements as shown in the figures above, the results can be checked using **beam theory** together with appropriate cross section and boundary conditions. We get (I = w h^3/12):

Pinned-pinned case, cross section base w = 0.5, height h = 1.0, modes 1 and 4: 144 Hz and 576 Hz.

Fixed-fixed case, cross section base w = 1.0, height h = 0.5, modes 2 and 3: 163 Hz and 450 Hz.

The table below summarizes these results.

Mode	Simulation (Hz)	Beam Theory (Hz)
1	144	144 (pinned)
2	166	163 (fixed)
3	458	450 (fixed)
4	570	576 (pinned)

The frequency differences are insignificantly small and are caused to some extent in modes 2 and 3 by the fact that the 3D cylindrical supports are not quite correctly modeled by fixed-fixed beam end conditions. A refined mesh produces only small changes in the computed frequencies.

9-4   TUTORIAL 9B – NATURAL FREQUENCIES OF A CHIME

Consider the wind chime shown in the figure to the right. We will use the frequency finder simulation tool to determine the natural frequencies of one of its components.

Figure 9-12 Wind chimes.

The shortest chime in the group used in this tutorial is an aluminum tube **10.5 inches** in length; it has an **outer diameter** of 29/32 = **0.90625 inch**, and a **wall thickness** of 1/16 = **0.0625 inch**.

1.   **Use DesignModeler** or another **CAD system** to create a **solid model of the tube** described above. **Open** this model in **DesignModeler**.

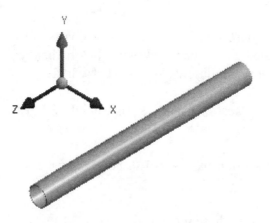

Figure 9-13 10.5 inch tube.

Because the tube very long in comparison to its thickness, we will create a **midsurface model** from this solid to use in the analysis.

2. **Tools > Mid-Surface > Click the outer surface > Ctrl Click the inner surface > Apply**

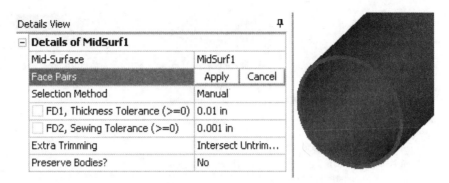

Figure 9-14 Surface pairs selection.

3. **Generate** ⚡ Generate

4. **Surface Body > Thickness > 0.0625**

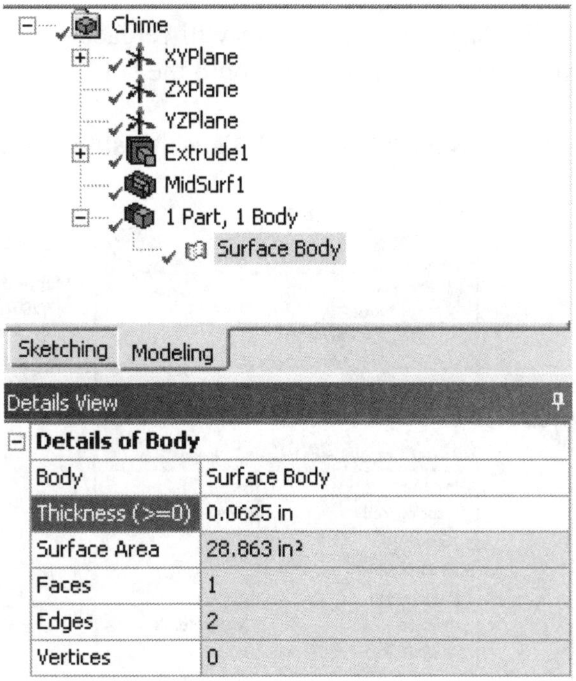

Figure 9-15 Surface body thickness.

Switch to the Simulation module and check to see that the **Units** are set correctly.

5. **Click on the Project Tab** 🔨 [Project] **> New Simulation > Units >** inches, etc.

6. **Geometry > Surface Body > Material > New Material**

7. **Right click on 'New Material' and rename to Aluminum. Enter the data shown below.**

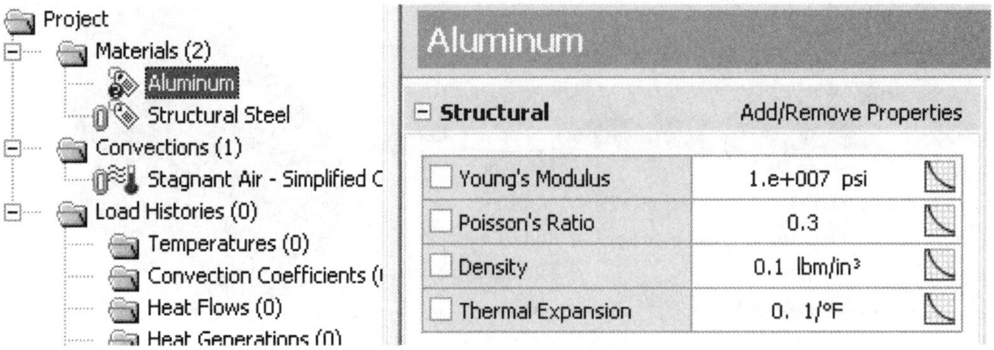

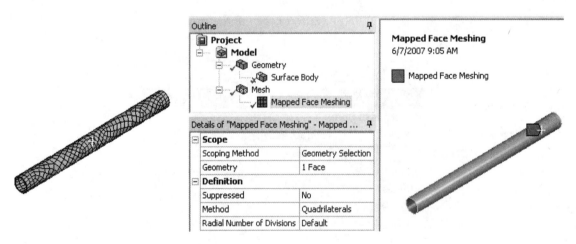

Figure 9-16 Properties of aluminum.

8. **Switch back to Simulation**.

9. **Right click Mesh > Generate Mesh**.

Since the default mesh is not very uniform, we will replace it with a **mapped mesh** in which a regular pattern of rectangles is mapped onto the surface.

10. **Right click Mesh > Insert > Mapped Face Meshing > Select the Surface > Apply**.

Figure 9-17 Meshing options.

11. **Right click > Generate Mesh**.

Note that the mapped mesh process produces a nice regular mesh of 1122 **shell elements**.

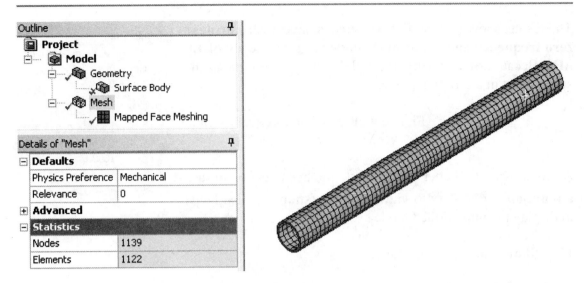

Figure 9-18 Mapped mesh.

12. New Analysis > Modal

When the tube is installed in the chime it is essentially in a free motion condition supported only by the cord from which it is suspended. For this reason we will not apply any displacement boundary conditions and will calculate the frequencies in a **free-free** condition as we would do for an aircraft or spacecraft in flight.

Because of the free-free boundary conditions, there will be **six zero-frequency, rigid body modes** corresponding to the six rigid body degrees of freedom. The chime sound is produced by the elastic vibration modes, so we set the number of modes to be calculated to 9 anticipating that the sounds we are interested in are contained in modes 7 – 9 and above.

13. Details of Analysis Settings > Max Modes to Find > 9

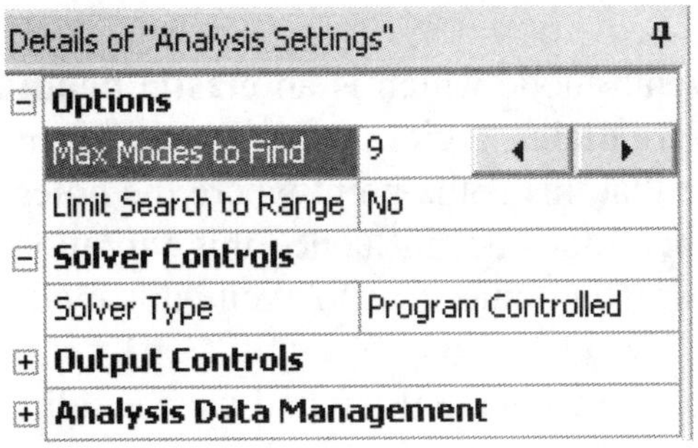

Figure 9-19 Max modes to find.

14. Solve Solve

The results show that the **first six modes** have **a zero or near zero frequency** and the **seventh mode** has a frequency of **1.8 kHz**. Because of symmetry, the eighth mode is the same as the seventh but in a different plane.

Tabular Data		
	Mode	✔ Frequency [Hz]
1	1.	0.
2	2.	0.
3	3.	0.
4	4.	1.4249e-003
5	5.	1.6286e-003
6	6.	1.7249e-003
7	7.	1883.8
8	8.	1883.8
9	9.	4822.

Figure 9-20 Tabulated frequency data.

A good way to better understand the behavior is to use **animation** Animation ▶ to view the **mode shape**. It also helps to display the undeformed model.

15. Show Undeformed Model

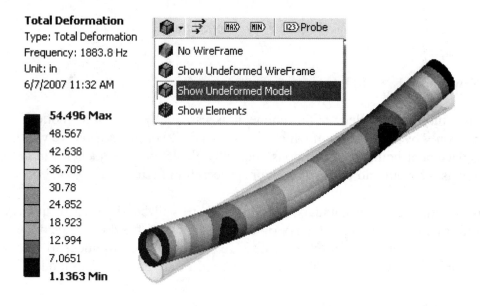

Total Deformation
Type: Total Deformation
Frequency: 1883.8 Hz
Unit: in
6/7/2007 11:32 AM

54.496 Max
48.567
42.638
36.709
30.78
24.852
18.923
12.994
7.0651
1.1363 Min

Figure 9-21 Seventh mode.

The figure shows the seventh mode which is an **elastic bending mode at 1.8 kHz**. The dark regions on the sides are **nodes**, regions of no displacement. Take a look at the photo of the chime and you note that this is the point where the holes are drilled for the support chord since a constraint here does not influence this vibration mode. Note also that the striker hits each chime near the middle so as to excite this mode of bending.

We would have gotten the same results if we had used a **solid model of brick elements** instead a surface model for this problem, but the calculation time is much longer owing to the large number of elements in the default mesh.

(If you have access to a chime, have a computer microphone and frequency analysis software installed, see www.relisoft.com; you can verify this type of analysis experimentally.)

9-5 TUTORIAL 9C – NATURAL FREQUENCIES OF AN ASSEMBLY

In this tutorial we determine the natural frequencies of an assembly of component parts. First create a **110 mm diameter rotor** that is **10 mm thick** and has an integral **axle 15 mm** in **diameter** and **42 mm** in over all **length**. A **20 mm diameter boss** protrudes **5 mm** on each side of the rotor.

Modify the bracket from Chapter 5 by eliminating the base holes and reducing the size of the bore to fit the 15 mm shaft. Create the assembly shown below.

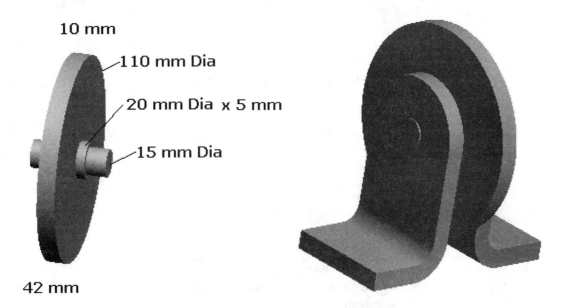

Figure 9-22 Rotor assembly.

1. **Start ANSYS. Begin a New Simulation; attach the geometry.** Check that the units are set for mm. We will use the default structural steel material.

A contact region is defined between the axle and the bore as well as the inside face of the bracket and the rotor boss on each side of the rotor. Define these contacts to be **No Separation**. This allows small relative motion between the surfaces so the disk rotates on its shaft.

To better visualize the contact regions, use the wireframe display option.

2. **View > Wireframe**

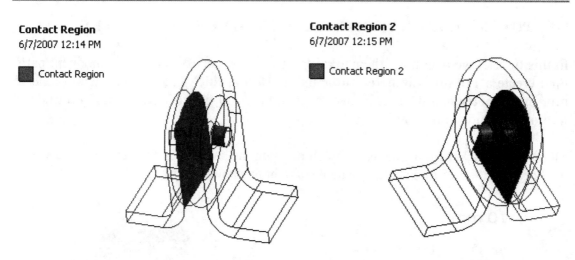

Figure 9-23 Rotor assembly.

3. **Contact > Contact Region > Type > No Separation**

Details of "Contact Region"	
Scope	
Scoping Method	Geometry Selection
Contact	3 Faces
Target	3 Faces
Contact Bodies	WHEEL2[39]
Target Bodies	LBRACK[40]
Definition	
Type	No Separation
Scope Mode	Automatic
Behavior	Symmetric
Suppressed	No

Figure 9-24 No Separation contacts.

Set the default mesh size

4. **Mesh > Details of Mesh > Advanced > Element Size; Enter 0, Press Return.**

5. **New Analysis > Modal**

6. **Environment > Supports > Fixed Support > Ctrl click base, two faces > Apply** (Fix the base from motion.)

Figure 9-25 Fixed supports.

7. **Details of Analysis Settings > Max Modes to Find > 6** (Default)

8. **Solve** Solve

The default mesh of 1578 elements is shown below together with a display of the first two modes computed.

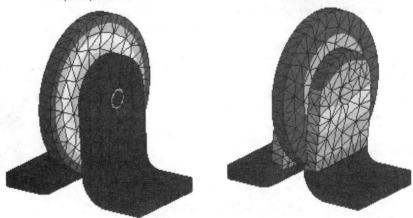

Figure 9-26 First two modes.

Use the **animation** option to examine each mode in turn. The table below summarizes the results.

Mode	Frequency (Hz)	Description
1	152	Not clear
2	1259	Side-to-side
3	1282	Twisting about vertical axis
4	1726	Fore-aft bracket bending
5	2067	Twisting about horizontal axis
6	4299	Symmetric bracket bending

Mode 4 clearly shows the relative motion of the axle and brackets. Mode 1 is not so clear however. Let's analyze the rotor alone. **Save your work.**

Copy and paste the model to create a new problem in the project. In the geometry object, right click and **suppress** the left and right support brackets. This results in a model consisting of only the **rotor**.

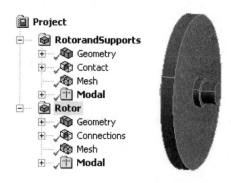

Modify the outline tree to apply a **Cylindrical Support** for the rotor axle. Fix the cylindrical support in the Radial and Axial directions, but set it to Free in the tangential direction.

Figure 9-27 Modify tree.

9.   **Environment > Structural > Cylindrical Support > Definition > Tangential > Free**

Figure 9-28 Rotor only model.

10.   **Solve** Solve

The first two modes are shown in the figure below. The first mode is a rigid body mode with a frequency that is zero. Turn on the element display and use animation to display this mode. (All modes are animated as oscillatory motions even though the rigid body modes are not actually cyclic.) The second mode is an elastic mode involving bending of the rotor on the axle.

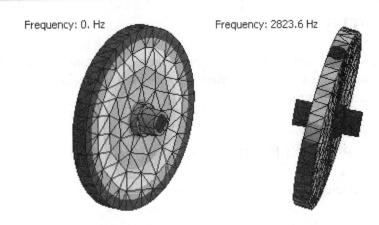

Figure 9-29 First two modes of the rotor alone.

Return to the assembly model.

The first mode frequency for the assembly calculated earlier was 152 Hz whereas we see from the mode shape analysis and animation of the rotor alone that this mode is really a rigid body mode and should be zero. Refine the mesh of the assembly model in order to define contact conditions more accurately.

11. Mesh > Global Control > Advanced > Element Size > 2.5 mm > Preview Mesh

12. Solve   ⁒ Solve

The computed frequencies are shown below.

Mode	Frequency (Hz)	Description
1	25	Rigid body
2	1209	Side-to-side
3	1230	Rotor twisting about vertical axis
4	1631	Fore-aft bracket bending
5	1959	Rotor twisting about horizontal axis
6	4064	Symmetric bracket bending

We see from these results that the both first mode (a rigid body mode) as well as the higher elastic modes are measurably influenced by the quality of the mesh. The contact description, as well as the distribution of both mass and stiffness, depends upon the mesh and thus the frequencies calculated are dependent upon the mesh. Refine the mesh further as your computer hardware and time budget permit and you may see a point at which the results **converge** to values somewhat smaller than those shown.

Start an animation and zoom in on the axle-bearing connection. You should be able to observe the small relative motion of the contact surfaces.

9-6   BUCKLING LOADS

ANSYS Simulation provides tools for computing buckling estimates of elastic structures. We start by considering two problems that can readily be checked, a fixed-free column and a pinned-pinned column.

9-7   TUTORIAL 9D – FIXED-FREE COLUMN (FLAGPOLE)

First use DesignModeler or another solid modeler to create geometry for a solid bar **0.5 x 1 x 25 inch**. See below.

Figure 9-30 25 x 1 x 0.5 inch solid.

1. **Start ANSYS. Begin a New Simulation; attach the geometry.** Check the units in Simulation. We will use the default structural steel material.

2. **New Analysis > Map of Analysis Types**

The Map of Analysis Types indicates that boundary conditions and loading need to be defined in a Static Structural solution prior to the Linear Buckling calculation.

3. **New Analysis > Static Structural**

Fix the left end completely.

4. **Environment > Supports > Fixed Support**

On the right end apply a unit load of 1.0 lbf in the **negative X Direction**. The computed buckling load will be a multiple of this unit load.

5. **Environment > Loads > Force > X Component > -1.0**

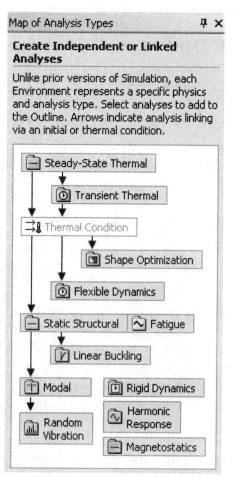

Figure 9-31 Map of Analysis Types.

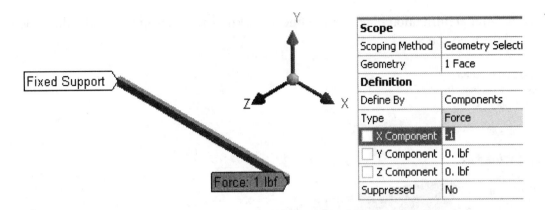

Figure 9-32 Boundary conditions and loading.

Next insert the Linear Buckling object.

6. New Analysis > Linear Buckling

Set the Initial Condition Environment to 'Static Structural'. The default number of buckling modes to find is set to 1.

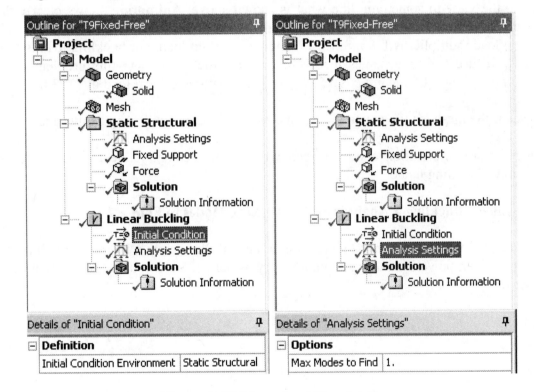

Figure 9-33 Linear buckling details.

7. Solve

Insert a Total Deformation object in the linear buckling solution and view the deformed and undeformed shape.

Total Deformation
Type: Total Deformation
Load Multiplier: 1195.2
Unit: in
6/7/2007 3:39 PM

0.13016 Max
0.1157
0.10124
0.086774
0.072312
0.05785
0.043387
0.028925
0.014462
0 Min

Figure 9-34 XZ Plane buckling.

Rotate the view to something like what is shown above. **Animation** shows clearly that the deformation is in the **XZ Plane** (the direction of weaker flexural stiffness). The critical load multiplier is 1195. Since we applied a 1.0 lbf load, our buckling load is **1195 lbf.** If we use solid mechanics theory to compute the solution to this problem (cross section base $w = 1.0$, height $h = 0.5$) we get a comparable critical load of **1193 lbf.**

To see if the mesh is influencing the results, reduce the element size and solve again.

To get more information about the behavior of this geometry, elect to solve for an additional buckling mode.

8.   Linear Buckling > Analysis Settings > Max Modes to Find > 2

The second mode corresponds to buckling in the **XY Plane** with a load of **4775 lbf**. This result also can be verified using column theory as before. Save your work before moving to the next tutorial.

9-8   TUTORIAL 9E – BUCKLING OF A PINNED-PINNED COLUMN

We can use the geometry of Tutorial 9A to consider buckling of a pinned-pinned column.

1.   **Start ANSYS. Begin a New Simulation; attach the 0.5 x 1 x 25 inch beam geometry.** Check the units in Simulation.

2.   **Geometry > From File** (Locate and attach the simply supported beam geometry.)

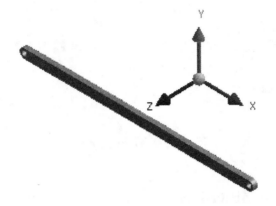

Figure 9-35 Pinned-pinned beam/column.

The column model requires the freedom to move along the X Axis in the direction of the applied load. If we use a cylindrical support at both ends as before, the radial constraint will prevent this. A 'work around' is as follows:

3.   **Return to DesignModeler** or your solid modeler and create a **0.5 inch diameter pin** for the hole in one end of the beam (the right end shown below) and **assemble the two components**.

4.   **Start a new simulation** and **attach the pin-beam assembly.**

5.   **Contact > Contact Region > Type > No Separation**

Figure 9-36 Pin contact with column.

We need Static Structural and Linear Buckling analyses as before.

6.   New Analysis > Static Structural

Apply loads and boundary conditions to the **near and far side faces of the pin: Unit load** in the **negative X Direction**, **No displacement** in the **Y or Z Direction**.

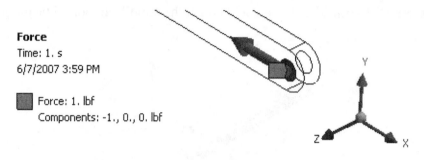

Force
Time: 1. s
6/7/2007 3:59 PM

■ Force: 1. lbf
Components: -1., 0., 0. lbf

Figure 9-37 Pin load.

7.   New Analysis > Linear Buckling

Set a **cylindrical support on the left** as before.

Set the mesh element size to 0.5 inch, request that two modes be computed, and **Solve** . The first mode is a **fixed-fixed XZ Plane mode**, and the second is the **pinned-pinned XY Plane mode** as shown below. (Pick two horizontal viewports.)

Figure 9-38 Fixed-fixed and Pinned-pinned column modes.

Once again the computed results can be verified using column theory from solid mechanics.

9-9 TUTORIAL 9F – BUCKLING OF A BUILT-UP STRUCTURE

The final example in this chapter considers the determination of the buckling load estimate for the built-up part shown in the figures below. The utility of finite element methods is evident for problems such as this one. It is a component of a truck dumping mechanism that is placed in compression when in service and is constructed by welding simple structural shapes together to produce the end result depicted. The construct is shown in two stages.

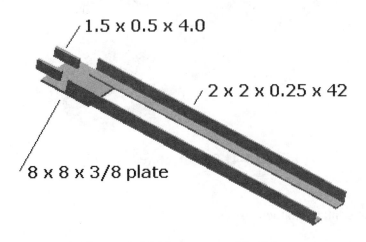

Figure 9-39 First stage of build up.

The left ends of the angle sections are placed at the center of the plate. The rectangular bars protrude 2 inches from the plate and are separated by 2 inches. The 0.25 x 2 x 8 braces shown below are equally spaced; the hole are centered 0.75 from the edges.

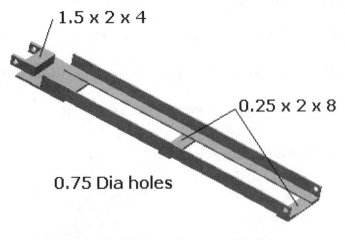

Figure 9-40 Second stage of build up.

As in Tutorial 9E above, we create an assembly that adds a **0.75 x 8 inch pin** at the right end to facilitate application of the boundary conditions.

1.   **Open the assembly** in **ANSYS Simulation.** Check the units.

2.   **Accept the default structural steel.**

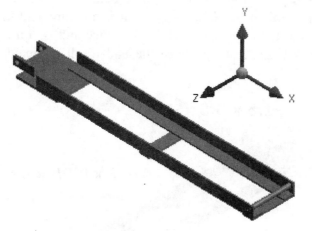

Figure 9-41 Pin-structure assembly.

Set the pin-frame contact characteristics

3.   **Contact > Contact Region > Type > No Separation**

Insert a new analysis.

4.   **New Analysis > Static Structural**

Set a cylindrical support condition for the bore on the left end.

5.   **Environment > Structural > Cylindrical Support**

6.   **Ctrl Select the Inside surfaces of the cylindrical holes at the left end.**

7.   **Radial > Fixed, Axial > Fixed, Tangential > Free**

Cylindrical Support
Time: 1. s
6/7/2007 4:33 PM

▨ Cylindrical Support: 0. in

Figure 9-42 Cylindrical support.

8.   Apply loads and boundary conditions to **both end faces of the pin: Unit load** in the **negative X Direction, No displacement** in the **Y Direction.**

The labels only show on one end of the pin but be sure to Ctrl-select both faces.

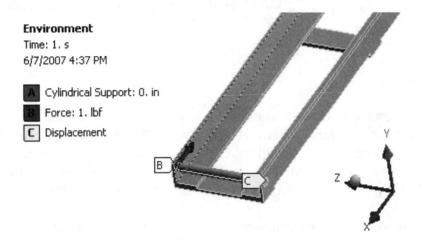

Figure 9-43 Loads and boundary condition at right end.

Insert a buckling calculation object in the solution.

9.   **New Analysis > Linear Buckling > Max Modes to Find > 1**

Set the element mesh size to 0.5 inch and Preview the mesh before solving.

10.   **Mesh > Advanced > Element Size > 0.5 > Generate Mesh, Solve**

The first mode of buckling is shown in the next illustration. The corresponding buckling load is about 71,000 lbf.

Figure 9-44 Buckling of the built-up frame.

Turn on the mesh display (show elements) and use animation to examine the deformation more closely, and you can observe the frame moving with respect to the pin.

The Euler buckling load for a pinned-pinned steel column 42 inches long with a cross section equivalent to two 2 x 2 x 0.25 angles is around 117 klbf, so the above result seems reasonable.

9-10 SUMMARY

Chapter 9 presents tutorials illustrating the computation of natural frequencies and buckling loads for structural parts and assemblies. We note that the results can be substantially influenced by the quality of the mesh and it is recommended that some **mesh refinement** exploration be conducted before final results are accepted. Alternatively a convergence object can be inserted as we saw in Chapter 4.

Small local features such as holes and rounds were not included in our models here since they usually have little effect on frequency and buckling results which are global in nature.

Finally note that **buckling load estimates** are just that, estimates. The results computed here are based on perfectly straight, unblemished items with loads perfectly aligned. The actual situation is often much different.

In addition, the finite element shape function modeling process places an additional constraint on the deformation the mathematical model is allowed to experience. For these reasons elastic buckling loads as computed in this chapter are likely to be **non-conservative upper bounds** on the actual loads that may cause instability and an additional nonlinear analysis may be necessary to obtain a better understanding of the stability limits.

9-11 PROBLEMS

9-1 Compute the first three natural frequencies of an aluminum cantilever beam of the same dimensions as used in Tutorial 9A. Compare your results with values calculated using beam theory.

9-2 Repeat Problem 9-1 but introduce a step change in the cross section at the beam mid-length. Judge the accuracy of your results by computing the frequencies for two beams, one of the smaller section and one of the large section, so as to bracket your computed results.

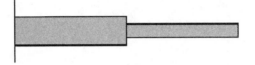

Figure P9-2

9-3 Find the elastic buckling load for a column such as used in Tutorial 9D but with fixed-pinned end conditions.

9-4 Compute the elastic buckling load for the beam of Problem 9-2.

NOTES:

NOTES:

NOTES: